MATTERS *of* LIFE *and* **DATA**

MATTERS
of LIFE *and*
DATA

—A MEMOIR—

The Remarkable Journey
of a Big Data Visionary
Whose Work Impacted Millions
(INCLUDING YOU)

CHARLES D. MORGAN

New York

MATTERS *of* LIFE *and* DATA
The Remarkable Journey of a Big Data Visionary

Whose Work Impacted Millions (INCLUDING YOU)

Published in New York, New York, by Morgan James Publishing. Morgan James and The Entrepreneurial Publisher are trademarks of Morgan James, LLC.
www.MorganJamesPublishing.com

The Morgan James Speakers Group can bring authors to your live event. For more information or to book an event visit The Morgan James Speakers Group at
www.TheMorganJamesSpeakersGroup.com.

Publisher's Note:

As a general rule, Morgan James does not publish works that contain profanity. In this specific case, however, we have deemed certain language integral to the proper understanding of particular personalities or situations being depicted. We apologize to any readers who may find some passages offensive.

A **free** eBook edition is available
with the purchase of this print book.

CLEARLY PRINT YOUR NAME ABOVE IN UPPER CASE

Instructions to claim your free eBook edition:
1. Download the BitLit app for Android or iOS
2. Write your name in **UPPER CASE** on the line
3. Use the BitLit app to submit a photo
4. Download your eBook to any device

ISBN 978-1-63047-465-2 paperback
ISBN 978-1-63047-466-9 eBook
ISBN 978-1-63047-467-6 hardcover
Library of Congress Control Number:
2014918265

Cover Design by:
Rachel Lopez
www.r2cdesign.com

Interior Design by:
Bonnie Bushman
bonnie@caboodlegraphics.com

In an effort to support local communities, raise awareness and funds, Morgan James Publishing donates a percentage of all book sales for the life of each book to Habitat for Humanity Peninsula and Greater Williamsburg.

Get involved today, visit
www.MorganJamesBuilds.com

Habitat
for Humanity®
Peninsula and
Greater Williamsburg
Building Partner

For Susie

CONTENTS

Prologue: The Bad Guys Database   ix

Part One: HARDWARE   **1**
   1 Drive, He Said   3
   2 The Boy Who Might Be Forgotten   22
   3 The Mathematics of Change   42

Part Two: SOFTWARE   **63**
   4 Men in Black   65
   5 Red Sea Change   86
   6 Do or Die   117
   7 Finding the Zone   135
   8 A Theory of Time   151

Part Three: BIG DATA   **169**
   9 Like a Weed   171
  10 Green Fields   191
  11 Marriage on My Mind   223
  12 Turning Points   240
  13 Theater of War   254
  14 Dawn of the Lost Decade   272
  15 The Long Goodbye   293

Epilogue: Full Circle   319
Acknowledgments   330
About the Author   331

PROLOGUE

THE BAD GUYS DATABASE

SEPTEMBER 14, 2001, three days after 9/11. Everybody in the country was still glued to the television, still struggling to comprehend the horrific images that now couldn't be shut off, even without the TV.

In my office at Acxiom in Little Rock I was going through the motions, trying to find normal in a world blown off its axis. A colleague knocked on my door. "Look at this," he said, and he seemed nervous. He handed me a computer printout. Data was our business, and these pages described a man who worked as a clerk at a Florida 7/11 store, had 14 credit cards, and had racked up $150,000 in credit-card debt.

"What is this?" I said.

"This guy," answered my colleague, "lived in the same apartment building as Mohamed Atta."

The name Mohamed Atta was now infamous worldwide, thanks to the recent FBI announcement identifying the 9/11 terrorists. Once these names had become public, some of our people jumped on our databases to see what we had on them.

They'd found Atta's address and cross-referenced it to pull up other names, including that of the free-spending 7/11 clerk. "We think this isn't a coincidence," my guy said. "We'd like your okay to look deeper. But it might be necessary to take a peek at Citibank's or Chase's data. Without permission, I mean."

Holy shit, I thought. Client trust was one of our most hallowed tenets, along with data privacy; legal liability was also up there in our concerns. But this was a unique situation.

They worked through the weekend, and on Monday they'd amassed enough tantalizing information that we knew we had to take it to the next level. Our company lawyer arranged for us to be subpoenaed by the U.S. Attorney's office, so we could hand over our findings. Soon a half-dozen wide-eyed FBI agents descended upon us. I personally called Bill Clinton, who would spend a couple of hours at Acxiom debriefing us on what we had uncovered.

But that was some three months later, after we'd gone to our buddies at TransUnion, one of the big three credit reporting agencies, and received permission to delve into their credit data. That was a breakthrough. Also vital was the fact that this terrible event occurred *after* we at Acxiom had developed revolutionary techniques in data processing and data matching, as well as our new grid computing system—essentially a private "cloud." Armed with these tools, we began putting the credit bureau data with all our info-based data, along with some data from Citibank—this time with their blessing—and a very shocking picture began to emerge.

That's when I decided to get a dedicated server and build a database so we could look harder and deeper. We outfitted an empty room in our headquarters building with computers and high security, and for a time I had 30 people working fulltime on what we now called The Bad Guys Database. I eventually made a presentation to Vice President Dick Cheney about our data-gathering capabilities.

□ □ □ □ □

DID WE CONTRIBUTE, inadvertently, to the NSA's clandestine activities? I have no idea. I am extremely proud of our work with the government following the events of September 11, but thanks partly to Edward Snowden and the NSA's excesses, today's ubiquitous Big Data is a concept that many people respond to with suspicion or outrage. It's absolutely true that some holders of information misuse it—I've met some of those people over the years—and others don't give a damn about your privacy—I've run across those types, too. But in telling my story, what I hope to show you is that data itself, as well as data gathering, is neither good nor bad; it's how it's used that matters.

I didn't set out to become a collector of your and your neighbors' information. When I was growing up, in the '40s, '50s, and '60s, nobody but egghead scientists talked about "data." It was the mechanical age, and I was a gadget geek, taking apart my cousin's toys and my mother's toaster and trying, unsuccessfully at first, to put them back together again. I was especially crazy about cars and engines, and had it not been for a fateful encounter during college recruiting season, I might've lived my life as a race car mechanic instead of learning about computers at IBM. As it turned out, pursuing Big Data allowed me the resources to become a professional race car driver on the side, competing against the likes of Paul Newman, who makes appearances in these pages as well.

Such are the wonders of this journey we're all on. Mine has taken me from the frontier of western Arkansas, where my ancestors owned a hardware store selling iron tools to westbound travelers, to the frontier of the digital age, where room-size computers have become eclipsed by the power of smart phones. But while much has changed in our world in these decades, even more has stayed the same. There is no software for reprogramming human nature—believe me, I've had ample reason to hope for such.

In a sense, then, the story you're about to read is not so different from those of the colorful adventurers who stocked up their wagons at my family's hardware emporium and headed west to make their fortunes. Data mining is the new gold rush, and we were there at first strike, dragging with us all our human frailties and foibles. In this book's cast of characters you'll find ambition, arrogance, jealousy, pride, fear, recklessness, anger, lust, viciousness, greed, revenge, betrayal—and then some. Of course love, or the lack of it, plays a part in this tale: I once traveled to Saudi Arabia to rescue an office sidetracked by love—a sad event that secured my own rise. Later, my own divorce was so overheated that Oprah invited me to be a guest on her show (I declined).

It is a messy story. In the big picture, this could be called a narrative of America since World War II. But in the micro telling, think of it this way: The man who opened your lives to Big Data finally bares his own.

Part One

HARDWARE

1

DRIVE, HE SAID

1001010010110010100010010110010101100 11

I GREW UP on the frontier's edge, at the jumping-off point for the Great Plains, where Indians, homesteaders, trappers, outlaws, and all manner of fortune seekers had vied for supremacy in the untidy settling of the West. All these people needed supplies, and so in the late 1800s my Arkansas River town of Fort Smith, Arkansas—last outpost of civilization before you crossed into the vast unknown—was a good place to own a hardware store. So good, in fact, that my maternal great-grandfather, Dave Speer Sr., moved all the way from far north Missouri to Fort Smith in 1887 to open Speer Hardware Company, a large retail operation located near the river and the rail line, perfectly situated to outfit the westbound hordes with wagon wheels, whips, cast-iron stoves, and tools.

Five years later, as the Oklahoma Territory moved toward statehood, he expanded to wholesale, becoming a major distributor for the entire region. My great-grandfather's five-story brick hardware store sat just across the street from the courthouse of Judge Isaac Parker, the legendary "hanging judge." Had Judge Parker still been alive for Speer Hardware's grand opening, I have no doubt that my great-grandfather would've supplied the lumber, nails, and rope that were at the heart of the judge's brand of frontier justice.

Hardware appeared to be my destiny from the start, thanks to the double whammy of genealogy and genes, which are not exactly the same thing. By the 1940s my great-uncle Fred Speer was running the hardware business and his brother, my grandfather Ralph Speer Sr., worked alongside him. Now enter my father, Charles Donald Morgan, a traveling salesman of dry goods. The year was 1941. Having been rejected by the military for his migraine headaches, he spent the war years working for Rice-Stix, a wholesaler and manufacturer in St. Louis; it was a major company—at the time of the 1904 St. Louis World's Fair, Rice-Stix was said to be the largest business in the city.

My father's territory was Northwest Arkansas and Eastern Oklahoma, an area that made Fort Smith a good base of operations. On this particular sales trip he was working out of the then-famous Goldman Hotel—center of Fort Smith society—and my mother, Betty Speer, Ralph's youngest daughter, ran the AAA desk in the Goldman lobby. So one day my future father dropped by her desk and said, "My, that's a lovely dress you're wearing. May I feel the material?" What a line! But Father's story, and he never abandoned it, was that he had to *feeeel* the fabric in order to decide if it was a cloth he should be carrying. Long story short, they got married on the Fourth of July, 1941, and I came along in February 1943. February 4, to be exact.

Don Morgan was a good salesman, and soon—I was probably 6 months old—he got promoted to a larger territory, working out of New Orleans. We lived in New Orleans for about two-and-a-half years, and then my father was promoted again—to Griffin, Georgia, just outside Atlanta. In January 1946 my brother Speer was born. He was a difficult pregnancy, and Mother went back to Fort Smith to have him. I think by this time she'd had enough of following a traveling salesman around from post to post, and she had no fondness for St. Louis, where he was likely to end up in the suffocating comfort of Rice-Stix middle management. Mother wanted to settle down in Fort Smith. And the way she managed that was to ask her dad to give Don a sales job in the family hardware business.

Everybody's road has its fateful forks, and this was the first of mine. My grandfather—whom we kids called Pop Speer—was a wonderful man, friendly and funny and unassuming, and he liked my father a lot. He also dearly loved my mother, his baby girl, youngest of his four children. We lived with my grandparents when we first moved back to Fort Smith. They had a comfortable two-story house on 14th Street, with several bedrooms, large living and dining rooms, and an ample kitchen with spacious pantry where I could always find something good to eat. My grandmother, Betty Black Speer—called "Woggie" by us kids, for reasons I've forgotten—was a spirited woman and I loved riding in the car with her. I remember her zooming down 14th Street in her 1940 Plymouth, me standing on the front seat while she tore through the intersections and I bounced up and down, bumping my head into the soft felt ceiling, laughing all the way. I probably got my love of racing cars from my grandmother. But our joyrides stopped being fun the day a car pulled out in front of us and Woggie slammed on the brakes, sending me head first into the windshield. I didn't go through it, but I cracked the thing, earning me a well-deserved reputation for hard-headedness.

Once Father and Mother found us a house of our own—a few blocks from my grandparents on North 21st Street—we still went over to see them every Sunday night for supper. Eventually Woggie fell and broke her hip, due to brittle bones from severe osteoporosis; she became an almost total invalid. But Pop Speer had an excellent cook, so we would go early and visit with him while the cook fixed supper. My grandfather was a shy man. His normal routine when company was present was to settle back in his easy chair and puff on his pipe and hardly say a word; he'd just listen, the way he listened to his big console radio. But my dad had a way of getting Pop to open up and tell about his days as a star pitcher for a semi-pro baseball team back in the 1920s; or about the times, in the early part of the century, when Grandfather would go with *his* father, Dave Speer Sr., and other men on two-week hunting trips to their camp in wildest Oklahoma. Camp Plenty, they called it, and my brother has photographs of one of those hunts; judging from the pictures, the "Plenty" in the camp's name refers as much to whisky and cards as to wild game.

In 1951 my grandfather would become president of Speer Hardware Company, so you would think that Don Morgan, his son-in-law, would be in a very favorable position. There was only one glitch in that scenario: Pop Speer's son, my uncle, Ralph Speer Jr.

□ □ □ □ □

HOW CAN I convey the character of my Uncle Ralph? I've consulted several relatives, who tend to remember him in monosyllables—"ass," "shit," "dick." Let me explain. Status, which Uncle Ralph had been handed at birth, was everything to him. He had been sent off to Sewanee, the University of the South, to acquire a gentleman's education, and he had accomplished that, in 1927, complete with Phi Beta Kappa key. In those days there weren't many people in our part of Arkansas who even had a college degree, much less one from a prestigious out-of-state university where students actually wore academic gowns to class, like budding oracles. So even as he worked in various junior positions in the hardware store, expanding his knowledge beyond the Silver Spoon Department, Uncle Ralph enjoyed a certain big dog status in Fort Smith. Then, at a summer resort in Winslow, Arkansas, where the Speers had a cabin, he met an oil heiress from Houston, Melanie Holt— pronounced Me-LAN-ie—and they got married. With her money fueling his social climbing, they were able, even in their 30s, to live in a big sprawling house— much grander than my Grandfather Speer's—on leafy Hendricks Boulevard, one of the city's best addresses. And of course they belonged to Fort Smith's venerable Hardscrabble Country Club, on whose manicured golf course Uncle Ralph regularly reinforced his position as an important man about town.

But there appeared to be one stubborn spot of tarnish in Uncle Ralph's otherwise golden life: his brother-in-law, my father, the—dare we say it?— "traveling salesman."

To Uncle Ralph, his sister Betty had scandalized the family by marrying beneath her station; Uncle Ralph had personally been humiliated by the union of this flower of the Fort Smith Speers with the cloth-peddling offspring of an itinerant West Virginia ne'er-do-well—if he knew that much about my father at all, which he probably didn't. The term "traveling salesman," with all its attendant jokes, was indictment enough. It must have galled Uncle Ralph when Grandfather Speer hired Don Morgan to work at the family hardware store. From that moment on, my uncle, a blustery redhead who started most sentences with "Goddammit," did his level best to make my father's life miserable.

Unfortunately, Dad was particularly susceptible to Ralph's bullying. My salesman father's gift of gab camouflaged a bundle of insecurities, not to mention contradictions. He was uncomfortable with personal relationships, especially with other men. Maybe that had to do with his upbringing—his own father, a tall, handsome, garrulous fellow, had never quite been able to find his calling, and consequently had moved from place to place and job to job. And even though my dad had managed to put himself through college, in Illinois, his position as traveling salesman clearly didn't bring him much respect. Dad had also been divorced—though I wouldn't know that for years—and divorce was very much a stigma in those days. Even if others didn't know about it, *he* was probably ashamed. He was a sensitive soul who loved theater and literature and writing; a religious man with an eye for the ladies; a Sunday School teacher who, until the kibosh of divorce, had hoped to become a preacher; an unabashed dreamer who never met an opportunity he didn't like. All in all, he was as unlike rich, swaggering, establishment Uncle Ralph and his cronies as it was possible to be. I don't know how much of all this Ralph knew, but surely, like a predator sensing an opponent's fear, he smelled my father's intimidation.

I remember many evenings when Father would come home from work feeling downtrodden, nursing yet another insult from Uncle Ralph. My mother would try to smooth it over, to urge him not to take things personally. But he did take personally the fact that he was given the worst sales territory—hole-in-the-wall general stores inevitably situated out in the farthest boondocks, five miles down a pock-marked dirt road; or that his commission plan was deliberately structured to be less lucrative than those of the other salesmen; or that Uncle Ralph had said something disparaging to him in front of the other men.

This last item was one of my uncle's favorite tactics for making people around him feel small. Though our family didn't spend a lot of time at the home of Uncle Ralph and Aunt Melanie, we were invited, apparently to keep up appearances, for most major holidays—Thanksgiving, Christmas, the Fourth of July. Sometimes other friends of my aunt and uncle would also be there with their kids, and my brother and I grew up swimming in our aunt and uncle's pool with our cousins and their rich friends. When I was young and less aware I looked forward to these outings, but now I know that my parents—at least my father—certainly didn't.

I'll never forget, nor forgive, one July 4 when Dad, never much of a drinker, was in a group of highball-swilling men gathered around Uncle Ralph, who was holding forth, as usual, on some subject of the day. My father ventured a comment, and Ralph turned on him with surprising venom, even for Uncle Ralph. "Goddammit, Don," he said, "why don't you just shut the fuck up, you don't know a goddammed thing."

My father was humiliated. And when Mother confronted Uncle Ralph about it—a rare occurrence—he was just as ugly to her.

The fact is, Uncle Ralph was congenitally rude to pretty much everyone. Which is why it's so surprising that he was always kind, even solicitous, to me. I appreciated that, but also came to resent it, wondering if it wasn't the ultimate insult to my father—trying to co-opt his eldest son. My cousin Margaret, Uncle Ralph's daughter, has said she thinks I was probably influenced in my business career by the pattern set by her dad. She's right, I was influenced by him, but not in the way she thinks. From very early on, some part of me burned to show him the meaning of a term that would never apply to him: *self-made*.

□ □ □ □ □

DOES THAT MAKE me sound like an angry boy? Nothing could be further from the truth. What I was, was determined. And consumed.

Earlier I said that hardware seemed to be my destiny. I was around it a lot, of course, given the family business, but mere proximity is never the point. Instinct and passion are the keys. Whenever I walked into Speer Hardware, I saw those thousands of mostly metal products not so much as items in and of themselves, but as bits of matter in a larger mechanical universe. As far back as I can remember, I've been fascinated by machines, especially engines. How in God's name do they work? What can I tweak to make them go faster, higher, farther?

But you have to begin somewhere, and I started with my cousin's toys. Whenever Mother would take me over to visit my cousin Reaves Lee, I would take apart his playthings—his music box, his whirring tin police car, his mechanical cash register—and try to put them back together. Unfortunately, I was still of an age—6 or 7—when I usually couldn't get them completely back the way they'd been. Reaves was a good sport, I have to say—though as time went on, he was increasingly careful about what toys he left out when I was around.

At home, I drove my mother nuts. She might walk in to find that I had cracked open the toaster, or the radio, or her mixer. I couldn't help myself—it was as though

I saw the world inside out: While others focused on the sleek exterior of things, I was drawn to the gears and springs and tubes inside. But the day Mother finally went over the edge, it wasn't—on the surface—due to my destroying anything mechanical. Her prize possession was a fancy gilded plate that she kept on a stand in the center of the mantel. That day I was playing with one of those '50s-era toy guns that shot darts tipped with suction cups, and I hit the bulls-eye. Holding my breath, I watched—seemingly in slow motion—as the cherished plate teetered on its stand, toppled from the mantel, and crashed into shards on the hearth. When Mother ran in and saw what had happened, she clasped her hand to her mouth... and then it was as though a switch had been tripped: Opening the china cabinet, she began flinging plates and cups and saucers like a mad woman. "You're going to tear up everything!" she screamed. "You're going to ruin everything I've got! I might as well *do it myself!*"

For a boy with a mind like mine, postwar America was a great time to be alive. The mechanical age had spread from the factory to the home, and the country was bursting with cool new products. To me, the coolest of the cool were cars—both inside and out. My dad still drove a '46 Plymouth sedan, with its small windows and a roof that sloped, like a claw hammer, down to the back bumper; in our part of the world, that was pretty much the status quo—even Uncle Ralph, never a car guy, drove a frumpy station wagon so he could haul his golf clubs and hunting gear. But cars were changing, and the magazines my parents read were full of splashy ads showing cars that were ever lower, ever longer, ever more streamlined. I was obsessed with cars, and by the time I was 8 or 9 I knew the specs of just about any model of automobile you could name.

It's no coincidence that, in 1952, when I was 9 years old, my father announced a plan so off the wall that the rest of us just stared at him in disbelief. The plan was for us, as a family, to build and operate a motel. Not only that, we would *live* in it. Apparently Dad had been taking note of the same car ads that I had salivated over, but he saw something beyond sleek lines and powerful engines. He saw restlessness, mobility, a country ready, after years of World War II belt-tightening, to get on the road and *go*. Yes, the Korean War was still hot, but it wasn't so all consuming as to restrict growth and movement; besides, the Korean War was a key part of Dad's scheme. Camp Chaffee, built as a training facility during World War II, was located a few miles southeast of Fort Smith on Highway 22. The camp was once again filled with soldiers, and there was a lot of coming and going, including visits from family and friends. As matters now stood, the closest place for those soldiers and their visitors to get together was all the way in downtown Fort Smith, at one of the hotels. Dad's idea was to build our motel out on mostly undeveloped Highway 22 between Fort Smith and Camp Chaffee.

No doubt part of the impetus for this plan was for Dad to forge a degree of independence from Uncle Ralph. He would still have to work at the hardware store, at least until the motel began making money, but no longer would he be completely beholden to his brother-in-law. We were also going to keep our existing house and rent it out, generating additional income. Dad couldn't wait to get going on the project, to buy the land and start construction. Sharpening his pitch like the salesman he was, he convinced the bank to lend him a portion of the $60,000 he needed; the rest he got from my grandfather. Did Uncle Ralph know that? I sincerely hope so.

We moved into our new motel home in 1953, when I was 10 and Speer was 7. It was a gutsy move for our parents, most especially for Mother. In Fort Smith, as in most places in America, there were the respectable areas of town to live in and the parts that were considered unacceptable for "nice" people. Being a Speer, Mother had always lived in respectable areas; for that matter, so had we all. But now, even though we were still within the Fort Smith city limits, we had crossed a line. In those days, you didn't want to live east of Waldron Avenue; our motel was three blocks into the no-go zone. Our neighbors included a gas station, a quarry, and a junkyard.

The motel was U-shaped, with 10 guest rooms configured in five freestanding duplex buildings—three on one arm of the U, two facing on the other—and the small office/residence, about 1,000 square feet of living space, centered in the U's base. And what do you think my dad named this attractive inn? *The Farm Motel.* Worst idea in the world! In those days, most farm families used privies, and so a lot of potential guests checked first to make sure we had indoor plumbing. I hate to think how many didn't stop at all.

But life at the motel turned out to be very good. My parents lived there for 16 years—eventually, in the late '50s, changing the name to "something classy," as my father put it, remembering the finest hotel in St. Louis, the Chase. That's how The Farm Motel became The Chase Motel. For me, though, and I suspect for Speer, what resonates about those days is a sense of adventure, of growing up slightly on the edge. For two young boys from historic Fort Smith, this untamed neighborhood was our own personal frontier.

□ □ □ □ □

WE HAD TO fight our way in. Not long after we moved to the motel, Speer and I were playing in a vacant strip of land behind our house when suddenly we were pummeled by rocks—jagged rocks, sharp and weighty. Our attackers were a whooping pair of boys whom we would eventually know as the Helms Brothers, but at this moment all we knew was that they were wild and loud and moving closer. Speer and I picked up rocks and hurled them back, but the Helmses didn't run away. The fight must've lasted five minutes, though it seemed like an hour, and we got the worst of it—especially me. I leaned over to pick up a rock and then spun back to face them, and *wham!* One incoming rock hit me square in the forehead, opening a nasty gash that spurted blood. I stood there dazed, knocked starry eyed. Blood was running down my face, dripping off my chin, soaking into my shirt. Time seemed to stop. Wide-eyed, the Helms boys stared at me for a long moment, then turned and hightailed it back to whatever hole they'd come out of. I headed for the house, where a friend of Mother's, Mrs. Cabel, was staying with us while our parents were away. I almost scared the poor lady to death.

There were other confrontations, various kinds of testing, as there always are in the world of kids. Outsiders have to prove themselves. But once Speer and I were accepted, we formed friendships—some more stable than others. Our closest and most reliable friend was a quiet, curly-headed boy named Junior Smotherman, real name Hoyt, who lived catty-cornered across Highway 22 in a three-room house with his mother; no father was in evidence. Even though Junior was a couple of years older, he and I spent a lot of time together, at his house and ours, and he was very protective of Speer with the rougher kids in the neighborhood. Junior was a responsible boy. He delivered newspapers to help his mother make ends meet. She worked two jobs and still had a hard time of it. We'd never seen that kind of struggling before.

Now it was all around us. Another pair of brothers, Jerry and Jimmy Prescott, lived in a tiny house at the other end of Holly's Junkyard, two blocks away. Jimmy, who was my age, was mostly mean to us, but his older brother Jerry was a friend—especially to Speer. The Prescotts had a garden out back, and Speer remembers that Jerry practically lived on tomatoes; in their house, there wasn't much else to eat. Speer and Jerry sometimes went fishing, and for Jerry it was more than just recreational—he really *needed* those fish.

Down a block from the Prescotts was where Ralph and Ronnie Ingram lived, again in a sad, miniscule house with a single mother. Ralph, a tall, skinny kid about five years older than me, was my neighborhood hero. His yard was strewn with the carcasses of old lawn mowers and other machines, which he either fixed up or scavenged parts from. But the thing that really impressed me about Ralph was his Harley Project—he was in the process of rebuilding not one but *two* Harley-Davidson motorcycles, and I couldn't get enough of it. I spent as much time as possible at the Ingrams' watching Ralph tinker with the Harleys and hanging onto his every word. Ralph Ingram was a mechanical genius, my personal guru of the internal combustion engine.

And then there were the Helms brothers—one was called Dub, and I can't for the life of me recall the other's name. Dub was a couple of years older than I was and his brother was a little younger. They lived about three blocks from us, down past that vacant lot where they'd attacked us with rocks. Their house was small, but nice—it was at the Helmses' that Speer and I first watched television. We called Dub and his brother "The TV Boys." Their dad was the main mechanic at Holly's Junkyard. At least they had a dad, and he had a job; that alone made them the best off in the neighborhood, after us.

Money and status weren't subjects we often spoke about, but they were as much in the air in our edgy world as if we'd lived west of Waldron Avenue. The neighborhood kids seemed to consider Speer and me "rich" because our parents owned a business and we had nicer, newer cars, and also because we were connected to a family whose name was emblazoned on a big building in the heart of downtown. And in a way we did live in two worlds. Every Sunday morning, our family would dress up and drive to the venerable St. John's Episcopal Church downtown, where Father taught Sunday School—I was in his class, along with the children of many of the city's most prominent families. Then we four attended church service together, always sitting in "our place"—third pew from the front, right of center aisle.

Speer and I also profited from Aunt Melanie's ongoing guilt over the boorishness of her husband, our Uncle Ralph. Bending over backwards to be nice to us, she invited us to spend many a summer afternoon swimming with Cousin Margaret and her privileged Hendricks Avenue friends—Ann Oglesby next door, whose father was a doctor; and the Dills girls across the street, Jane and Nancy, daughters of the owner of Arkhola Sand & Gravel. Jane Dills, by the way, will play a very important role in my story, but for now I'll just say that she was an older girl (by two years) whom I seemingly always knew. In fact, continuing the "two worlds" theme of this narrative, it was at the Dillses' house that I got my first taste of Champagne, at the tender age of 12, when my cousin Ewell Lee—Reaves' older brother—married Jane's sister. At the reception, the Dillses had a Champagne fountain on a table with a skirt around it, and I hid under the skirt and drank way more than my share.

By age 12, I was, at Mother's insistence, also attending cotillion—what they called "Tea Dances" in Fort Smith—and so I learned to waltz and foxtrot and dance the Lindy Hop with many of the proper young ladies in town. "He was a great dancer!" says my former cotillion partner, Jan Whitcomb—now Jan Phillips. But I deemed it wise to keep mum about Tea Dancing around the neighborhood guys, with whom I was spending more and more time the older I got. With the motel and Father's job at Speer Hardware, my parents were now too busy to chauffeur me around to visit my old pals on the other side of town, and in fact I was often busy at the motel myself. But this surface shift in domestic gravity coincided with that first major sea change in every school child's life, when he leaves behind his familiar friends from elementary grades and faces the uncertainty of the new, and the large, and the scarily unknown—junior high school. In Fort Smith, there were two junior highs, and many of my old buddies were bound for the other one. So for a period of time in these years, the neighborhood east of Waldron gradually became my primary turf.

Junior Smotherman never made much of Speer's and my somewhat heightened circumstances. Junior was perfectly happy to enjoy our air conditioning—to this day he remembers being welcome at our house even when Speer and I weren't around, and he would come over and stretch out on the living room floor and soak up the cool. He was a smart, easygoing kid who maintained a joking relationship with my mother, butchering the King's English to drive her crazy. But others in the neighborhood sometimes couldn't contain their resentment. One day when I said something that the Prescotts and Helmses took exception to, Jimmy Prescott started needling me: "Is your name *King Charles*, or just Charles?" The others joined in and it got pretty ugly, pretty pointed, and I was mad and didn't handle it well. *"King Charles! King Charles!"* I probably ended up stomping off while they laughed and jeered.

On other days we played together like the best of friends. The quarry was across the highway on the other side of Waldron, and all summer long we would swim in the deep quarry lake, which we called the strip pit. These are dangerous places, with treacherous ledges and sharp, underwater outcroppings that you could break your neck on if you dove in head first—local legend had it that several people had either died or become paralyzed after doing just that. For this reason, the entire quarry was cordoned off by a high chain link fence, topped by barbed wire. We would climb up and over it, and swim for hours. I even took my little brother there. That's where I learned to swim underwater. Without goggles you could still see 10 or 15 feet.

But I was never reckless, at least as I defined it. Even as a young boy I was an odds kind of guy: risk/reward, risk/reward. For example, I wouldn't dive off the cliffs head first, a reluctance that often elicited catcalls and dares from the usual suspects. I hated their taunts, but they couldn't make me cave to the pressure. What would be my reward—becoming a dead stud? And when we staged BB wars in the woods below the quarry, shooting at one another with our Daisy Red Ryder air rifles, I participated a few times. But always, and increasingly, there was this nagging thought: *The more I do this, the better the chance I'll get my eye shot out.* I was, as my parents always said, their grown-up little boy. I was too analytical to be a hot head.

□ □ □ □ □

THE MOTEL WAS a life laboratory for me. I started working there at age 10, handling repairs, cleaning bathrooms, checking in guests after school on weekdays. It was at the motel that I learned about managing money—I bought my first car at age 12 from the wages my parents paid me (and they *always* paid me). I also learned to talk to grown-ups one-on-one. Most kids don't get to do that, but you meet a lot of people working in a motel—some friendly, some crabby, some demanding, some weird as hell. Fielding their requests while maintaining control was a balancing act that helped me greatly later in life. And speaking of weird, it was at the motel where I was introduced, after a fashion, to sex.

To help us around the place, Father and Mother had hired a wonderful black woman named Earline McBeath, from Mississippi. Earline, whom Speer eloquently and accurately remembers as "a figure of order and grace and intelligence," was with us from the very beginning to the very end, when my parents finally sold the place. "Charles and I tried to talk Earline into making wine for us," recalls Junior Smotherman. Predictably, she would have none of it.

Earline's husband, Willie, used to drive her to work every morning, and when Speer was in junior high, Willie would take him to school. Willie McBeath was a powerful presence in my young life. He'd been in the war, on an aircraft carrier, and his foot had been nearly shot off. It was all but destroyed. He could get around, but he walked with a terrible limp, and with excruciating pain. For me, that mangled foot opened all kinds of windows into the way of the world back then. The government had done nothing whatsoever to help Willie. He'd had several operations that he had to pay for himself. Speer remembers Willie working at a dime store, in a job that didn't require him to be on his feet, during that period when Willie was driving Speer to school. After that, I think he worked at a drive-in theater. Earline and Willie sometimes stayed with Speer and me when our parents were out of town. They were very much a part of our family.

At the motel, weekends were the busiest times for soldier traffic—in the early days we were nearly always full on Friday, Saturday, and Sunday nights. Father generally ran the office on weekends, while Earline and Mother cleaned the rooms and made up the beds. I mowed the grass around the units and did repairs—fixing doors and screens, keeping the lawnmower in running condition, doing maintenance on the washer and dryer. When there was no grass to mow, I cleaned bathrooms; on a busy weekend, I might have to clean the bathrooms 15 or 20 times for our guests. Not only that, we had two septic tanks out back, and in the rainy season they would sometimes overflow. Guess who got to wade in and handle sewer system maintenance.

When you work in a motel, you can't help being confronted by some of the most basic facts of human nature—one being that these soldiers weren't just visiting their maiden aunts. Quite often when I was at the front desk, an eager young artillery sergeant would pop into the office with a beautiful girl on his arm. Maybe she was only seven or eight years older than I was, though she looked like she came from a different planet. I would check them in, give them the key, and they would go off into the night hand in hand.

What likely happened next was the subject of considerable curiosity between Junior Smotherman and me—we were probably 12 and 14 at the time. Most evenings after supper the two of us would get together on the front stoop of my house and talk until we were called in for the night. Sometimes Speer would join us. Occasionally we would climb the thick willow tree by Highway 22 and, unseen, watch the goings on—both at the motel and on the road. It was on one such evening that our curiosity got the best of us. From our vantage point in the willow tree, we could see dim light emanating from some of the guest rooms. Of course I knew who was in each one. One thing led to another, and soon the three of us—9-year-old Speer included—quietly descended the tree and, holding our collective breath, tiptoed around behind the guest room of greatest interest.

Each motel room had a big window fan to help fight the stifling Arkansas heat, and that night all the fans were running hard. We stood far back at first, squinting to see through the whirring blades; we detected motion, but couldn't make out more than that. We edged closer. Finally we were right outside the window, noses all but touching the screen. Through the stop-action strobing of the fan blades, the scene inside the room looked positively surreal—but then it would've been strange enough had we been standing right next to the couple in question. They were both naked, with the bedside lamp on low. He was on his back propped up by a pillow, and she was on her back too, sprawled partly over him looking at the ceiling, one leg splayed across both of his. And what he was doing was idly brushing her breasts and belly with a Gideon Bible. I swear to God. My family was Episcopalian, and I was even an acolyte in the church. I had never been so confused in my life.

□ □ □ □ □

ONE DAY IN 1955, my Grandfather Speer made a shocking, and courageous, decision. He had been president of Speer Hardware Company for four years, but the truth was, he didn't like the job. He didn't like managing people and didn't especially enjoy all the administrative duties that now filled his days. He was in his heart a *sportsman*—a hunter and fisherman, an outdoorsman, a man most at home on the lakes and streams and in the hunting woods, if no longer on the playing field. What he wanted to do, he announced, was to head up Speer Hardware's sporting goods department. And he was turning over the running of the overall company to a new president, his son, Ralph Speer Jr.

That must've been a horrible day at work for my father. Now there was no higher appeal—the buck, and Dad's luck, stopped with Uncle Ralph. The situation was even worse because things weren't going well at the motel. With the end of the Korean War in 1953, training at Camp Chaffee had steadily dwindled. My father had worked at Speer Hardware for close to eight years, and he was more vulnerable now than he'd ever been.

He had another big idea, though. Ever since the end of World War II, America had been on a building spree—subdivisions, shopping centers, new schools to accommodate all the babies made when hundreds of thousands of randy GIs had come marching home. This was an opportunity for Speer Hardware, Dad thought: Instead of continuing to focus solely on its core business of home hardware, the company should branch out into *builders' hardware*—residential and commercial hardware for doors, windows, cabinets, bathrooms, kitchens and the like. And Dad knew just the guy to run this exciting new division—himself.

"Go fuck yourself, Don"—that was basically Uncle Ralph's response. "You're going to be a salesman as long as you work here. So just goddam forget it."

My father tried running the idea by Ralph a few more times, but he remained a brick wall. So one day Dad came home and announced that we were going to start a builders' hardware business ourselves—he believed that much in this growing market, one that would lead, eventually, to the ubiquitous Home Depot chain. "We'll call it Morgan Supply Company," he said, breathlessly pitching to his dumbfounded family, "and we already have a location for it—our old house on 21st Street." It was true, zoning was lax in those days—our house already backed up to a cleaners. "We can fit out the living and dining room and kitchen and back porch with display shelving," Dad continued. "Later we can build a metal warehouse in the back yard." In his plan, Mother would become the bookkeeper for Morgan Supply, and Earline would run the motel—with Speer's and my help. Finally, this: Dad would quit Speer Hardware.

We probably stood speechless for a few moments while the enormity of this scheme sank in. In later years, I would come to realize that as a businessman, my father scored about a C-. Everything was reward with him—forget about the risk. But at least he was enthusiastic, and he did have vision. And unlike my Uncle Ralph, what he accomplished was totally of his own making. Uncle Ralph was probably a C- businessman himself, but for different reasons. He didn't seem to realize that the world was changing. His main competitor, Williams Hardware, had a builders' hardware division, but Ralph didn't see the point. His plan was to keep pushing the same old whips and wagon wheels that Speer Hardware had been selling for nearly 70 years. Eventually, he would use his wife's money to buy Williams Hardware. After which, he would congratulate himself for outdoing his father and his grandfather before him.

In our house, those were tense days, the mid-'50s. It seemed that everything was up in the air. Soon Father left for New York for an intensive course in the very specialized field of builders' hardware—the intricacies of building codes, how to spec jobs, all of that. While he was gone, I found myself retreating even more to my default pastime—cars and engines. For me, it was heaven having a humongous junkyard a block away. Out back, behind our house, sat the clunker of an automobile that I, age 12, had just bought—for $25—and with Ralph Ingram's help was attempting to rebuild. My yard was beginning to look like Ralph's. There was my Cushman Eagle motor scooter, which I planned to ride to school in the fall, when I started seventh grade. There too was my first motorcycle—homemade. I had bolted a lawnmower engine to a bicycle frame. Ralph and I attached it where the frame Vs right behind the seat, then linked the engine by double pulley to the bicycle wheel. I could reach behind me and run the throttle and the thing would get up to 20, 30 miles per hour.

From my earliest childhood, I always wanted to make machines do amazing things. One result of all this ambitious tinkering was that it captured the imagination of the neighborhood boys. "Charles' experiments made him a kind of leader in the neighborhood," Speer says. More and more, even the hostile kids would show up in our yard to watch me work—to see what wild idea I would come up with next. What I was doing was beyond them. They were like I had been one summer when we visited my mother's sister, Aunt Mary Olive, after she and her family had moved to Denver. My older cousin, Keith, was smarter than God, and one crystal clear Colorado night he and I lay out under the stars and he pointed to the sky. "You ever wondered what's beyond the stars?" he said. I was knocked out by the very thought. It was a concept I'd never even considered. Keith went on to get his Ph.D in Aeronautical Engineering. Then he became a bigwig engineer at General Dynamics, where he helped to create weapon systems he could never talk about.

I had decided, probably by the age of 12, that I might want to be an engineer too. But I wanted to work with cars. On those nights that Junior, Speer, and I sat in the willow tree watching the world pass by, we would play a game—as a car headed toward us, we had to guess its make and model from the headlights and the dark shape of the body behind them. I got 99 percent of them right. I had internalized cars, had absorbed them into my being. Whether I ended up driving them or engineering them, I intended to be ready when the time came.

That was a lesson my dad had impressed on me years before.

During the summer that I was 9 years old, before we owned the motel, I accompanied Father on one of his week-long business trips, calling on small general stores along his route. As if Father didn't have enough to worry about during these grueling trips, I was engaged in an ongoing sales campaign of my own. Whenever we were on a decent road, I would beg him to let me drive. "Please, Father. Just a little way. Please. *Please.*"

We weren't on good roads very often, though. As I've said, his territory was the worst of any salesman's at Speer Hardware—we drove up into the Boston Mountains, then swung southwest into Oklahoma in a wide, lazy, ultimately eastward-leaning loop, ending up in Mena, Arkansas, about two-thirds down the state near the Arkansas-Oklahoma line. But within that broad arc we traveled scores of narrow dirt and gravel roads to reach Father's customers—general store operators serving the little dirt farmers tucked here and there in the middle of nowhere. That was the way the world still worked in 1952. Most of these farmers, if they ran out of nails, or horseshoes, or if their plow broke, they couldn't just crank up their car and go to the store. Cars, especially reliable cars, were few and far between back there in the boondocks. Some farmers might've had a rickety old Model T or something, but nothing they could drive very far in. These people were still using horses and wagons to go fetch their supplies. And so the general stores were located off the beaten path, in the proximity of the farm communities. Sometimes the general store *was* the town.

Father and I were in his 1946 Plymouth, which might as well have been a rocket ship when we pulled up to these stores. It was like we had come from another galaxy, which in a way we had. Father would get out and glad-hand his customer a little bit, exchanging views about crops and the weather, and maybe I would get a Nu-Grape soda as a treat while I waited for Father to write up his order. Then we would head the Plymouth back up the perilous little roadway, tires crunching and slipping on the rocks. Pretty soon I would start in again. "*Please*, can I drive? Please, Dad. *Please?*"

I thought at first that I'd just worn him down. Because when we got to Mena, he said, "Son, I've got some paperwork to do before we get home. We've had a good week, took a lot of orders, and I'd like to get everything written up today. So I would like you to drive me home while I'm doing that."

Home was 80 miles north on narrow, curvy Highway 71. *Narrow* was the word that suddenly set my pulse to racing: Highway 71 was the main, and very *narrow*, north-south truck route on the west side of the state. It was a busy highway studded with *narrow* bridges, on which I was bound to meet big trucks that were *not narrow*. "Are you sure, Dad?" I said. "It's a long way home."

"Yes, son, I need you to drive. I've got a lot of work to do." He pulled over and got his order file out of the back seat, then went around to the front passenger side. I slid into the driver's seat. My hands on the steering wheel were higher than my head—I was maybe five-foot-two, if that. Father got one of his catalogs for me to sit on. Even then, my view of the road was through that half-moon between the horn and the top arc of the steering wheel. I could barely reach the pedals.

I gripped the wheel in the 10/2 position and eased the Plymouth onto the highway. It was already late afternoon, on a Friday, and a lot of people would be in a hurry to get home. There were long stretches of highway that dropped off steeply on the sides, no room for error. I edged to the right as far as possible when I saw the first truck coming at us, a white block seemingly as big as a house. I may have closed my eyes as it passed. "Father, it's really narrow here, and there's a lot of trucks. Maybe you—"

He didn't let me get the words out. "Son, I told you, I need you to drive. I have to get this work done."

I tried it again when I saw us coming down a long hill with a curve—and a *narrow* bridge—at the bottom. I just knew I was going to kill the both of us. By then I had driven maybe 25 miles, almost a third of the way. "Dad," I whined, "I'm really tired…."

He didn't even look up from his work. "Charles, I'm not finished yet. I need you to keep driving."

And so I did—white knuckled, wrung out, petrified, all the way home. The last hour was in the dark; Father even turned on the ceiling light so he could see his paperwork. When we pulled into our driveway, a welcoming lamp was on in the window. I stepped out on rubber legs, my knees nearly buckling. We gathered up our things and went into the house. When Father told Mother that I had driven home from Mena, she was livid. I had never seen her so angry at him—she was waving her arms and screaming. Mother suffered from narcolepsy, though she refused to admit it. She fell asleep in church, zonked out in the middle of conversations, nodded off at stoplights when she was driving. The idea of my driving 80 miles was no doubt particularly horrifying to her.

Father was totally calm. "I needed to get some work done, Betty," he explained. "So Charles drove us home."

Later, after I stopped shaking, I was proud of what I had done. A day or so later, Father said, "Son, let that be a lesson to you. Never ask for something unless you're sure you really want it. And if you *really* want it, prepare yourself to take it on."

2

THE BOY WHO MIGHT BE FORGOTTEN

1001010010110010100010010110010101110011

I HEARD THE coach screaming at me: "Morgan, *get up*! Quit your *faking*! *Get up like a man*!"

His voice sounded light-years away. I was flat on my back, my nose spewing blood, Coach Malone and Bill Booker standing over me like buzzards over road kill. Coach looked apoplectic, eyes and neck muscles bulging; Booker had a smirk on his face.

This was my first day of football try-outs—August 1955, seventh grade, Ramsey Junior High. Back in the neighborhood, we kids often played football in that big empty lot behind our house, and I'd tasted my share of gridiron glory. I was getting tall and could throw the ball over the heads of others; my longer arms also gave me an advantage at pass catching. I'd thought it would be fun to play football at school.

Clearly, I was wrong.

I was trying out for end or guard, but Coach Malone seemed to have it in for me already. He'd issued me a helmet without a face mask; these were traditionally given to the youngest players, the ones Coach thought were a waste of his time. Then he'd lined me up in down stance to try to block Bill Booker, the biggest and baddest of ninth-grade jocks. Just before the snap, Booker had eyed me across the line of scrimmage and said, "See this elbow? It's about to take you out." And it did. Nearly 60 years later, my nose still bears evidence of the reshaping that Bill Booker gave me that day.

This wasn't just my introduction to organized football; in a way it was my introduction to junior high itself. The fact that I'd been knocked on my ass by a jock upperclassman carried a certain symbolic weight, as I would soon discover. Very quickly I learned all I needed to know about junior high's social castes—jocks, socialites, and hoods; upperclassmen and underclassmen; cool kids and geeks—and my puny place in the pecking order. I can't recall if the thought actually crystallized in my head during those first days at Ramsey, but on some level I was certainly feeling it: *Engines are easier than people.*

I stayed with football, despite Coach Malone's disdain—despite my own awareness that I was a total bust as a jock. Once I start something, I have a hard time quitting it—even if it's patently absurd, not to mention crazy and dangerous, as this certainly was. I just didn't want to admit defeat. So every autumn afternoon for that year, as well as for the next, I suited up and hit the practice field, where I dropped passes, missed tackles, got knocked down, and ran an astounding number of punitive laps. My goal—my *hope*—was to make one of the B teams. I never did.

Looking back now on that period of my life, my overwhelming impression is this: For three years I was enrolled at Ramsey Junior High School, but in a sense I was never really there. I was a shadow figure, a peripheral presence, a kind of ghost. I felt that most of the other kids looked right through me, never seeing me at all. And I didn't know how to connect with them. The jocks, especially, were impossible. They ran in a pack—and so did the girls who adored them. None of my concerns seemed to mesh with anyone else's. I didn't care about clubs or cliques or campus kings and queens, and at the junior high level there weren't even math or science classes that piqued my interest. More and more, I found myself daydreaming about the neighborhood, about shooting the shit with Junior Smotherman, and especially about getting lost in my latest engine project—rebuilding the transmission of my '46 Ford.

Even though this car was only nine years old, it was a mess. I had bought it off a used car lot in downtown Fort Smith and driven it all the way home, illegally, in second gear—third gear didn't work. I put in new piston rings and thought everything would be fine. But it still ran rough. That's when I learned about timing lights, to calibrate the spark with the pistons.

While I had worked on many engines, I had never been inside a transmission. Lying on my back beneath the car, I'd tried to figure out the best way to remove the transmission so I could take it apart and make third gear work again. The car really needed to be up on jacks, but my risk/reward calculations made me cautious: What if while I was tugging on the transmission, the damn car were to fall and crush me?

Such were my secret musings as I sat in Civics class, or English, or History. I pondered the problem at my locker as I changed classes, amid the posturings of the football stars and their chattering cheerleaders. I carried it with me to ball practice after school, turning it over and over in my mind while I did my jumping jacks and ran my laps.

I can't recall where I was when the solution came to me. Probably in some class, pencil in hand. I began to see the Ford on an incline—on that slight hill behind our house. I saw concrete blocks chocking the wheels, keeping the car steady and still. I drew it out, the car and the ground a diagonal line rising from left to right, the Ford's front wheels firmly grounded at the top of the hill. Then I drew a 90-degree notch in the earth beneath the car, starting well left of the front wheels. That would be the trench I would dig for me to lie or kneel in while I wrestled down the transmission.

In the early fall, it was still light enough after supper for me to go out back and work. Marking the section of hill to be excavated, I set to with my shovel. Occasionally I would glance back toward the house to see my mother's face at the kitchen window. She was concerned about me. She wanted me to like school, to fit in with the other kids, to feel comfortable moving from this phase of my life to the wider world—instead of digging in even deeper.

□ □ □ □ □

WHEN I WAS in the eighth grade, Mother insisted that I take a typing class. "Everybody needs to learn to type," she said, and this wasn't a negotiation. It was humiliating—I was the only boy in the class. It was 1956 and I hadn't a clue what knowing how to type would ever do for me. I wasn't going to be a secretary. I wasn't going to be a journalist.

But Mother was just getting started. I was apparently her new pet project, the project *she* daydreamed about while keeping the books for Morgan Supply Company.

I worked for Morgan Supply on weekends and in the summers. For me, builders' hardware was a better fit than the motel. I felt totally at home there, and with good cause. Behind the yards of new shelving were the walls of my old house, our family's first, where I had lived between the ages of 4 and 10. That's a long time in a kid's life. Now, even though I might be stocking those shelves with doorknobs, faucets, window locks, and cabinet pulls, I worked in rooms surrounded by memories. Other times, Dad might send me outside to fix something on the delivery truck—even more like home. He also wanted me to help him spec jobs, which entailed learning the ins and outs of hollow metal fabrication—you could buy these sticks of steel and cut them into frames for doors and windows, which would then be glazed. Soon I was designing and building door and window frames for schools and small office buildings. It was precise work—the measuring, the cutting, the fitting—with the added engineering challenge of figuring out how few frames you could use to adequately cover a given space. I even designed and made my own cutting saw.

The only job I didn't enjoy was telephoning business people whom I didn't know and talking with them about an order. I dreaded those calls and found myself procrastinating. I wondered if Mother noticed that.

In the summer that I was 14, between eighth and ninth grades, my two big personal projects were selling my car and upgrading my motorcycle. The old Ford had taught me all it could, so I gladly parted with it; there was always another car on the horizon. I also sold my Cushman Eagle scooter and bought a brand new Mustang motorcycle. This I planned to ride to school for the next two years, until I could get my driver's license and legally drive a car.

The Mustang became my newest obsession. I spent untold hours hopping it up by putting a great big carburetor on it and, later, rigging the bike to run on alcohol.

Once I had everything ready, I wanted to give it a time trial. Since my little brother weighed some 30 pounds less than I did, I roped Speer in for the trial run. On the day of the test, the bike didn't run smoothly because it didn't much like alcohol. But, boy, was it fast. Speer was flying along at 80 miles an hour. I *loved* this about engines: that with a little strategic tweaking—new camshaft, bigger carburetor, larger pistons—I could alter a machine's performance. To me, at my young age, the rush of that experience held the promise of a fulfilling life.

I should interject here that my parents—*our* parents—weren't like the parents of anyone we knew. Did my father get upset when I drove the '46 Ford home from the used-car lot at age 12? No, he didn't. Did Mother wring her hands when I sent her baby boy careening down the highway at 80 miles an hour on a motorcycle without a helmet? No, she didn't. Did they forbid us to swim in the strip pit even after a boy we knew actually did break his neck diving in? They absolutely did not. There was something about our parents that was impervious to overprotectiveness.

"Father didn't seem to believe in death," says Speer. "It was irrelevant to him. He didn't worry about whether we had guns or motorcycles or cars or accidents."

The truth is, he and Mother trusted us. They trusted our judgment. They were willing to let us make, and learn from, our own mistakes—even if those mistakes resulted in broken bones. This same attitude carried over into the family business. They told us everything, both good and bad. I can't recall a time when I wasn't a full partner in the business, be it the motel or the builders' hardware. On any big decision, they always asked my opinion. And because of the way they raised us, I had come to trust my own judgment on pretty much everything.

So I was a bit taken aback when, during the last weeks of my ninth grade year, Mother sat me down and suggested I channel my life in a new direction. She said that if I ever wanted to get into a good college, I needed to show that I was well rounded. "It's just logic, son," she told me. "You need to have some things on your resume other than that you took apart an engine and put it back together." What this boiled down to was that, next year in high school, I should "join some clubs."

She had been watching closely, of course. And she didn't have to look far afield to see that something was askew. Right there in our little motel house were prime examples of the two poles of adolescent development: my brother, Speer, outgoing, popular with girls, easy in groups—he was already on the path that would lead him to high school elective office; and at the other extreme, there was me—

uncomfortable with the opposite sex, petrified at the thought of public speaking, a geek whose best friend—now that age and different schools had increasingly separated me from Junior Smotherman—was probably a socket wrench.

Mother empathized. Even though she'd been popular as a girl, she too had feared expressing herself in public. So *now* she worried: There were worse hurts than broken bones.

□ □ □ □ □

IN 10TH GRADE, at Fort Smith High School, I joined the Science Club, as well as the better of the two high school fraternities—Delta Sigma. I say "high school fraternities," but not only were these organizations not sponsored by the school, we weren't allowed to conduct any fraternity functions on school property. Even so, the fraternities—and sororities—cast a large shadow on official high school life. In any *Bruin* yearbook from Fort Smith High, you'll see people writing the usual "don't-ever-change" and "stay-as-sweet-as-you-are" sentiments, but they'll also include the Greek letters of their extracurricular affiliation—a prestigious addition. My fraternity, Delta Sig, was the choice of "clean young guys," as a new frat brother of mine put it. The other—Kappa Alpha Phi—was for "the hoods." Some hoods, joining a fraternity.

Science Club was my initial foray into the "well-roundedness" that I would eventually document on my college application. Not wanting to become too well rounded too fast, I decided to go slow and maybe add a club a year. Joining Science Club first was pretty much a "birds-of-a-feather" decision. Even though I never cared a whit for Science Fair—the club's main yearly event—at least I got to know my fellow geeks. There's something to be said for looking around and realizing you're not alone in the world.

But of my two sudden affiliations, it was Delta Sig that most changed my life. Not only did it provide me a framework for belonging, it gave me back, at age 15, a part of myself that had nearly gone missing. I want to be very careful how I say this: For the past five years I had largely immersed myself in the "other-side-of-Waldron" part of my life, and I had loved it, and profited from it, in many, many ways. I will never forget summer evenings sitting in the willow tree watching cars with Junior Smotherman. And Ralph Ingram will never cease to be my mechanical hero. But

Delta Sigma attracted boys from the more prominent, more established families in town, and I, being one-half Speer, had no trouble getting invited to join. Now I was becoming reacquainted with boys whose birthday parties I had attended during elementary school, when my family lived on 21ˢᵗ Street. Many of them had gone to the other junior high in town, and we had almost lost touch. Now we picked up where we'd left off.

It was a much more social life than I was used to, and I found that I liked it. Suddenly I was part of a crowd of cool kids. Curtis Hawkins, the son of a very wealthy surgeon, was a fraternity brother. Bob Taylor was another pal; also Jim Barton. But by far my closest friend was a boy named James Hampton Rutledge, whom I called "Jimbo," and then, eventually, just "Bo." Besides the fraternity, Bo and I had geekdom in common. Bo was in many of my classes on the pre-college engineering track—chemistry, science, and advanced math—and so he spoke my language. He also loved cars, though he wasn't as much into the workings of engines as I was. In high school, I owned a couple of cars—a 1951 Studebaker, and a strange little French car, a Renault Dauphine. Whenever Bo would come over to my house, he would usually stand around and talk while I mumbled back from under a car hood. I don't really like to talk when I'm concentrating on mechanics.

The fraternity was a strong antidote to the jock culture, which—it's still high school—was obnoxiously pervasive. But I had finally walked away from all that. Now I had my fraternity brothers to run with, and we had some crazy times. We would have our meetings at someone's house, then all go out and drive around town, or go somewhere and have a party.

One night I found myself in a car driven by a boy named Sammy Phillips. Sammy requires a bit of background. I had known him for years. He was from a well-to-do Fort Smith family and knew many of the boys in Delta Sig, but he wasn't always in town because his parents had shipped him off to military school when he was maybe 12. He was a wild child, no doubt about it. Sammy's dad owned a very successful insurance agency, and they had a big house with woods and a two-acre lake within bicycle distance from our motel. So during junior high summers, Sammy was someone from my other world whom I had stayed in touch with. I would ride my bike over to his place and we would spend the day fishing or just messing around. The family also had a party house on the property—a separate cottage with tables and chairs and a well-stocked refrigerator. Once we all reached high school, this party house made Sammy especially popular. So whenever he was in town, he was kind of an honorary fraternity member.

But you really had to be careful around Sammy—he hadn't been sent to military school for nothing. Once, during junior high, when he and Bob Taylor and I were over at his place tromping through the woods, we stopped for a minute to rest. I sat down and leaned against a tree, about eight feet from Sammy. Sammy did not sit down. Nearly vibrating with nervous energy, he pulled out a Bowie knife and started horsing around with it—acting like he was going to throw it at us. "Damn it, Sammy, put that thing away," I said. Sammy Phillips with a Bowie knife was a frightening concept.

"I'm an expert with this knife," he said, a wild gleam in his eye. "I can throw it with pinpoint accuracy." I was just about to say something else when he spun around and hurled the knife at me. *Bam!* It stuck in the tree about an inch from my head. I'm sure I went ballistic, cursing Sammy while he cackled maniacally.

He was equally berserk in cars, and I tried never to ride with him. But one night we'd had a fraternity meeting at the house of a boy named Marshall Yantis, and Sammy was there. Not only was he there, he was now 16, and he was driving his dad's new 1957 Ford Fairlane. That's the way with insurance people—they don't want their clients to think they're getting too rich off of them, which is why you seldom see them driving fancy cars like Cadillacs or Lincolns. So after the meeting, Sammy wanted to take us for a ride, and then we could all go over to his party house. I knew better, but went anyway. This is one of the flip sides of fraternity solidarity: peer pressure. And it comes at a dangerous time in a boy's life—when he's starting to drink, starting to drive, and is out with other fledglings in the dark of night.

There were six of us jammed into Sammy's car, headed for his place. But first, Sammy had to show us how quick this Ford Fairlane was. We were *wailing* down a hill, way too fast for comfort, and I started screaming at Sammy from the back seat—"Sammy, goddammit, slow down! *Slow down!*" I can still hear his laugh, the aural definition of "out of control." At the bottom of this hill was an S turn, and right in the middle of that S was a telephone pole. As Sammy approached the turn, we were all trying to hold on—to the dash, to the ceiling, to the terror handles above the rear doors. Sammy sped into the turn much too fast to negotiate the S without rolling. In fact, he couldn't make the turn at all—we kept going straight, flying into the field with the telephone pole, which we missed by inches. In seconds, it was all over. Then we were just six high school boys and a new Ford sitting in an Arkansas field with weeds up to the door handles. Miraculously, nobody was hurt. The car wasn't even seriously damaged. As Sammy's cackle rose into the night, I swore I would never again ride in a car with him—a vow I unfortunately wouldn't keep. But at least it would be years.

The coda to that tale is that today, at age 69, Sammy—a much-decorated Vietnam war helicopter pilot who's now married to my old cotillion dance partner, Jan Whitcomb—contends that he purposely drove into that field "to scare you guys." That's his story, and, being Sammy, he won't budge from it. But I don't believe it for a second.

☐ ☐ ☐ ☐ ☐

DESPITE MY INITIAL euphoria over fraternity membership, I soon began to see the gradations and demarcations present in all groups. Take the country club, for example. Many of my new fraternity friends' parents belonged to Fort Smith's Hardscrabble Country Club, and so my friends had swimming and tennis and golf privileges there. But Bo Rutledge's parents weren't members, and neither were mine. I don't actually recall anything about Bo's situation—his dad, a feisty civil engineer, typically went his own way and didn't like being beholden to others; he couldn't even tolerate working for anyone else, so clearly he wasn't temperamentally suited to prostrating himself before some hoity-toity country club screening committee.

It was different in my house. I remember country club membership being a matter of considerable discussion during my high school years. It wasn't that important to me—I could swim at the club anyway, as a guest of my well-heeled friends. Who it really mattered to was my father. Membership was expensive, of course, but Mother and Father thought it would be a worthwhile investment for all of us—for greasing the wheels of commerce for Morgan Supply Company, and for Speer's and my social development. Despite the high cost of club membership, our parents were prepared to come up with the money.

The problem, once again, was Uncle Ralph. A bigwig at the country club, Uncle Ralph was dead set against Don Morgan being a member, and so he blackballed our family's application. Mother was furious at her brother for blocking the rest of us just because he despised Father.

So within the larger Delta Sigma fraternity there were sub-fraternities—the ones who belonged to the country club and the ones who didn't; those who worked after school, like me, and those who didn't, like most of the rest; and then there was the girlfriend divide—those who had steady girlfriends and those who didn't. Curtis Hawkins dated the same girl all through high school; Bo went with a couple of girls, including, in senior year, the daughter of the Episcopalian rector, Eleanor Shoemaker, with whom he was madly in love.

In some ways, this was the hardest dividing line of all for me. I had crushes on some of the most popular girls in school, but I knew they wouldn't go out with me in a million years. It was an era before geeks were cool, and I could live with that, at least most of the time. You just come to accept your place, which brings its own peace of mind.

I did occasionally spend time with a girl in my college-track classes—Davida Moore was her name, and I considered her a kind of soul mate. We liked to drink whiskey together and laugh about the absurdity of high school, all its ridiculous social pressures. She thought I was funny and admired my smile, which made me smile even more. The great thing about my time with Davida was that we never tried to impress each other. I once picked her up for a date in a car with the whole insides stripped out, except for the driver's seat; she laughed and crawled in the back, and off we went. Another time—this was in summer—we were out together, walking, and it started pouring down rain. We just kept walking, and the wetter we got, the harder we laughed. Finally, she jumped under a downspout and got completely drenched; it was like she was standing under a waterfall. So I ducked under a downspout, too. In high school, it was relaxing—and very, very rare—to be with someone with whom you could just be your weird self.

As 10th grade came to a close and everyone was signing their friends' 1959 *Bruin*, I flipped through the pages of mine. There was my cousin Margaret, graduating as Miss Everything—by her name was a list of credits a mile long: Columbians; Sock and Buskin; Bruin Hall of Fame; Junior and Student Councils; Senior Council President; Spanish National Honor Society; Girls State. I didn't even know what some of those credentials meant. Jane Dills was as decorated as Margaret: Junior-Senior Student Councils; Bruin Hall of Fame; Columbians, president; Girls State; Office; National Honor Society; Spanish National Honor Society.

How had they had the *time*? I didn't think of myself as anti-social; I was just preoccupied. As I thumbed through the book looking for my picture in Science Club, I accidentally landed on the pages devoted to football. God, there were a lot of them—all those grainy Friday night action photos, the quarterback dropping back, the spiraling ball in mid-air, the star receiver about to reel it in. And then, from the upper left-hand corner, a familiar face diverted my attention. It was Bill Booker, his dark, stark flattop evoking a helmet itself, his tiny eyes beady beneath lowered brows. But it was his smile that gave me the creeps. Maybe this was his most engaging Senior Smile, but to me it still looked like a smirk.

□ □ □ □ □

I WORKED AT Morgan Supply during my high school summers, and so did Speer. I was building and installing windows and doors, and Speer was the muscle. We would go out on jobs together in the bob truck, our cube-shaped cargo truck with a sliding garage-type door, and Speer would climb up in the back and wrestle down the parts for me to put together. Then he would help me with the assembly.

One summer—I can't recall exactly which one—we had a hollow metal job in Booneville, a little town about 40 miles southeast of Fort Smith. After we'd built and installed the doors and windows, the customer had improperly primed the metal, and now the paint was peeling off. Father sent Speer and me out to investigate.

I was now 16, able to drive, and since we weren't delivering anything, we took my current automobile, a Renault Dauphine. This wasn't a car you saw every day on the roads of Arkansas. It was small and sleek in a stodgy sort of way, a rear-engine sedan with four doors and a sporty scoop on the side. The Renault reflected my present automotive leanings, toward the kinds of fast and powerful European sports cars you might see in Grand Prix races. This wasn't that, but at least it was European. It also had a sun roof, which was fun. I had enjoyed tinkering with the Renault's engine and transmission system, and on some level I was now thinking I might want to do more than just engineer fast cars—I might also want to drive them. To that end, I had bought and installed seat belts in the Renault. Nobody but auto racers used seat belts back then. Most people who saw the belts didn't even know what they were for.

Late that afternoon, after Speer and I had finished our business in Booneville, we were headed back to Fort Smith when we came up behind an old red pickup poking along at about 40 miles an hour. The road was a winding two-lane, so I began looking for an opportunity to pass. When the moment came, I pulled out into the passing lane, and as we got even with the truck, the driver—a Bubba if I've ever seen one, complete with beer in hand—looked over and saw this strange little foreign job trying to overtake him. He laughed and pointed, and immediately sped up. As I dropped back behind him, I could hear, through my open sun roof, Bubba and the Yahoo riding shotgun hooting like they'd just run over somebody's cat.

A few minutes later, I tried again—out in the passing lane, up beside the red truck, Bubba guffawing as he floored the accelerator. Once more I dropped back behind him—which was Bubba's cue to slow down again to 40 mph.

This went on for 10 miles, maybe more. I was boiling. These guys were cretins—I could see them laughing in the cab ahead. Yahoo would wheel around and look at us through the back window, then say something to Bubba, and the two of them would howl like hyenas. Occasionally Yahoo would eject an empty beer can from his passenger-side window.

I knew this highway well, and coming up in about two miles was a 90-degree left curve which then turned into a long straightaway. It was a gamble, but I was angry enough to try it—to shoot by them in the curve, then leave them on the straightaway. The key was to get up speed. Dropping back farther behind them, I waited till I had some room and then gunned it, moving into the passing lane just as we both entered the curve. Fortunately, there was no car coming; unfortunately, Bubba got pissed that I was about to get by him, and he swerved left and ran me off the road, where I hit some loose gravel and started spinning; then the Renault flipped up and over and we landed roof first on the shoulder, Speer and I dangling upside down from our seat belts. Thank God for my aversion to risk. Well, at least I installed the seat belts.

We were shocked, but not hurt. Bubba and Yahoo turned the truck around and came back to see if we were alive. When they saw we were okay, they had a big belly laugh, popped another couple of brews, and drove off.

It was the first time I'd ever flipped a car, though it wouldn't be the last. The Renault was also my first experience with automotive body work. Before the summer was out, I bought a new top and taught myself to weld it on. And I drove the new, improved Renault to school for the start of 11th grade.

□ □ □ □ □

IN JUNIOR YEAR, I continued my march toward well-roundedness by joining the German Club. My thinking was that German, much more than Spanish or French, would be a very useful language when I became an engineer.

By this time I had traveled with friends to the automobile races in Stuttgart, Arkansas, down in the Delta. They were SCCA races, Sports Car Club of America, featuring cars like MGBs and Austin-Healeys on a three-mile airport circuit with 2,800 feet of straightaway. Very exciting stuff. Now my big goal was to go to the 12-hour endurance race in Sebring, Florida—America's version of the yearly 24-hour race in Le Mans, France. In 1959, Sebring had hosted the Formula One United States Grand Prix, which had attracted the absolute top drivers in the world—England's Stirling Moss, New Zealand's Jack Brabham and Bruce McLaren, the U.S.'s Phil Hill, Germany's Wolfgang von Trips. You could have your movie stars—these guys were my high school heroes. And the cars they drove—Ferraris, Porsches, Coopers, Lotuses—gave me goose bumps with their high-speed whine.

Eleventh grade is hard to remember, there being nobody special to remember it by. Mainly what I remember is building my boat. Otherwise, I took advanced math and science, dated rarely, attended German and Science Club meetings, and hung out with my Delta Sig brothers. I played some bridge, drank Jim Beam and Coke—Bo Rutledge, who abstained in high school, once had to drive me home and put me to bed—and dreamed about my future. When I wasn't with my frat brothers, I worried a little about how my classmates might view me. I don't know why I worried about that. Looked at logically—which is how I always tried to approach things—it didn't make sense. I was in clubs. I was a *fraternity* man. I had a lot of popular and well-connected friends, both male and female. I was included in many events at the country club, membership or not. I wasn't *un*popular. I was even liked.

But I also knew that my very formidable focus was on subjects alien to most of my classmates, and I couldn't help that. It was just who I was. In my mind that put me on the fringe, out in the no man's land beyond the reliable sweep of the social radar. It made me wonder, when I encountered the popular girls and guys in the halls between classes, just what they thought when they saw me. What I knew, on some level, was this: If someone in the in-crowd was having a party, I was the boy they just might forget to invite.

My boat project, highlight of my junior year, came about as a result of water skiing. Our family had some dear friends, the Altmans, who had once lived in Fort Smith but had moved, when I was probably starting third grade, to Spiro, Oklahoma, about 20 miles away. Marvin Altman was the administrator of Sparks Hospital, the region's most important medical facility; Marvin's wife, Betsy, was the daughter of a very prominent doctor, had family money, and was herself on the board at Sparks; it was thanks to Betsy that Marvin had landed this very plum job. Marvin and Betsy had three children—two daughters, Gail and Sally, and a son, Mike. As Marvin and Betsy had been my parents' closest friends, so Mike—until they moved away—had been mine. We'd gone to the same elementary school, attended the same church, and even lived near each other back when we were in the 21st Street house. And even after the Altmans traded their nice city life in Fort Smith for a 600-acre ranch in Oklahoma, I would occasionally go visit Mike after school on Friday, catching a ride with Marvin, who still commuted to Fort Smith for work. Then on Sunday my parents would come pick me up. They would stay for hamburgers at the ranch before we all headed back home to Fort Smith.

The ranch in Spiro was an amazing place. Mike had horses, a well-stocked fishing lake, and was near the river so we could go duck hunting. The problem with that was that I *hated* duck hunting. The one time I went with Mike, he got me up in the dark of night and we trudged out to the river and froze our asses off; I told him, *Never again*. But what I did like, and Mike also was equipped for this, was water skiing. Not far from the Altman ranch was Tenkiller Lake, a 20-square-mile reservoir created by damming the Illinois River. It was one of the best skiing lakes in the world, and now, by the time we were in high school, Mike had his own ski boat and a trailer to pull it on. His was a magical world, and several of us guys—Bo Rutledge had also been a friend of Mike's in elementary school—would pile into my car and we would light out to Spiro on the weekends. There we would hook up the boat and head for Tenkiller, where we would ski all day long. Bo reminds me that one day even my father showed up, wanting to see what all the fuss was about. Dad hadn't brought a swim suit, so he took off his shoes and shirt and rolled up his pants legs, and we taught him to water ski.

Soon I yearned for my own ski boat. They were very expensive, however, and we couldn't afford one. Even the trailer would've been a stretch. So I came up with this crazy idea to build a flat-bottom hydroplane powerful enough to pull a skier behind it. My plan was to take it to the strip pit and we could run up and down the strip pit on water skis.

I'd never built a boat, so I got hold of a *Popular Mechanics* magazine and found an advertisement in it: "Build a Hydroplane in Your Garage!" I ordered the plans, but I didn't have a garage, just a shed out behind the motel house. The problem with the shed was that it was a little small. Also, it was winter and not very pleasant spending long hours out there. So I came up with another idea—to build it in one of the motel rooms. The hard fact was that the motel business had slowed to a crawl by then. Earline was renting some rooms, but not all that many. And so my parents reluctantly allowed me to take over one of the rooms for a while.

I'm happiest when I have a project. More than that, when I'm *not* designing something, I feel a little insecure, like I've misplaced some vital part of myself. In that sense, the boat kept me afloat that year. I wouldn't go to parties, I wouldn't play golf with Dad even after he begged me to, "so we can do something together." Golf bored me. Parties bored me. What *didn't* bore me was my boat. So whenever I wasn't working at Morgan Supply, I would dash home from school and go right to my motel laboratory, where I had set up saw horses and a big board to lay everything out on. I built the boat out of four-by-eight-foot pieces of quarter-inch marine plywood, glued together and curved up slightly in the front. At the back was a transom where I planned to put a 15-horsepower motor. I sealed the whole thing with epoxy.

By the time school was out, the boat was ready. I bought an old pickup truck to haul it in, and that's how Speer and I transported it to the strip pit. With the motor it weighed about 200 pounds, so it was a little tough hoisting it over the fence. But after that, it was a breeze. The driver drove it kneeling down—I'd installed pads for that—and he guided the boat by steering the outboard behind him. It would pull a medium-size skier at about 20 miles per hour, which was plenty fast for the strip pit.

□ □ □ □ □

BY THE SUMMER before 12th grade, I had developed a core confidence, at least in regard to what I thought and what I believed and what I could do. Surely, part of this personal confidence came from the way my parents treated me, both at home and at Morgan Supply, where I had become a key member of the operation.

Father was now a distributor for Andersen Windows, the largest window and door manufacturer in North America. While installing the windows on some job, I had made a suggestion for a change in the way the windows were made, to provide more flexibility in the installation. I can't even recall the specific idea, but I know it was simple—and, to me, just a matter of logic. Father was very impressed.

But I wasn't prepared for what happened next. One day in the late summer of 1960 he told me he wanted me to take the bob truck and, with my brother, Speer, drive it to Andersen Windows, where we were to pick up a new load of windows. Andersen Windows was in Philadelphia, Pennsylvania. "And I've arranged for you to meet with the Andersen engineers to explain your idea. After that, I've booked you boys into a hotel in New York for a couple of nights and reserved Broadway tickets for you."

Was this a joke? I was 17, my brother 14. Speer wasn't even old enough to drive without an adult in the vehicle. But Dad was serious. He loved New York, especially Broadway plays, and he wanted us to have that mind-expanding experience, too. It was another example of his instinct for empowerment, like when he'd made me drive him home from Mena when I was 9. He always got you to do more than you thought you could.

And so we set out, armed with cash, a gas card, and the stamina of youth, along with a very good map. The interstate highway system had been started by then, but progress was spotty. So on mostly two-lane highways we drove straight through from Fort Smith to Philadelphia, some 1,300 miles, arriving at Andersen Windows in the gray of an early morning. We were expected. The Andersen people filled our truck with new supplies, and then invited us into their boardroom, where five or six executives, including their top engineers, quizzed me about my idea—which to them apparently seemed just short of miraculous. "You're one smart son of a bitch," one of the execs said, clapping me on the back. "We just may have to hire you." After which, they took Speer and me on a guided tour of their manufacturing plant.

Then, leaving the bob truck inside the secure gates of Andersen Windows, we were driven to the depot where we boarded the train for New York's Penn Station. We'd hardly slept for a day and a half, and even the stamina of youth has its limits. But when we arrived at our hotel off Times Square, we were informed that our room wouldn't be ready for nearly three hours more. So we sucked it up, stowed our bags, and started walking around midtown Manhattan. Finally, thankfully, we got into the room and slept for four or five hours. Then we had to get showered and dressed to go see "Bye Bye Birdie" at the Martin Beck Theater, a musical about the Army draft of a teen heartthrob, based on Elvis Presley, and the effect on his heartbroken fans.

It was a perfect show for two boys from Fort Smith. After all, the real Elvis had been stationed at Camp Chaffee in 1958, and that's where he'd received his famous first Army haircut. The photo of a shorn Elvis, his iconic ducktails vulnerable after all, was published in newspapers and magazines around the world, to the dismay of his legions of fans. Girls actually wept at the loss of his hair. It would've been great if Elvis could've been a customer of The Chase Motel, but he was at Chaffee only three days before he shipped out to Texas for basic training.

After another 36 hours in New York, Speer and I shipped out, too. We caught the train back to Philadelphia, cranked up the bob truck, and hightailed it back to Fort Smith. It had been a great adventure, but we were glad to be home. And like after that drive from Mena when I was 9, once the adrenalin of this New York/Philly excursion had subsided, I felt incredibly proud of what we had done. None of my fraternity pals, even the most worldly ones, had experienced anything even remotely comparable to that trip, and indeed I did feel empowered by it—by the responsibility of driving Father's truck halfway across America; by the respect accorded me at Andersen Windows; by having taken care of my little brother in a city the size of New York; and by the faith Dad showed in me by entrusting me with the entire mission.

I started my senior year strong, feeling good about myself. I added the third leg of my incipient well-roundedness by joining Mu Alpha Theta, the mathematics society, and I also made a strategic upgrade to my Science Club affiliation by accepting the club vice-presidency. Appearing well rounded was a project, like any other, and I was determined to see it through to successful completion.

I also began lobbying my parents for a particular graduation present. Though I'd owned four or five cars over the past six years, not one of them had been new—an understatement if ever I'd heard one. But now, in less than a year, I would be heading off to college, ironically to Uncle Ralph's alma mater, The University of the South at Sewanee—a gentleman's school of the liberal arts, as Mother repeatedly pointed out. There I would expand my world and meet boys from all over the country. But to me, the selling point of Sewanee was that it had a connection to Georgia Tech, so I could get a liberal arts education *and* an engineering degree. In any case, a brand new automobile would not only be a nice acknowledgment of my hard work and success at Fort Smith High, it would also be the *only* proper means for transporting me into this next crucial phase of life.

I was working it hard. The car I wanted was an Austin-Healey Sprite. In the past year, I had become obsessed with English sports cars—Jaguars, Aston-Martins, Healeys, MGs, Morgans. All of them were expensive, but I thought the Sprite, being a smaller roadster, was probably doable. And I could race it! Mother and Father seemed to be listening.

So the year was starting out very well indeed.

□ □ □ □ □

THEN SOMETHING TERRIBLE happened—I received an honor. Every month, the Fort Smith Lions Club chose a promising high school student to be its Student of the Month. Someone from the church had probably nominated me, and when the Lions Club selection committee had looked into my record, what had they found? *A well-rounded boy.*

The drill, as outlined in the letter they sent me, was that the Student of the Month would attend one of the weekly Lions Club luncheon meetings, during which he or she would be presented with a certificate attesting to the honor being bestowed. And then the honoree would give a speech to the assembled members.

I dropped the letter on the floor. I was sick to my stomach. I could hardly breathe. It was my worst fear realized, my deepest insecurity laid bare. Suddenly all self-confidence, all faith in my mechanical genius, vanished into thin air. Could I turn this down? Was there a graceful way to sidestep this accolade?

There was not. Mother and Father made that clear. Proud of me, they began telephoning their friends to announce my selection. And I retreated to my room and stared at the ceiling.

The good news was that I had a few weeks; that was also the bad news. I had plenty of time to stew, to worry, to fret, to dread. Mother kept a close eye on me during that interminable anguish. She watched me mope around, look off into space, push back my supper and retreat to my room.

Finally, I summoned the courage to start writing down some thoughts. At first they seemed not bad, but the more I pored over them, the more inane they became. I tried again, and again, and again. Then one day I looked up and all that blessed, cursed time had suddenly drained away. In mere days I would be standing before 100 of the most prominent business leaders in the city—people who knew my father and mother, who knew my *uncle*, who knew my entire extended family. Some of these businesspeople had children my age, my classmates even, and when they returned to their homes that evening after the Lions Club luncheon they would tell their families about their day, and about me, and how well—or not—I had represented myself before the pillars of the community.

I was sick, sick, sick.

On the appointed day, I put on my dark suit and tie and went to school. The morning was a blur. Then it was time to sign out and drive downtown to the meeting. I thought of just keeping going, over the bridge into Oklahoma, maybe on across the Plains and over the Rockies until I reached the Pacific Ocean. But no. Instead, I pulled my car into the parking place and got out, patting my heart to check the note cards in my inside pocket. Then I took a deep breath and walked into the room.

At first, the atmosphere felt warm and friendly, reassuringly cordial. Men I knew waved from across the room, or, if they could, stopped by the head table to shake my hand. Lunch was served. I pushed my food around and tried to pay attention to my host, the man who would soon present my honor. I sipped iced tea and nodded as he told me all sorts of things I hardly heard.

Then he picked up his spoon and tapped his glass. It was time. He stood and talked about the fine young people in our community, about leadership, about exemplary character, about the importance of well-roundedness. Then he spoke my name and summoned me to stand with him at the lectern.

The room burst into applause as he presented my certificate as Student of the Month. We shook hands and held the pose as a photographer captured the moment. Then he sat down and I took my note cards from my pocket and placed them on the lectern. I faced the audience.

In the room there was a settling into silence. Someone cleared his throat; another coughed. I surveyed the crowd, glanced at my first note card, then looked back at the waiting faces. I opened my mouth to speak.

Nothing came out. I was moving my mouth like a fish out of water. I looked down again, then glanced at the man who'd presented me. I saw his stricken face. Once more I eyed the crowd, these civic leaders, and felt their growing alarm. I tried again to speak, and this time I did get out a few halting words, but *eloquent* and *coherent* weren't among them. Very soon I scrapped the rest of my speech and sat down to a smattering of applause. I couldn't look beyond my plate. I was mortified, and everyone in the room was mortified for me.

3

THE
MATHEMATICS
OF CHANGE

100101001011001010001001011001010110011

THE GREYHOUND BUS was cruising along south of Nashville on old U.S. 41, through towns called Smyrna and Murfreesboro, Beechgrove and Manchester—alien country. Bo was napping, head against the window, but I was too keyed up to sleep. I watched the road and took note of the signs to unfamiliar places out there in this new unknown: Tullahoma, Lynchburg, Cumberland Heights. Tennessee didn't even *sound* like Arkansas. We'd spent a couple of days in Nashville with relatives of Bo's; gracious people, beautiful house, a last connection to home before we landed at Sewanee and whatever waited for us there. How would we know where to go? How would we find our way? Who would be there when we did?

I thought of my sporty white Austin-Healey Sprite just sitting out behind The Chase Motel in Fort Smith. What a waste. I had loved driving it all summer long. It made me feel special. But it's just as well that we weren't allowed a car at Sewanee freshman year; my steamer trunk was stored somewhere below us in the Greyhound's cargo hold, and I sure couldn't have gotten that in the Healey, much less Bo's trunk too. You bring a lot of baggage to college—some of us more than others.

After that horrible day at the Lions Club luncheon, I couldn't sleep for a month. I was so humiliated that I didn't even tell Bo what had happened. But people *knew*, I was sure of that. I felt like I could see it in the eyes of classmates all through senior year. That Lions Club event really set me back.

In time, the Greyhound left Highway 41 and continued on a smaller, very mountainous road. A sign said Monteagle, and I held my breath and tried not to look at the precipitous drop-off just beyond the window. I exhaled when we arrived on the campus of The University of the South. It was a Sunday afternoon in August and the place looked empty, desolate, not so much unwelcoming as indifferent, which amounts to the same thing. Finally the bus chugged to a stop before a tiny building that appeared to be no more than an uninhabited waiting room with a public john. I heard the Greyhound door whoosh open and nudged Bo. "We're here," I said, and we gathered our things and went outside, where the driver was opening the bus's belly so we could retrieve our trunks.

We pulled them out and plopped them down in the deserted parking lot, then looked around trying to get our bearings. The tiny building turned out to be the Student Union, which I took as a bad sign. As the driver closed the cargo door, we heard a voice behind us. "Mr. Morgan, I believe?" he said. "Mr. Rutledge? I'm John Ransom, head of admissions. Welcome to Sewanee. I'm here to see you and your things to your dorm room." I'd never been so relieved in my life. Knowing that our parents weren't bringing us to school, this man had *personally* come down on a summer Sunday to meet two nervous freshmen. That's what you call hands-on admissions work. As the Greyhound crept away, my trepidation seemed to disappear with it.

We piled our bags and trunks into Mr. Ransom's car, and he drove us to our new home—Selden Hall, a run-down old structure that had been built to house GI Bill students after World War II. Our room was small, containing a couple of desks and a set of bunk beds. Mr. Ransom apologized profusely for the appearance of the place. He needn't have; despite my earlier foreboding, I suddenly had the strange feeling that everything was going to be okay.

The next day was even better. It was the start of rush, which at Sewanee was largely a concentrated three-day event. Unlike at other universities, where rushees are invited to the various fraternity houses, at Sewanee the rushees stay in their dorm rooms and the various fraternity interview teams visit there at 15-minute intervals. It's a very efficient system. And of course you've filled out your relevant information prior to rush, so the fraternities know what high school and extracurricular activities you participated in. They probably also had access to your grades, so they know if you're a smart guy or a dolt. Finally, there are the legacy letters, which can carry significant weight. Uncle Ralph, who'd been a Kappa Sigma at Sewanee, as well as a university regent, had consented to write a letter on my behalf.

But I was very surprised by the reception I received. One of the first teams to visit me was headed up by none other than Roy Flynn, president of the Sewanee chapter of Kappa Sigma fraternity—the top guy *himself*, a senior, a very important man on campus. We got along famously. I don't remember a single thing we talked about, but this is one of the many times when my motel training paid off. I might be anxious about speaking to large groups, but from a very early age I knew I could talk one-on-one with anybody. If I could've delivered that Lions Club speech a hundred times to each person in that room, or even to pods of three or four at a time, that day would've been a different story.

And now, apparently, Roy Flynn was very impressed. Soon other Kappa Sigs were showing up, as well as teams from other fraternities. The word, whatever it was, was getting out; we felt the heat of competition. They wanted Bo, too—we'd made it clear that we were a package deal—but Bo was a little shy during the interviews. Thankfully, not me—I just plunged in. Next thing I knew, guys were saying hello to me all over campus, going out of their way to come shake my hand. Nothing like this had ever happened to me. It was like I, the geek, had miraculously been transformed into the star of the pledge class.

Had that Greyhound bus driven through some social time warp into an improbable age where Science Club was *cool?* Such were my delirious ramblings before fitful sleep. But in the clearer light of day, I decided that the difference was as simple as context. Here in the beautiful, isolated mountains of Tennessee, I was no longer vulnerable to being judged by a lifetime of externals: who my parents were, where we lived, whether or not we belonged to the country club, if I had a girlfriend. Here was a fresh start, a place where—despite Uncle Ralph's letter—I could be judged mostly on me alone, and at Sewanee brains counted. I had not proved wanting.

By the time Bo and I had pledged Kappa Sigma, I had somehow been transformed from the boy on the outside of the circle to the boy in the center. In a matter of weeks, my self image had been altered. I'd long been confident about business, about studying, about intelligence; now my insecurity about social matters—about how I was viewed socially by others—faded away. And I never looked back at the boy I'd been before.

At the end of rush all pledges attended parties at their respective fraternity houses, where copious quantities of beer were consumed. I was standing in the Kappa Sig house talking with an upperclassman when suddenly a young guy came sailing across the room and dropped into a full split at my feet. "Hi, Jerry Adams," he said. Then, closing himself up like a pair of scissors, he stuck out his hand for a shake. Bo came over and I introduced him to Jerry. The next morning at breakfast, Jerry asked me a strange question. "What are your parents' first names?" he said.

"Don and Betty," I said.

"Well," he said, explaining that he'd told his mother about meeting Bo and me, "my dad and your mother have known each other since childhood. And my dad gave your dad a job at Rice-Stix—in Griffin, Georgia. You and your little brother have spent the night at our house in St. Louis. Not only that, my dad is your brother's godfather."

A friendship with Jerry Adams seemed preordained.

□ □ □ □ □

THE UNIVERSITY OF the South was like a piece of old Europe dropped onto the Cumberland Plateau. Our dorm notwithstanding, most of the university buildings were gothic gems, heavy on stone, stained glass, and flying buttresses. Upperclassmen strolled to class in black gowns, which camouflaged a multitude of sins. For example, one of the guys who roomed next door to Bo and me got drunk one night and, finding our door locked, simply broke it down. The next morning, he slipped on his academic gown and made his way to class, looking for all the world like a scholar and a gentleman.

My curriculum was a mixture of Liberal Arts and Pre-Engineering, based on Sewanee's "three/two" arrangement with Georgia Tech. That meant, according to the pre-enrollment hype, that I could finish in five years with double degrees—a Master of Science, say, from Sewanee, and a Mechanical Engineering degree from Georgia Tech. I chose German for my language requirement and took as much math as possible. And while I'd been fortunate to have very good math teachers at Fort Smith High, at Sewanee my mathematics professor took teaching to a whole new level.

Dr. Stephen Puckette was a young guy, a newly minted Ph.D who'd been at Sewanee for only a year or so. Today, I think of him as someone who could've stepped out of a *Harry Potter* book—a brilliant professor who created magic in the classroom. He made Differential Equations seem like the most exciting thing in the world.

It's been said that arithmetic is to mathematics as spelling is to writing. I'm actually terrible at arithmetic, which is all about adding and subtracting and multiplying. Math is about logic, and I like to think I'm a logic guy all the way. So was Dr. Puckette. "I could care less if you get the right answer in my class," he said at our first class meeting. "But you'd better understand what you're doing. I'm looking to you to demonstrate an understanding of the concepts."

I'll never forget the day he devoted an entire hour to the derivation of pi. He was a whirlwind in his black academic gown, starting at the far left of the blackboard and jotting numbers so fast that he practically became a blur, moving steadily right around the room, his chalk *click-click-clicking* on the board so that if you closed your eyes, you might mistake it for a flamenco dancer. But nobody closed their eyes. Puckette's performance was too thrilling to miss.

Inspired by such professors as Dr. Puckette, I became restless at Sewanee. Instead of being content to settle comfortably into my college years enjoying the camaraderie and the hijinks, of which there were many, I embraced the idea of change, welcomed the inevitability of it, looked forward to reaping its benefits. Mainly, I was eager to get on with the business of being a mechanical engineer, but that was essentially a means to an end. I wore blinders during college, and here was the thread of my tunnel-vision logic: *I don't have the money to race good cars in college, so I need to make good grades, so I can get a mechanical engineering degree, so I can land a better job, so I can afford to race good cars.*

Seriously, at that time of my life it was as simple as that. I had hoped to equip my Austin-Healey Sprite for racing, but it was just too expensive. I couldn't buy racing tires, I couldn't put roll cages in it, and if by some trick of fate I *had* converted the Sprite to a race car, it would've then been really hard to drive on the street. And if I wrecked it, I'd be screwed. I never tried to do something I knew was crazy. So the only answer was to get out of school, earn some money, and *then* start racing.

Bo remembers me as being especially diligent during our time at Sewanee. He loved movies and often tried to get me to go with him; usually I declined. Movies weren't a priority with me. Instead, I studied hard, staying up late and rising early. It was this regimen that brought about one of Bo's and my first conflicts.

The fact is, my dear friend Bo liked to sleep in, and when I got out of bed to hit the books, I shaved with an electric razor. The sound of the razor drove Bo crazy. He would toss and turn, making a show of his exasperation. "Dammit, Charles," he would moan, "I can't sleep with that thing on." Eventually I started going down the hall to the common bathroom to shave, but even then the buzz of the razor cut through the morning stillness like a saw cutting ice.

You learn new things about old friends when you room together. Bo was moody. Maybe I knew that back in Fort Smith, but we weren't always together then; now I couldn't miss it. Not only was he moody, he had a tendency to pinch pennies. One day in our room at Selden Hall, these two facets of his personality converged to cause another conflict between us. Bo wrote with a fountain pen, but instead of buying replacement cartridges for it, he bought a syringe and a bottle of ink. When his pen ran dry, he would use the syringe to siphon ink from the bottle, and then he would refill the used cartridge. On this particular day, he was already in a foul mood. I was at my desk trying to study, but he was cursing under his breath and slamming things; apparently, he was having trouble refilling the pen cartridge. Suddenly he reared back and threw the syringe across the room, where it slammed into the wall just above my head. "Goddammit, Bo!" I said, leaping from my chair. "What the hell!" It really infuriated me; fortunately, the ink didn't get all over my clothes. Today we laugh about it; Bo says he was so caught up in his bad mood that he hardly noticed I was there.

But we had good times, too. Jerry Adams, our English-major friend, recalls that both Bo and I did very well academically while participating in our share of partying: "We introduced Bo to alcohol," Jerry says, "and projectile vomiting."

Bo and I roomed together for two years, but I was on a self-imposed fast track to graduate. After we finished our spring semester of sophomore year, I drove my Austin-Healey down to Atlanta to talk with a dean at Georgia Tech about my curriculum. Looking ahead, I'd decided that I should actually go to Georgia Tech instead of Sewanee for the remaining two years of my three/two program, and I wanted to make sure I was taking the proper courses and would have the necessary credits. The Georgia Tech dean studied my record and gave me bad news: The only way I could graduate in a three-year/two-year plan was to go straight through for 24 months, which meant three summers, and during the regular year I would have to carry a crazy class load—at one of the toughest engineering schools in the world. I wouldn't even get to go home for two years. I couldn't earn money at Morgan Supply, couldn't hop up my Healey for racing, couldn't do anything but work myself to the bone. What kind of life was that? For students who wanted an engineering degree, Sewanee's vaunted three/two deal with Georgia Tech had just been a bait-and-switch.

I drove back to Fort Smith in a funk, knowing I had serious decisions to make. On the way, Dr. Puckette came to mind, and from there it was a short leap to thoughts of calculus, the mathematics of change. *Puckette would be proud of me,* I thought. *I may not know which change is coming, but I'm getting mighty familiar with the concept.*

□ □ □ □ □

I DIDN'T RETURN to Sewanee. In the fall of 1963, my junior year, I entered the University of Arkansas at Fayetteville. Most people take five-and-a-half years to graduate from engineering school, but I figured out that I could earn my degree at Arkansas—*without* going to summer school—in two-and-a-half more years. It would be tough—I'd have to carry 21 hours a semester—but it could be done. And if it could be done, I was determined to do it. By now, my primary goal was to get out of school.

And after that? Cars, in some form or fashion. In the spring of my second year at Sewanee, some friends and I had driven down to Sebring, Florida, for the 12-hour endurance race. We had no plush seats in the grandstand; instead, we stood by the fence watching these beautiful sports cars whiz by. I was mesmerized. And even though they didn't finish at Sebring that year, Hap Sharp and Jim Hall's new Chaparral cars, based in Midland, Texas, were one of the most exciting aspects of the race to me. Sharp, a race car driver, and Hall, an oilman, engineer, *and* talented driver, had just joined forces to design and build revolutionary race cars. Two years later, in 1965, they would win the 12 hours of Sebring.

What Sharp and Hall were doing was exactly what I'd been dreaming of. This is from Wikipedia:

"The development of the Chaparral chronicles the key changes in race cars in the 1960s and 1970s in both aerodynamics and tires. Jim Hall's training as an engineer taught him to approach problems in a methodical manner and his access to the engineering team at Chevrolet as well as at Firestone changed aerodynamics and race car handling from an art to empirical science."

Race cars, engineering, empirical science—what could be better than that? More than once during college I thought of just packing up my Austin-Healey, driving to Texas, and throwing myself on the mercy of Sharp and Hall for a job—any job. But that would've been dangerously premature, because I probably would've gotten hired. And if I had, I have no doubt that I would've ended up a poor race-crew tinkerer because I would've loved the job so much. Not that I ever spent much time thinking of getting rich; money itself was never the point. But by giving myself the chance to mature, I gained the self-awareness to see beyond the dream. I gained empirical wisdom.

Mechanical engineering is a fascinating filter on the natural world. I never could get excited about chemical or electrical engineering. In the former, you can't see anything—it's just some reaction happening inside a fluid or a gas. In the latter, all you can actually see is the light switch that causes the bulb to glow. But with mechanical engineering, you study things like material properties, bending strength, how fluids flow through pipes, the myriad effects of vibration.

At Fayetteville, we would have labs in which we did various incendiary experiments—measuring heat transfer, or trying to demonstrate the practical application of strength of materials, or seeing how gases pass over a wing. I loved that stuff. Thirty years later, I ran into one of my old engineering professors, and he said, "You were the only person within a two- or three-year span who actually did original lab work. Everybody else copied it—I could tell. I was always amazed. You actually *did* the lab work."

Sometimes, though, despite my determination, the workload began to feel oppressive. Whenever that happened, I looked for ways to blow off steam. This usually involved automobiles. Once, I left Fayetteville after class on Friday and drove to the SCCA races in Stuttgart. I had a Thermodynamics test the following Monday at 8 a.m., but I wasn't worried—I was, in fact, acing the course. So I went off to Stuttgart in the heat of an Arkansas Delta spring and drank beer and watched car races all weekend. Returning to Fayetteville on Sunday night with a throbbing sunburn, I tried to study, but my head wasn't in it.

The next morning I took the test, which was a killer. Two days later, the professor, Dr. Wolf, handed back our papers. "Mr. Morgan," he said to me, "I hope you had a great time last weekend. Because you sure didn't study." And he dropped my D+ test on my desk. I'd been one of few students heading for an A in that class, but at the end of the year I was lucky to salvage a B-. I was crushed. I really looked up to Dr. Wolf, who now made it clear that I had let both him and myself down. As someone who's always wanted approval for my accomplishments, I still feel the sting of his disappointment.

Another night, a friend and I had downed a goodly number of bourbon and Cokes when, at about 1 a.m. I decided I *really* needed some female companionship. The girl I had in mind was a high school student in Fort Smith, 60 miles to the south. She was a very affectionate young lady with noteworthy charms, and she was especially fond of college boys. It's amazing how such an idea can seem so brilliant in the wee hours of a college morning. So in short order, my pal and I had fixed fresh drinks and were barreling south on Highway 71 toward Fort Smith.

This is hilly terrain, in the foothills of the Ozark Mountains, and the two-lane highway dipped and rose, twisted and turned. Besides that, it was raining. We made it pretty far, considering. But on a curve just outside Mountainburg, I lost control of the car. Suddenly we were airborne, the Jim Beam and Coke between my legs raining down onto the Healey's dashboard. We landed upside down hanging—

once again—from seatbelts I had installed. It's a miracle we weren't hurt. I ended up walking to a gas station and phoning Dad. "Please come get me," I said. "I really screwed up."

□ □ □ □ □

THE WINTER OF 1964 marked the start of major turning points for me. Actually, that doesn't quite capture the magnitude of the changes that began presenting themselves. It was more like I rounded a curve in my Austin-Healey Sprite and suddenly encountered a veritable convergence of forks in the road.

First, I landed a job with Humble Oil (soon to become Exxon) in Houston, for the following summer. So instead of looking forward to working at Morgan Supply, which had been my summer mainstay since I was 12, I began making plans to spend the summer of 1965 in Texas doing production research for Humble. This development also presented a turning point for my father, who still harbored the hope that when I graduated I would join him fulltime at Morgan Supply. "Dad," I said, "I'm sorry, but it's just not happening. I'm not making a career in builders' hardware." He would smile and shrug, but I could tell that the salesman in him wasn't ready to give up.

I didn't know Houston, or any person in it. As fate would have it, however, when I was home from school for Christmas 1964, I spent some time with Jane Dills. Remember Jane, the girl who lived across the street from my cousin Margaret? After receiving her business degree (with honors) from the University of Arkansas in 1963, Jane had first stayed home a few months to help her parents with some unexpected health problems. Then she'd taken a job as a statistical specialist—"a glorified statistical clerk," she says today—for Humble Oil in Houston. She lived there about a year and then came home again. What I wouldn't know for some time was that there was a man involved—a bombardier on a B-52 in Vietnam whom she'd met in Texas; they had become serious, and he was now stationed in Montana. She had come home apparently as a precursor to joining him somewhere, somehow, sometime.

And this is when we reconnected. As I was trying to find out where to live and who I might hook up with in Houston, Mother suggested I phone Jane Dills about it.

I hadn't seen Jane in a number of years. The truth is, the last time I'd been around her, I had found her a bit stuck up—a cool girl with a tight blonde bob who had little time for younger, unimportant boys. But now we were 21 and 23; even viewing it from the outside, the gap between us no longer seemed so cavernous. And sure enough, when I called Jane, she seemed very accessible. She said she'd be happy to talk with me about Houston, and invited me to meet her at a Christmas party being given by a friend of hers.

We did discuss Houston that evening, but only in the most general terms. Surprisingly, we seemed more preoccupied with catching up—what we'd each been doing, what our mutual friends were up to, what latest life calamity had befallen my cousins, the children of Uncle Ralph, whose abrasive, controlling personality had inflicted considerable pain on his children; they were already running into problems, which Jane and I, over holiday cocktails and against a backdrop of twinkling Christmas lights, now commiserated about. When we finally said our good-byes that night, I came away with a new impression of Jane. Instead of being the ice queen of our high school days, she was nice, fun, easy to talk with. Jane also saw me in a new light—tall, confident, funny, a young man with a plan and the determination to see it through.

We had several dates over the next few months. I came back to Fort Smith a few weekends, including Easter, and Jane even visited me in Fayetteville once. I think we were both surprised at this unexpected development. Maybe everybody was. Bo was now in St. Louis, finishing up his electrical engineering degree at Washington University, and when I told him I was dating Jane Dills, he almost fell out of his chair. Bo had remembered Jane the way I had, as aloof and unapproachable. Bo and Jane had always had an odd connection based on, of all things, an electric train. Bo's father and Jane's father were business friends, and years earlier, when we were all very young, Mr. Dills, who had no sons, had bought Jane an electric train. Maybe she didn't play with it enough, but eventually, when Mr. Rutledge decided to buy an electric train for Bo, Mr. Dills said he'd sell him Jane's. From then on, Jane thought of Bo—when she thought of him at all—as "the boy who got my train." On the rare occasions when they saw each other, she sometimes joked about it—but Bo always detected a slight edge to the humor.

Jane gave me the names of several people in Houston, including girls, but I didn't call any of them. As it turned out, an acquaintance from Theta Tau, the engineering fraternity, was also working for Humble Oil in Houston that summer. Jim Womble was his name, and he and I decided to room together. There was also a third roommate, Louis Hageman, but we didn't know him prior to rooming together, and he pretty much went his own way.

In hindsight, this was a pivotal summer for me, for two very different reasons. The more important one was that I actually got to know Womble, a civil engineering student with whom I had no classes, just a casual friendship through the engineering fraternity. But Jim would go on to play a major role in my life, and I in his; our bond began that summer of 1965 in Houston.

"We lived together out on the Southwest Freeway," Jim recalls, and he's already laughing. "On Thursday, the *Houston Chronicle* would publish beer ads. You couldn't do that in Arkansas—back then, they couldn't advertise liquor in our newspaper. So we would see 'Budweiser, $3.50 a case,' and Charles was like, 'Oh, my God. This is gonna be great!' We were twenty-two years old, and our feeling was, 'Boy, this beer's so cheap, you're losing money if you're not drinking it!'"

The other reason that summer was so important for me was that I finally acquired the car of my dreams.

Soon after we arrived in Houston, I saw an ad for a Jaguar XKE. It was practically new—had something like 2,300 miles on it—but it had been wrecked, and the salvage yard was asking less than $2,000 for it. New E-Types went for $6,000 or $7,000 back then, so this sounded to me like a once-in-a-lifetime opportunity. I had to go check it out.

The damage was concentrated in the left front corner of the car. The Jag had hit something, or something had hit it. Whatever had happened, the left front wheel was bent over to the right, and the whole front frame was busted up. The hood was destroyed.

Other than that, it was in great shape.

As I recall, I paid $1,600 for it, trading in my Sprite to get the money. Then I found a shop that would rent me space and had the car towed to the shop. And for the entire summer, I worked on my car weekdays from 6 p.m. to midnight, and all weekend long. I couldn't believe I actually owned an XKE.

My day job with Humble Oil's production research division involved trying to improve the efficiency of oil-gas separation in pumping wells. Oil wells often have a lot of gas mixed in with the oil, but, at the time, there wasn't enough well pressure to push the oil out. In which case, the oil had to be pumped out. But pumping efficiency was terrible because the gas compresses, making it impossible to pump out as much oil as was theoretically possible. So Humble was trying to figure out a way to remove gas from the oil, and they had hired a University of Houston engineering professor to study the problem on a long-term consulting contract. I was assigned to work with him.

The professor had built a test rig on the lawn outside of the University of Houston engineering school where we were working. The idea was to simulate an oil well, but instead of the drill going into the earth, everything was above ground. The top of the rig rose probably 40 feet in the air, but the bottom—which would normally be underground—was encased in clear plastic so we could watch all the devices we were testing and see how they performed.

That, then, was my Houston routine—oil rig by day, XKE by night, sale beer with Womble on weekends. Sometime that summer, Jane came down for a short visit. I showed her my Jag and we all—she and Womble and I—went to a couple of parties. Then she headed back to Fort Smith.

It wasn't a bad existence, except that I was making more progress with the Jaguar than we were making in oil-gas separation. We'd been concentrating on all these funky separator ideas, strange gadgets with holes in them that the professor hoped would mechanically separate the gas from the oil. Nothing was working. I found myself mulling the problem even as I rebuilt my car.

One day I arrived at work with an idea. "Professor," I said, "it would be real easy to separate the gas from the oil if we could do it with a centrifugal separator."

He looked at me like I was crazy. "Why would we do that?"

"We've got gas pressure," I said. "Let's build a little turbine that's driven either on gas pressure or by electric motor, and have it drive a mechanically dry centrifugal separator and extract the fluid from the outside of the separator that's inputted in the pump."

"I don't know how you do that."

"I don't think it's that hard," I said. "What if I build one?"

"How?"

"Well, we've got a machine shop here," I said. Right in the next building we had lathes and other tools to build things for the test rig. There was also a part-time machinist there who could be called on if we needed help with the lathe.

The professor thought about it a minute. He knew as well as I did that any improvement in separation capacity we'd made was microscopic at best. Finally, he said, "Okay. Give it a shot."

For the next week or two I worked on building the separator. First I drew it out according to the idea I'd had while working on the Jaguar. Then I built it, largely on a lathe, though I did go buy a few parts at a machine shop. I got some lathe help from the machinist, but mostly I did the whole job myself. Finally I figured out a crude drive mechanism that sort of worked.

It took a little fiddling to install it, but once we did, the results were dramatic. It worked 10 times better than anything we'd ever tested before. "Wow," the professor said. "Holy smokes!"

After we tweaked it so that the separator was working really well, the professor invited the head engineer for the production department to come take a look. This guy was old and salty, and you could tell he didn't much believe in college professors or green young guys. He showed up angry, with a chip the size of my Jag on his shoulder.

"What kind of nonsense is this?" he said. "I've been working with gas separators for thirty-five years and I've never heard such crap." He didn't even really *look* at the separator, he just argued. I tried to explain the concept to him. "You don't know what you're talking about," he said. "This is bullshit. It can't possibly work."

And he left.

"Jeez," said the professor. He tried to get some other Humble Oil people to come look at it, but without much luck. And that's the way it went until about a week before my summer term was to end. By then, I had rebuilt my XKE and even installed a fiberglass hood on it. I couldn't afford metal, and the hood wasn't yet painted. I planned to drive the Jag back to Fayetteville and have the whole car painted there—racing green was the color in my mind. I couldn't wait to drive this magnificent machine onto campus in the fall.

Then one day the professor showed up with some people from the production department. We did our dog and pony for them and they thanked us and left; I figured that was that, which was fine with me. I was already out of there in my mind. But later that day, the professor called me over. "They want you downtown in the morning," he said.

"What for?"

"They want to talk to you."

So the next day I drove to the main Humble Oil building—the very building where Jane had worked during her time in Houston—and gave my name to the receptionist. I was escorted into a conference room, where several executives were waiting for me. They were really, *really* nice, telling me how impressed they were with my work in general—"quality work," they called it. Then they brought up the separator. "A lot of people are skeptical about whether this thing would ever work in the real world," the lead guy said, "but just to show we like what you've done, we want to offer you a really good job. When you finish your last semester, come back and work for us in the production department. We're ready to offer you an above-grade salary...."

Wow, I thought. *Cool.*

"As a matter of fact, what we'd like to do is get you to accept the job now and we'll pay you a bonus."

Now they were forcing an answer. Did I want to work for the Humble Oil production department? I'd already met the head engineer. I couldn't imagine working for that guy.

"Look," I said, "I'm very flattered, but I'm not ready to accept a job. But this is *so* nice of you...."

"Well," their spokesman said, getting to the real point of this meeting, "we just want you to know you have a standing job offer here. But we realize we didn't get you to sign all the normal paperwork when you came to work...."

Aha, I thought. I had already done a bit of math, because I knew how many wells they had. If this separator worked, it could move a lot of oil—hundreds of millions of dollars worth. Maybe billions in today's world.

They were trying to be nonchalant, but using considerable lawyer terminology. "Normally, all our engineers have to sign releases to anything they develop while they're in our employ. But since you're not an employee, since you're temporary, you didn't sign all the normal stuff. We still want you to come to work for us, we really do. But we really need you to sign this now."

By now I was more amused than anything. "Look, guys," I said, "I know where you're going with this. And yeah, maybe I could sue you or something, but that would be crazy, not to mention bullshit. It wouldn't be *right*. So I'll be glad to sign away my rights on this because I think that's the right thing to do."

They were beside themselves. "Oh, my God, you really will? That's great, Charles. Thank you so much." They clearly had a whole list of tricks they were going to try if necessary, but they were relieved that it wasn't.

Did they ever use my separator? For years I hadn't even thought about it, but one day after I'd started working on this book I decided to Google "centrifugal in well oil gas separators" and see what I could find. The result was astounding: Nearly 40 years later, the diagram that appeared on my computer screen looked an awful lot like what I designed in Houston in that strange summer of 1965.

□ □ □ □ □

LIFE SEEMED TO hit warp speed as graduation loomed. And after years of rushing the moment, I suddenly felt unready. So much was happening so fast, yet so much was still up in the air.

The thing with Jane was not only heating up, it was being played out largely on the 50-yard line of Razorback Stadium in Fayetteville. Nineteen-sixty-five was a surreal year for football in Arkansas. Back on January 1, the 1964 Razorbacks team had beaten the Nebraska Cornhuskers in the Cotton Bowl and ended up the only undefeated college team in the nation, winning the 1964 national championship. As the new season got underway, everybody in Arkansas celebrated all over again, turning Saturdays into a wild statewide party. Jane's dad, Bob Dills, had 50-yard-line seats for the Fayetteville and Little Rock games, and now I was invited to join the family in their personal cheering section.

It was nice, I have to say. I liked Jane's parents, Bob and Lucille, and of course her sister, Nancy, was married to my cousin Ewell, brother of Reaves, whose toys I had taken apart as a youngster; Reaves was now a close friend of Jane's. It felt natural being with this family, and Bob and I talked easily with each other, man to man. But my 50-yard-line seat also afforded me views of more than football—various facets of the family dynamic came into play as well, especially between Jane and her father. He was controlling, and she prized her sovereignty. Jane *really* bridled against perceived authority of any stripe, but particularly from her father. If Bob ordered her to do something, she did just the opposite, and with greater intensity. In hindsight, I might've paid more attention to that, but that's hindsight for you.

Even on those drunken game days my mind sometimes wandered far from the red-and-white sea of Razorback mania to deeper, more private concerns. It was four months until January 1966, when I would finish my course work for my degree. Where was I going to work? And what about my dad, who still held out hope that I would take over the family business? He had persuaded me—as a kind of "payback" for all his and Mother's generosity during my college years—to work for him for a few months in the spring of 1966, before graduation in June. He wanted me to help with a major hollow metal fabrication job at a high school in Fayetteville. This was an important, lucrative piece of business for Father, so how could I refuse? And besides, what else was I going to do?

Looking forward to things is a great pleasure—maybe *the* great pleasure. For some 15 years I had looked forward to becoming a mechanical engineer so I could spend my life doing something I love. But so far, I hadn't been offered anything I thought could sustain my interest. Most of the interviewing takes place in the spring semester, and I had seen my share of big company interviewers. IBM flew me down to Cape Canaveral to talk about a rocket job. When I got there they put me with a very junior guy, who explained that IBM was doing a lot of computer work on the early rocket launches, and they needed a mechanical engineer mainly to design frames to support their banks of computers. They offered me the job, but I turned it down. It could've been interesting for a while, but not for the long haul. And I worried that I'd be stuck in a beautiful backwater already overrun with engineers. I also interviewed with Mobil, again in Texas, and they were offering maybe 40 percent higher pay than I could expect from most starting engineer jobs. But pay wasn't my main motivation; the job itself felt like a glorified sales job. Then, of course, there was the standing Humble Oil offer, which came with the standing jerk of a head engineer.

My big hope was Texas Instruments, which was doing interesting things in those days. They invited me down to see them and I liked their building—very modern, sleek partitions, an elegant solution to an office problem. I met with the engineering team and we were having a stimulating conversation. "So how would you solve *this* problem?" they would say, and I would explain how I would go about it. I was getting excited about these guys, about being part of their team. Then a bell rang somewhere in the office. "Coffee break!" they said. "We go to coffee now."

"What?" I said. "You have a coffee bell?"

"Yeah, we get exactly fifteen minutes, then we have to be back."

Just like elementary school. Later I found out they also had a lunch bell and a time-to-go-home bell. It was too depressing to think about.

I was really getting worried now, because I couldn't summon up an iota of excitement about any of these jobs. I had always expected to find my dream engineering job without any problem—engineering paired with cars. Once again, I thought about jumping into my Jag and going down to see Hap Sharp and Jim Hall at Chaparral. I didn't know of anybody else on the planet using engineers to design exciting cars, except for the big manufacturers in Detroit. I wouldn't have a clue about how to get in with them. And besides, now I figured all those mainstream behemoths would have ringing bells, just like TI.

Reality was not pretty.

One day late in the fall semester I was sitting in the front room of the Theta Tau house, the engineering fraternity, telling a buddy my tale of woe—how I had all these job offers and didn't want any of them. "Well," he said, "I've just made my decision—I'm going to work for IBM in Little Rock."

"What'll you do for them?" Even though I'd interviewed for that engineering spot with IBM at Cape Canaveral, I really didn't know much about the company.

"They sell and install computers," he said, "and I'm going to be a computer systems engineer. Writing programs, developing software, stuff like that."

This came as a revelation. No doubt I paid special attention because the guy talking, Randy Stewart, had a formidable brain—he was a starting Razorback football player but also an Academic All-American, and I respected him greatly. Because of that, something about his words *computer systems engineer* hit me like a bolt of lightning, instantly incinerating my blinders. For years I'd been pursuing a single-minded hardware dream, allowing no alien options into my line of vision. Now, thanks to Randy, I felt like I was seeing in cinemascope.

"How'd you get hooked up with them?"

"They interviewed on campus twice last spring. In fact, they're here today, probably for the last time this year. I just stopped by the interview room to check in with them."

If this book were a movie, this next scene would be the chase—the point in the narrative where the main character realizes he's been a total boob and runs his heart out to make amends. I sprang from my chair and dashed out the door, sprinting across campus as fast as I could. I was dressed like a slob, but there was no time to change. I had to catch the IBM recruiter and get in on this new thing, the only stimulating idea I'd heard in months.

When I reached the interview room, there was only one IBM rep still there—but he was the top guy; all his colleagues had already packed up and gone. A secretary was there, too. But if I'd been five minutes later, all I would've found was an empty room. "I was just about to walk out the door," said Bob Oliver. His briefcase was already buckled shut.

Out of breath, I blurted Randy Stewart's name and said Randy had urged me to see him. "I never even thought about working for IBM," I said. "But will you talk to me?"

Bob looked at his watch. "Yeah, okay, I've got a few minutes," and he sat back down at the desk.

The conversation went well, though when I told him about my commitment to my dad's hollow metal project through the next spring, he said, "That could be a problem." They were hiring several young engineers to start in January, to be trained on something called the IBM 360. "But first things first," he said. "You've got to take the aptitude test." He asked the young woman if she could stay behind and administer the test to me, and she did.

And that's the story of how I stumbled into my life's work. I shudder to think how close I came to missing it.

□ □ □ □ □

FORT SMITH WAS like a ghost town in those months after I finished my course work. All my friends were gone off to jobs elsewhere, and it was the same for Jane. Stay home too long and you get left behind. But at least I had a future now, at IBM in Little Rock, starting in June 1966 after I finished this assignment for my dad.

It was a big, hot, hard project, designing and building windows and doors for a new high school in Fayetteville, and then installing them. By now Speer was away at Sewanee, so he wasn't there to help me. I worked at Morgan Supply from 8 to 5 every day. Occasionally, I experienced a wave of strangeness at not being in school anymore—almost like playing hooky.

Most evenings, I would see Jane. Once she was sure I was going to be in Fort Smith this semester, she moved out of her parents' house and into an apartment so we could be together without her dad constantly looking over her shoulder. Much later, Jane would tell me that Bob Dills didn't approve of me at first. "Why are you spending time with this younger guy?" he asked. He should've known that that question would become its own answer.

Jane and I played a lot of bridge that winter and spring; we also played house. It seemed there was nobody around but us, like we were in a bubble. She cooked for me, fussed over me. In time, we said we loved each other, and it was obvious to me that Jane wanted to get married. But I was reluctant because I'd always had an unspoken plan about marriage—that I should wait until I was 30. I was now just 23. The truth is, I was young and naïve, not mature enough to marry. But since when has that stopped anybody?

I used to kid Jane about her brazen plots to snag me. She would be 25 in September, and it was a different era; people got married much earlier than they do today. They were *expected* to marry early. The apartment was an early part of her scheme; so were the 50-yard-line seats, where I got another taste of the nice world she'd grown up in: big house, plenty of money, traveling in style. I respected her dad's business success and was impressed that he seemed to know every important person in the state. Her mother was a gracious lady from a fine Pennsylvania family, and her only fault, as far as I could see, was that she smoked too much. Jane smoked too—a couple of packs a day. I never liked excessive smoking.

But the ballgames, the apartment, the candlelight dinners were only a prelude. Jane's coup de grace came in May, about two weeks before I was to leave to start work at IBM in Little Rock. Once I was gone, I wouldn't see Jane for quite a while, because after my first week at the Little Rock office I would immediately go to New Orleans for a six-week IBM school there. Jane knew she needed to close the deal before I left town. "I've got to go in the hospital," she said, in mid-May. "I have to have my wisdom teeth out."

She was in *such* misery! I would go visit her each evening and comfort her while she put up a brave front, like in a scene from a movie, wincing at the shooting pain while squeezing my hand. I was very concerned, and greatly impressed. Later she admitted that this was one of her entrapment plots, to look helpless while I took care of her. God, she knew so much more than I did!

I proposed right after she was released from the hospital. In a nanosecond the Dills women shifted into wedding mode, while I packed for IBM and tried to keep my head down. I would be gone from early June to the end of July, and we would marry in August. In retrospect, we both went into the marriage with secret doubts. I worried that I wasn't ready, and wondered how I'd gotten so turned around. Jane suspected that the real reason I married her was because my draft classification was now 1-A, and marriage would keep me out of Vietnam.

But like so many other young couples, we tamped down our misgivings. The Wedding took on a life of its own, silencing everything in its path.

Part Two

SOFTWARE

4

MEN IN BLACK

1001010010110010100010010110010101100011

FINALLY I UNDERSTOOD why Mother made me take typing in eighth grade. At IBM, I was one of very few engineers who could use a keyboard with more than my index fingers.

Today, when our lives are so intertwined with computers, it's hard to fathom just how early 1966 was in terms of computer knowledge. I'd taken no computer course in engineering school, and only one at Sewanee—a useless class whose instructor was teaching it out of a book; every day he was maybe one chapter more knowledgeable than his students.

No wonder IBM was recruiting young engineers—mechanical, civil, chemical, electrical, what-have-you. There were no computer experts to recruit. Engineers were at least problem-solvers with a tech turn of mind, so the company was hiring the best they could get and training them to become computer whizzes. IBM in Little Rock recruited five of the top 10 engineering students at University of Arkansas the year I graduated, including me.

But my steep learning curve wasn't restricted to the office in that autumn of 1966. Marriage, I was finding, was even more complex than computers. Looking back today at Jane's and my wedding pictures, I see two young people playing roles that society prescribed for them then. There we are, Jane in her beautiful white wedding dress and me in my black tux, posing for the requisite "feed-the-groom-the-cake" photo—me hamming it up for the camera. Then there's the "groom-wiping-his-brow-while-the-best-man-points-to-his-watch" shot—in this case, Speer counting the minutes left in my bachelorhood while I sweat my impending fate. It's all so packaged, so elbow-in-the-ribs jocular.

Our first real moment of marriage occurred the next day, on the way to our honeymoon. We had spent our wedding night in Fort Smith, and now were in the XKE between there and Heber Springs, where we planned to spend a leisurely week at The Red Apple Inn, an elegant, cozy resort on Greers Ferry Lake. We were excited, and for me it was a heady moment: great job, new wife, sporty car, bright future. I was speeding, as I tend to do—why have a fast car if you don't drive it fast?—when suddenly we heard the deflating wail of a highway patrol siren behind us. The cop gave me a ticket and a stern talking-to; he'd clocked me at 90 miles per hour.

I was furious, and embarrassed. As soon as the policeman made a U-turn and disappeared in the opposite direction, I floored the accelerator again. I was probably back to 90 when Jane started screaming at me. She was absolutely irate. This was something new. Throughout our whole courtship, she hadn't argued with me a single time. She'd always deferred to me; I was always right. I remember thinking: *The perfect woman.*

I know, I know. But as I say, I was on a steep learning curve. And I was shocked that my sweet bride of less than a day could've metamorphosed into this ballistic creature sitting beside me. "I lost it," she says today. "I was just ugly—but it didn't do any good."

She was still mad when we reached the resort, and I had to really work the charm to get her calmed down. At long last we were lying on top of the bed, completely naked, getting down to what honeymooners are supposed to do. Then the door opened and there stood a bellman holding a bucket of Champagne. If he had knocked, I certainly hadn't heard him. He seemed more shocked than we were, if that's possible. "Oh! *Oh!*" he said, and ran out the door. The mood broken, I had to dial room service to get them to bring back the Champagne.

In jokes, the punch line usually comes on the third beat. So it was with our honeymoon. After a couple of days, I got a phone call from my new boss. "I need you back here," he said, even as I protested that I was on my honeymoon. He couldn't be swayed. So after only three nights and two days of our planned weeklong vacation, Jane and I packed up and drove to our new apartment in Little Rock. The digital future beckoned.

◻ ◻ ◻ ◻ ◻

CORPORATE CULTURE WAS a concept I'd never considered before joining IBM; I probably didn't even know about it. There were no Texas Instrument-type bells to tell us when we were allowed to take breaks or eat lunch, but the company did have some strict rules, especially regarding appearance. Everyone was expected to wear dark suits and white shirts, and the men had to wear ties. When I saw the movie *Men In Black*, I thought of our office. On my first day at IBM in Little Rock, two of my classmates showed up in sport coats and were sent back home to change.

Later I would learn about various time-card and expense-account practices that I found silly and picayunish. Once, when I'd been out to visit a client, I rounded off the mileage to 26 miles; my boss tossed my expense account back, saying he'd driven that route himself and I had exaggerated the distance by four miles. And even though I worked long hours, he didn't want to pay for overtime. "Don't tell me how late you stay," he said, which was fine with me. I didn't care about the money—I was just riveted to the projects I was working on.

AT IBM school that first summer, most of our classwork had focused on mechanical accounting machines—even at IBM we weren't yet fully in the computer age. We learned that data processing had started back in the 1890s with the U.S. Census Bureau, which desperately needed a faster, easier way to tabulate stats on an increasingly large and complex population; that before automation, it was taking up to eight years to process census findings; and that a man named Herman Hollerith had invented a punch-card system that allowed the number-crunchers to do their work in a year. Hollerith had gone on to establish, in 1896, a company that would eventually become part of IBM.

My class was comprised mostly of men, with a handful of women, the majority of us coming from Arkansas, Mississippi, and Alabama. Tech and sales were lumped together—whether selling or installing, we all needed to understand accounting, which was, in one form or another, our clients' interest in buying a computer. From 8 to 5 every day we had classes on basic accounting—debits and credits, general ledgers, that kind of thing; we also learned other basic business applications, such as payroll and inventory control, from the ground up. Finally, we were required to give presentations. IBM's hiring philosophy was to recruit the best people they could get, and then, over the next six weeks or so, wash out 10 to 20 percent of them. My roommate that summer just disappeared one day; I never saw him again. The instructors observed us very closely, and if they decided someone wasn't going to cut it, they called his boss back home, who would tell the student he'd been terminated. The only part of the schooling I worried about was the presentation. I was violently nervous about having to stand up before everyone. When the day finally came, my branch manager from Arkansas was there to watch me. I didn't knock it out of the park, but at least I didn't freeze. I did okay.

Now, back in Little Rock, they had us installing computers we hadn't even been trained on yet. It was a time of playing catch-up—computers were very much in the wind, the infinite *possibility* of these machines. As problems to solve, I found them fascinating. While IBM still hadn't set up classes on the various machines, they did have manuals called *Principles of Operations*, which described in great technical detail how the various computers and software worked. These were my new Bibles; I would take one or two home every night and study them. Realizing that we were operating far ahead of our training, I told my boss that whenever there was something new in the office, a problem he needed solving, to give it to me and I would try to figure it out. He welcomed the help and threw all kinds of challenges my way.

One time he came to me about a new computer called the IBM 1130. We'd sold it to Vogel's, a local frozen food wholesale company, to do inventory management, payroll, and general ledger. The only problem was, this was what's called a "floating-point computer." It was for scientific applications only—it didn't do digital. I could explain the ins and outs of that, but unless you're a hopeless geek it would bore you to tears and you would stop reading. The bottom line was, with this computer, none of the numbers ever rounded off right. Our customer would add up a column of figures in floating point and also on his calculator, and the computer would be off one or two pennies. You can see why the client was upset.

Another systems engineer in the office, Ron Eddy, had been charged with getting this thing to add the numbers up right, and he had developed various new software tools to fix that problem. But now there was a *new* problem. Vogel's was trying to use this computer for billing, which meant they needed to print the bill for every individual truckload of goods before the truck was even loaded. But the only printer IBM made to work with this computer had but one speed, and it was so slow that the printer was still laboring away after the trucks were supposed to have left the plant. This new, very expensive computer was throwing our customer's business way behind schedule.

This is when my boss dropped the problem in my lap. "I'd like you to make this printer print faster," he said. *Are you fucking kidding me?* I didn't actually say that, but he could see the incredulity on my face. "Maybe you can fix the software so it goes faster."

And that's essentially what I did. The 1130 had a spinning wheel—think of it as a spinning drum with 120 full character sets, both numbers and letters. As the paper went by the drum, an electromagnetic hammer came down and made an imprint of whatever letter or number was called for. The wheel did a full revolution with each imprint to make sure all available letters and numbers had time to be applied. That was the flaw—every line took exactly the same amount of time to print, whether it contained three digits or 120.

It was a very unsophisticated machine. It didn't have many of what are called "interrupt levels." So what I did was rework the program to make sure the paper advanced to the next line just as soon as the last thing on each line printed. In that way, I almost doubled the print speed.

That machine was set up to operate through a machine-level language that IBM didn't even teach to guys like me. Nor were there manuals for it—I had to teach myself. The software for increasing the speed of that printer was the first software I wrote that was distributed nationally. IBM had mixed emotions about that. It wasn't something I should've been doing—it wasn't in my job description— but in fact I did do it, and IBM did finally let me publish the program.

I loved solving problems like that, despite my initial reaction when the job was handed to me. More and more, I found myself immersed in these new computers trying to learn everything I could about them. It was like falling into Alice's rabbit hole, where I could become deliriously lost for hours on end.

Today, Jane recalls that in those early years I sometimes came home from work at 2 or 3 in the morning, slept a couple of hours, showered, and went back to the office. And on a handful of occasions, I looked up from my desk and it was 8 a.m. My colleagues would be coming to work, and I hadn't gone home at all.

□ □ □ □ □

OUR LITTLE ROCK years weren't happy for Jane. We first lived in a spacious one-bedroom apartment in the Hillcrest section of the city, an area where it was possible to walk to stores and restaurants. But too often she was there alone, without anyone to talk to. She wasn't used to being anonymous. In Fort Smith she'd been an active member of the Junior League, and when we moved she transferred her membership to Little Rock. But at her first meeting there—a buffet luncheon preceded by a social hour with sherry and followed by a fashion show—no one even spoke to her. "I was a funny duck," she recalls, because she was so much younger than everyone else there—Fort Smith inducted members at an earlier age than Little Rock did. Still, the treatment was rude, and Jane read it as "just Little Rock."

Though Jane did have some college friends in town, when we socialized it was mostly with people from IBM. We sometimes played bridge with one of my fellow engineers, Don Barrett, and his wife, Nelma, and Jane enjoyed that; on other occasions we went out to dinner with various friends from my office. But most of the time I was working. I've often said that I inherited a bad gene from my father—the 80-hour gene. I also traveled quite a bit—in that first year alone IBM sent me to three different training schools: the six-week New Orleans one, another week in Poughkeepsie, New York, and six or seven weeks in Chicago. I also had to make overnight trips to New Orleans occasionally, because that was IBM's regional headquarters. My absences were hard on Jane.

In addition to these internal adjustments that all newlyweds face, couples of our era also contended with a major external factor: the draft. Jane was wrong when she suspected that I married her because my draft status had become 1-A after college—in fact, IBM employees were deferred for the first year of service with the company. We went to school so much, it was like working toward a master's degree.

So I wasn't going to be drafted at least until the summer of 1967. But the war in Vietnam was heating up fast—from 112,386 inductions in 1964, the quota in 1966 had more than tripled, to 382,010. So pressing was the need for fresh troops that in October 1965, the Selective Service had quit deferring married men without children.

This subject was much on my mind that fall of 1966. Finally, four months after our wedding—I remember it was nearly Christmas—I got up the nerve to sit Jane down and lay out the situation. "I'll be drafted next year," I said. "I *will* be drafted and I'll spend two years in Vietnam—unless we have a child now." We'd already decided we wanted children, but the plan was to wait two or three years to get started; the looming draft, however, was a plan-changer, and it put Jane on the spot. Today, she recalls being against having a baby right away—she wasn't ready, she says; and she thought we needed more time to get to know each other. On the other hand, she didn't want me to go off to war, with who-knows-what outcome.

She was pregnant before the month was out. Am I proud of this moment in my life? No, but I'm not ashamed of it either. I didn't believe in that war, and my risk/ reward instinct required me to take preventive action.

Jane hadn't been pregnant long when we realized we had to move from our apartment. The couple below us used to get into ferocious fights—we often heard them screaming, vases shattering, the woman sobbing. But late one night their fighting took a dangerous turn. The man was outside in the parking lot shouting insults—"You fucking bitch!"—to the woman, who was standing at their apartment window. She was cursing right back at him, but something he said tipped her over the edge. Suddenly we heard gunshots—she'd grabbed a pistol and was firing out the window at him. Jane and I jumped out of bed and rushed to look. The way the apartments were built, this wild woman waving the live gun was probably three feet below us, and here Jane was pregnant—what if bullets started ripping through our floor?

The next day we went out and found a house to buy. Jane always joked that the real reason we moved was because I was afraid our crazy neighbor would shoot up my XKE.

The new place, in tonier Pulaski Heights, was a two-bedroom bungalow sitting on a little hill, with a pretty park view and a garage for the Jag. The price was around $17,000, as I recall, with a $3,000 down payment that we didn't have. What we did have were contacts in Fort Smith, and through them we talked with a banker who assured us he would lend us the down payment. But the day before closing, he reneged—he said we must've misunderstood him. Fortunately, Jane's parents were due to drive through Little Rock that day on a trip to Florida, and they brought us the money.

The house had been built in 1950 and probably hadn't been painted since. So I painted it myself, mostly on weekends. Jane was getting bigger and couldn't do much to help, though I think she did paint the window trim while I was standing high on the ladder, the rungs killing the balls of my feet. It was a sweet domestic time for us—Jane pregnant with our first child, the two of us working together to spruce up our first house. Jane seemed content then; she was always happier when she had a project. We definitely had that in common.

My projects were as many, and as varied, as IBM had customers. Jacuzzi, based in Little Rock, was one of them, and I was assigned to go out to their headquarters and help them with their manufacturing processes. I also worked with a printing plant and a milk producer. But one of my most fascinating projects was for a potential client I wasn't even assigned to.

One of our salesmen was trying to convince the owner of a textile company in south Arkansas that our computers could help him with his piecework payroll. The people in his plant were paid by the piece—by what they produced—and some pieces had a higher rate than others. The payroll also had to include bonuses based on how many pieces employees produced over their quota, and if they fell below certain levels, they got docked. It was a very complicated payroll.

The plant owner didn't believe a computer could keep track of all this, so in my spare time I set out to prove him wrong. By then I had worked on payroll projects for a couple of other companies that were using the older IBM 1401 series computer, and I had studied the auto-coder manual and learned to write code in the 1401 RPG language. That stands for "Report Program Generator," and it was a sophisticated language for the time—more like the language of modern computers. You could compartmentalize types of data, which streamlined the programs tremendously; you could simply write in "A" or "B" instead of writing individual code for each piece of data in those categories. But even so, for a program that today might require you to write 10,000 lines of code, back then you would have to write millions.

It was very labor intensive, and I couldn't get enough of it. I did manage to produce a demonstration program for the textile plant's piecework payroll, but I don't think we ever sold them the computer. The guy just couldn't drag himself into the modern world.

□ □ □ □ □

FATE OFTEN COMES disguised as mundane occurrences. If, in the late 1960s, you had asked me what life-changing events happened to us during our two-and-a-half years in Little Rock, I would've said, "Our daughter." Caroline was born in September 1967, and now we were three. Jane and I would never again be the people we were before her arrival.

But I wouldn't have thought to mention Alex Dietz. He was just a guy I met in the break room at work. Alex had graduated from Tulane and then gone off to do his military service, after which he'd joined IBM in his hometown of Little Rock. I liked him immediately. He told me he and some buddies often rode their motorcycles in the woods south of town. He wondered if I'd like to join them the following weekend; if so, he could borrow a motorcycle for me. How could I say no?

Jane was not enamored of the idea. On the Saturday morning that Alex arrived at our house with two bikes on his trailer, he knocked on our door and Jane opened it. She would eventually be crazy about Alex, but they got off to a rocky start. After introducing herself, Jane told Alex, "Charles is *not* going to buy a motorcycle."

"Fine," he said. "I'm not selling one."

"And *no racing*," she said.

"You're safe on that," Alex said, and I kissed Jane good-bye and we got into Alex's truck. It took one week for me to buy a bike, and six weeks until our first race.

We never intended for things to work out that way. The original plan was just for us to roam off-road in the woods around Bryant, a few miles south of Little Rock. Alex had a 125-cc Yamaha and I bought a Spanish bike, a 260-cc Bultaco.

It was fun riding our motorcycles up and down gravelly ravines and jumping them over downed trees. We explored miles of wilderness trails, and one day we came upon an old closed-circuit track apparently laid out for motocross racing—it was dirt, with twists and turns and hills and valleys. We could see fresh tracks left by other bikes. "Let's ride around this thing for a while," I said.

Even then we weren't really planning to race. I had decided, after less than a month of owning the Bultaco, that it wasn't the right bike for riding in the woods; for one thing, it had poor suspension. So I sold the Bultaco and bought what was called an "Enduro bike"—a Yamaha DT1, which was a combination on-road/off-road motorcycle. I convinced Alex to trade his old bike in and buy one too. Then we took both new bikes to my garage and stripped off the lights and fenders and anything else we didn't need for off-road biking. Alex says he recalls thinking, *This is crazy.* "It was a brand-new beautiful bike, straight off the showroom floor."

But that's what we did. And after that, we went to our hidden track and raced each other—and whoever else showed up.

I was hooked, and Jane wasn't happy. She threatened to do everything except vaporize me, which I guess she thought I'd likely do on my own. But while she didn't want me to get hurt, she also realized she couldn't dissuade me from something I was so passionate about. Soon Alex and I were doing motocross every weekend. "'No racing,'" Jane says; "I lived to eat those words."

"I had a great relationship with Jane," Alex recalls. "She became a really good friend of mine. She knew this motocross racing was really important to Charles, and she supported it as best I could tell. She went to almost all the races with him—it wasn't just Charles and me. Jane and Charles were kind of the stabilizing influence in my life at that time. I was sewing wild oats right and left back then, so they met all my wild girlfriends. Whatever girlfriend I could bring with me would go, and we would race, stay overnight, drink too much, go to bed, and wake up and race again the next day."

In 1968, IBM transferred me to Fayetteville to oversee the installation of the biggest computer in the state, at the University of Arkansas. It was a plum assignment for me, and Jane was thrilled—she was very close to her mother, who was her confidante and comforter. And our families were glad to be nearer their granddaughter. I have pictures of us at Christmas 1968 in the living room of Mother and Father's motel home. Everyone is doting on Caroline, a precious dark-haired toddler tripping through the Christmas wrapping carrying her new doll.

I loved working in Fayetteville. It was an office of about 20 people, but only two of us were in computers; the rest were in the services group or the typewriter section. This meant I was essentially my own boss on a day-to-day basis; my time was now free for *me* to allocate as I saw fit, with no interference from my anal boss in the Little Rock office.

It was in Fayetteville that I traded in the XKE for a 390ci Ford Mustang. No one who's owned a Jaguar—especially an E-Type—will be surprised to hear that my car was having significant mechanical problems. I finally faced the fact that it was a machine meant more to be looked at than to be driven daily, and at IBM, especially in Fayetteville, I was putting a lot of miles on a car. By this time I had changed my work style: Instead of working hard, like I had in Little Rock, I now made a point of working smart. They didn't need to know the ins and outs of my day—all they needed to see were results. IBM had decided at one point they were going to make guys like me available for hire if a customer wanted us as a consultant. As it turned out, I was the top-billing systems engineer in the state, and more customers wanted to hire me. So in addition to doing a good job for the University on its computer installation, I made sure I took care of my clients, and I occasionally accompanied the other computer guy, sales rep Jim Hefley, to call on prospective customers—after which, I often knocked off early and took my motorcycle out to the motocross course.

And what was the fallout from that? Two years in a row—1969 and 1970—I was named IBM's Top Systems Engineer in all of Arkansas. They presented the award at a big banquet in Little Rock. Even though I knew I was taking care of business, I was totally surprised when they called my name that first year. IBM had also nearly doubled my salary over the time I'd been with them. To me, it just reinforced this evolving philosophy of mine—that results are all that matter.

It was during our years in Fayetteville that I also became a formidable motocross racer. Alex often came up to ride with me, but it killed him that I could now out-ride him. I figured it was poetic justice. Alex had been a star football player, and I'd never been any good at football, basketball, baseball, or any of those sports. I couldn't run fast at all. But what I had was exceptional hand-eye coordination, and no fear of crashing. "You can't be too cautious," says Alex today, "and I think I was a little too cautious." I raced in Arkansas, Texas, even in Kansas City, winning numerous trophies, and Jane was usually there—with Caroline—to watch me ride. I did crash a few times, resulting in two knee surgeries. To her everlasting credit—and my relief—Jane didn't lord it over me for that. "Instead," she says, "I took care of him." And she absolutely did.

But our relationship also suffered blows in Fayetteville. We lived in town when we first moved there; then we decided it would be nice to be in the country, so we bought a house a few miles beyond the city limits. Jane was excited at first, but gradually she started feeling isolated. She smoked too much, and I complained; we started arguing a lot. One night she packed her bag and went home to her mother in Fort Smith. Her father was furious at her. She could stay overnight, he said, but the next morning she needed to go back to Fayetteville "and beg Charles for forgiveness." She didn't beg, but I forgave her anyway.

With an up-and-down situation like we had, I really appreciated the ups. One evening when she was in a particularly happy mood and we were enjoying our cocktails, I suddenly felt so good about our relationship that I really screwed things up. I started out telling her that I knew she was going to be all right, and if I'd stopped there, maybe *we* would've been all right. But in the glow of the moment, I went too far. I told her I loved her and that I wanted no secrets between us. I had been totally faithful to her, I said…except for one little transgression, which I had regretted for years. Then I told her that on that IBM trip to Chicago in 1967, I had gotten drunk in a Rush Street bar and taken a girl back to my dorm room. I emphasized that it had meant nothing, that I'd felt like a dog about it, and that I would never do anything like that again. I said I hoped she would forgive me.

What was I thinking—that she would give me a medal for my honesty? The misguided confession was one regrettable mistake on top of another, and Jane was devastated; she said she could never trust me again. It's only fair to let her tell it her way: "After that, I didn't want to have anything to do with Charles. I didn't want to see him the next day, when he left on an overnight business trip. That was the day I got a call saying that Mother had had an aneurysm and was hemorrhaging and I had better get to Fort Smith right away. I did, and she died five days later. She was 60 years old. My shrink would later tell me that I lost my mother and my marriage at the same time."

□ □ □ □ □

IN 1970, ALEX left IBM to take a leadership role in a small service bureau called Demographics in Conway, Arkansas, 30 miles north of Little Rock. Service bureaus rent time on their computers to various clients, processing their bookkeeping, inventory, payroll—whatever the client needs. A few years earlier, H. Ross Perot had made a big splash with *his* service bureau, Electronic Data Systems, known as EDS, so service bureaus were kind of a hot idea at the time.

The owner of Demographics was a wealthy man named Charles Ward, whose family owned one of the three largest school bus manufacturing companies in the world—right there in Conway. Ward and his school bus company had been Alex's client at IBM, and one day Ward told Alex he was thinking of spinning off the bus company's data processing department into a service bureau, which he intended to name Demographics; he wondered if Alex might be interested in coming to work for him. The new service bureau's first client would of course be Ward School Bus Company itself.

Over the next year or so, Alex often talked to me about Demographics. It was a scrappy little company and he was having a good time at it. Occasionally he suggested that I might enjoy it too. "I know we'd work well together," he said. "I think we could build this into a nice business."

I wasn't interested. "I love my job at IBM," I told him. What I didn't say was that in my world, service bureaus were considered the bottom of the barrel.

Besides the exciting computer project I was working on for the University, I had interesting clients with fascinating problems to solve. Daisy Air Rifles was one of my customers; another was an up-and-coming retail chain called Walmart; at this point, they had five stores open and two under construction, and anything beyond that was just a dream.

Usually I called on Walmart in concert with Jim Hefley, but one day when we had a scheduled meeting, Jim had to go out of town at the last minute; he was interviewing for a bigger job with IBM in New York. So I had to handle the Walmart meeting by myself. It was a very important occasion. Walmart was considering ordering its first computer, and now I had to close the deal with a presentation.

You can imagine how I felt about that—sick to my stomach. But I had little time to wallow in my insecurities. At this meeting, which took place in the boardroom of a new bank building on the square in nearby Bentonville, there were six representatives from Walmart and me. The six from their company included Ron Mayer, then the Chief Financial Officer, and Sam Walton himself.

This was the culmination of many months of meetings, and I had met Sam Walton before. Usually, he said nothing—just listened like a Sphinx. At that time IBM didn't sell computers, they only rented them; you couldn't buy one if you wanted to. So now I gave my flip-chart spiel, extolling all the wonderful things our computer could do for their company and how much it would cost per month.

At the end of the presentation, Mr. Walton said, "Son, you know we don't pay retail. As a matter of fact, I always insist that we pay fifteen percent less than any price we're given. According to my figuring, *this*"—and here he glanced down at a pad on which he'd scribbled some numbers—"is what we'll pay monthly for this computer." He read out a figure that was astonishingly short of my quote, and rested his case with, "And we're ready to go ahead."

IBM didn't discount computers for God or GM. "Uh, Mr. Walton," I said, "IBM doesn't offer discounts to its customers."

"I know, son," he said, "but you'll figure it out. Thank you very much." And the meeting was over.

We did figure it out. We'd included some nice but unnecessary add-ons in our price, so those were easy to trim out; we also ended up pairing the computer with a less expensive printer. After a few such adjustments, we went back to Walmart with the price Mr. Walton had wanted to pay, and he gladly signed the order.

It turned out to be a fine deal for both parties. Who knew, at that juncture, how many stores Sam Walton would someday own? Not us, but we were glad to be along for the ride. And it was largely due to those computers that Walmart grew to such a size. I didn't install the computers at Walmart—by then an ex-engineering-school acquaintance of mine named Rodger Kline had finished his military duty and joined IBM, and Rodger was the technical point man in dealing with Walmart. Rodger and I still laugh about what we discovered the first time we called on Sam Walton in his office: Everyone there, including Sam, worked on unfinished plywood desks. Sam Walton had his strict business priorities, and office furnishings couldn't hold a candle to information.

I often worked with the company to help them maximize their computer functions, and I was amazed at how savvy Sam was at using computer-generated data. Actually, never mind "computer-generated"; it was an eye-opening lesson to see how he used data at all. When we started working with him, Sam wanted cash register tapes from every one of his stores on his desk at 8 o'clock every morning. With those tapes, he could see what every department in every store had sold the day before. The reason he wanted this information is that he didn't have any cash, and that's part of the brilliance of Sam Walton's story—he knew that if he had really good information, he didn't have to keep so much merchandise in inventory. What he really wanted was sales at the per-item level, but that was impossible in those days.

Prior to our computers, they were using NCR cash registers that produced a continuous stream of punch-hole tape indicating each department's sales. Employees would install new tapes every morning, and those same rolls would run until the stores closed. Back then most stores didn't stay open late like they do today, and after they had shut down someone would hand the day's NCR tapes to a courier, who would then deliver them to Sam Walton's office.

Rodger Kline used those tapes as the basis for the program he wrote. It showed the store number, the department number, and the number of items sold.

He couldn't put an actual product number on it, but Walmart categorized everything—for example, the report might read "Sporting goods: $2.95; soft goods: $1.98." They probably had 20 category buttons listed, so even though they couldn't tell exactly what was selling, they could kind of figure it out. If Sam and his buyers knew that they had run a big special on basketballs, and they knew those basketballs cost $6.95, when they saw a lot of sporting goods sales for $6.95, they knew those basketballs were selling and that they'd better order more before they ran out.

This was groundbreaking retail practice—nobody else was doing anything remotely like this. But then they took it a step further. Sam had no money, so his buyers would go to Spalding Sporting Goods and say, "Spalding, we're going to buy ten thousand dollars worth of basketballs, but we want four weeks from the time we get them in our distribution center to pay you for them." Because of his tight inventory research, Sam knew he could sell that many basketballs in about three weeks, and he got *his* money the day they were sold. So by the time they were all sold, he would have money in his bank account and still didn't have to pay Spalding for another week. By this business model, he turned inventory into cash on hand. And if he could get 45- or 60-day terms, all the better.

Sam's competitors, like Kmart and Sears, regularly bought $10,000 worth of basketballs from Spalding and paid for them right away; they didn't care if they were financing hundreds of millions of dollars' worth of inventory, because they had the cash to do it. Sam was forced to be smarter. His great idea was to have good enough information that he could sell the goods before he had to pay for them.

Sam Walton and Walmart would go on to *define* Big Data for retail and distribution, using data to crush their competition.

But even back then, his strategic reliance on information made an indelible impression on me.

□ □ □ □ □

AT THE BEGINNING of 1971, IBM sent me to a three-month school in New York City. Called the Systems Research Institute, it was a sort of master's degree program that only a few IBM people worldwide were invited to attend. It was mostly for non-management professionals who planned to stay with the company, as well as for younger guys like me on the road to promotion. It was quite an honor to be asked to go.

The idea of SRI was to give attendees a chance to get away from everyday concerns and turn their minds to Big Thoughts. The company brought in high-priced talent to teach the courses, which ranged from logic to the future of computing to the future of the *world*. They wanted smart, big-thinking people working for IBM—people who could make a difference for the company long term—and this course was a chance to get smart people together in the same room and let the synergy happen. You get a little philosophical at times like this. For three months, I didn't think motorcycle racing; I didn't think Walmart. I was like, "Wow, hmm, what does *this* mean? What does it mean to the world? What does it mean to *me*?"

Adding to the aura of profundity was the fact that we were in New York, living almost like natives. Our school was right across the street from U.N. headquarters, and we lived at the Hotel McAlpin on Herald Square. We walked to class when it wasn't too cold, which wasn't often, and otherwise we took the subway. We learned New York on five or 10 dollars a day and ate our meals at little dives that were cheap and good. We were off on weekends. I saw plays. I went to the opera for the first time. We could attend class in khakis and sweaters, and I even grew a beard. It was a memorable, mind-expanding period of my life.

They allowed each student one ticket home over the three months, which was smart. If the idea is to escape your daily problems, that had better include your domestic life. I had plenty of concerns on that front. More and more, Jane seemed depressed and withdrawn. Lighting cigarette after cigarette, she all but faded into the smoke.

About two months into the program, I got a call from my boss in Little Rock. "I'm coming up to see you," he said.

"Really? What's the problem?"

"We've got some stuff we need to discuss."

I couldn't imagine why he would fly all the way to New York to talk with me. Why couldn't he just tell me on the phone?

When he arrived, we went out to get a bite to eat. I was dying to hear what he had to say, but first we had to go through the usual chit-chat about my school and what was going on back at the office. Finally: "Charles, I'm going to have to ask you… to shave off your beard."

I couldn't believe what I was hearing.

"There's a *reason*," he quickly added, and he told me I'd been invited to the annual sales and systems engineers symposium in Atlanta. All the top systems engineers from around the country would be there, and it was a big deal to be invited. It was important enough for me to miss a couple of days at SRI.

But he was really concerned about my beard. "I can't tell you why," he said, "but I've got to plead with you to shave off your beard. Will you do that for me?"

"Listen, Bob," I said, "I don't even like this fucking beard. If it means that much to you, of course I'll shave it off."

"Oh, thank you," he said. "I've been worried *sick* about this. And it's for a good reason—nothing bad."

A few days later I walked into an auditorium in Atlanta that was filled with IBM people—probably a thousand of them, from all over the U.S. and Canada.

My boss was there, saving a place for me. But I was the only systems engineer from Arkansas.

As they started the program, a sign flashed on a big screen: *The Difference Is You.* Maybe it was because I'd been in New York expanding my mind, but suddenly I had an epiphany about IBM. During my five years with them, I had occasionally wondered how they happened to be the hot company to work for, how they'd had such a track record of success. Now I saw it—it was because they hired the best people. But that wasn't the totality of it. Success came to IBM because the company *itself* realized that topnotch people made all the difference. That was a central tenet of their corporate culture. It wasn't to make the most money or even the best products; it was to hire the very best people and put them to work on a good idea, and all the rest would follow. It may not sound like much of a revelation, but to me it was. IBM didn't just *happen* to have all these smart people—they did it on purpose. Smart people were the ultimate software. And for IBM, that was the bottom line below the bottom line.

The program started in the morning and consisted of a series of speakers, with a break for lunch. Then more speakers in the afternoon and, finally, the award presentations. Suddenly I heard my name called from the podium—I was being summoned to come accept one of the top national awards for systems engineering. I turned to my boss, who was beaming. No wonder he'd been so pleased that I'd agreed to shave; he knew it would never do for me to appear on an IBM stage wearing a beard.

A day later I was back in New York, back in my comfortable khakis and sweater. The Atlanta interlude had seemed like a dream. And in an odd way, it had made me slightly uneasy. The whole idea of this Systems Research Institute was to think outside the box, which requires asking yourself hard questions. I had loved the work at IBM—I *still* loved it. But these awards I'd won had had an unexpected effect on me—I was starting to feel a subtle pressure about my future, a topic I hadn't thought much about. Now I felt a twinge of urgency: Was IBM where I wanted to be for the long haul?

SRI was over at the end of March. Before flying home I took the train to Connecticut to spend a weekend with Jim Hefley and his wife, Judy. Jim had worked with me when I first transferred to Fayetteville, and Judy was the sister of my old high school pal Bob Taylor. The day that Jim had no-showed and I'd had to make the pivotal presentation to Walmart, he was finalizing his next move up the corporate ladder, to IBM data processing headquarters in White Plains, New York. I wanted to hear what life was like in that rarefied atmosphere.

It was fun catching up with them, but what I heard from Jim was anything but inspiring. He told me he spent most of his time running around making presentations to divisions *within* IBM, trying to get them to support data processing's latest product—to write software for it, to agree to market it, to get behind it at the expense, perhaps, of some other division's product. It was all about internal politics. He was basically a lobbyist at his own company.

I thought I'd rather have my toenails extracted.

□ □ □ □ □

I RETURNED TO Fayetteville a wiser man, but not in the way IBM had intended. I'd turned 28 in New York—time was slipping by. I'd always had a propensity for projecting myself into the future. Now I applied the template of time to everything around me: *Do I want to be lugging this briefcase to meetings with Walmart 20 years from now?* It was an unanswerable question.

But time is elastic. Some days I felt an imminent worry, other days I could banish the questions from my mind. I lived that way for the next six months. Then, in mid-October 1971, I received word that I'd been selected to attend a two-day class in New Orleans. It was a class about how to plan your career, and everyone at IBM knew it was a precursor to promotion. You might not get promoted immediately, but this "career class" was a tip-off that you were on the fast track and would likely receive a promotion within a year or so.

The class was held right before Thanksgiving. I remember nothing substantive about the class itself, but the instructor's opening words have never left me: "You've got to think about the rest of your life," he said. "All of you are likely to be promoted within the next few years, and you really need to decide what you want to do. You need to have a strategic planning session with yourself. This isn't a group session, but you do need to coordinate it with your family. Family wishes are key here. So I suggest that the only good way to do this is to get away by yourself for at least one day, with a pen and a note pad, and write down what's important to you, what the issues are in your life. You've got to write stuff down, and you have to articulate it, or it's not real."

So here it was, no more time for drifting. One thing I feared was being promoted out of the work I loved, and it occurred to me to tell IBM I wanted to stay in the field a few more years and *then* I would move up the ladder. But would I be ready then? Was I just procrastinating?

The instructor's admonitions about family really hit home with me. The joke was that IBM stood for I've Been Moved—climbing the corporate ladder meant that you had to be willing to relocate every couple of years for up to a decade. I knew Jane would have trouble with that. She was a good soldier, she would go, but she wouldn't do well at it. She was struggling internally, trying to fight off a feeling that I can only imagine as emptiness. She didn't want to go back to work. She didn't know *what* she wanted to do. And, frequently, she seemed angry at me about it.

I was at another crossroads. Staying with IBM was a domestic disaster in the making. If IBM was my choice, Jane and I might as well get divorced right now, because divorce would be inevitable.

Then I thought: *Alex Dietz*. We still raced motocross together, still talked all the time. Six months prior to this, Alex's immediate superior at Demographics had been fired and Alex was now running the business. It was a lean young company, entrepreneurial in spirit, still making it up as they went. Hadn't I flourished in Fayetteville, where I was basically my own boss? In this new light, the service bureau looked vastly more attractive.

Over the Thanksgiving holiday, I told Jane I was thinking of leaving IBM. She seemed open to the idea—though she was understandably nervous about it too. I also broached the subject with her dad, Bob Dills, who was totally flummoxed. "You're going to throw away this brilliant career?" I explained to him that I couldn't stay at IBM forever, and it was high time that I figured out what I was going to do with my life. "Charles," he said, "I think it's a terrible idea."

But I had reached that point that I sometimes do, when a decision had been made and there was no changing my mind. I'd been like that all my life—I could roll on, and roll on, and roll on with some situation or another, and then I would reach my limit. Then there was no talking me out of it.

Just after Thanksgiving I phoned Alex. "I've got to leave IBM," I said.

"Why? What happened?"

I told him the story and said I wanted to come talk with him about working at Demographics. He said great—but Charles Ward was on an extended trip to Mexico. It would be better to wait until he was back.

No problem, I said.

A day later I got a call from my boss in Little Rock. "You need to fly to New Orleans tomorrow," he said. "They want to talk with you about a job teaching the career class. It's a great opportunity."

My heart sank, and I called Alex again. "Everything's changed," I said, and explained the situation. "They're going to want an answer soon. And I need one before that."

5

RED SEA
CHANGE

1 0 0 1 0 1 0 0 1 0 1 1 0 0 1 0 1 0 0 0 1 0 0 1 0 1 1 0 0 1 0 1 0 1 1 0 0 1 1

CHARLES WARD DID fly home from Mexico to meet with Alex and me. In his mid-30s, Ward was a big, exuberant man with his own airplane. When I got to know him better, I heard stories of his escapades, many of which took place in bars with attractive women who were not his wife. "Want to go to Mexico?" he'd say to the disbelieving young lady. "Come on, *we're going to Cozumel!*" Whereupon he would phone his pilots and tell them to have the plane ready. Jane used to say she couldn't understand how Charles Ward's wife, Sharon, could stay married to the man.

Charles was—as I would also later learn—a bit of a visionary, albeit one with a tendency to take his eye off the ball. He tossed ideas into the air and hoped someone else would run with them while he was busy jetting around. Years later when Demographics had grown enough to need more space, Charles decreed that we would buy the adjacent parcel of land. Soon he found that he already owned that; what he *didn't* own was the parcel we'd been occupying for nearly 14 years. Fortunately, nobody had bought that land out from under us.

But he did have vision—he could see disparate events in the wider world, connect them, and imagine new possibilities. When he observed the success that Ross Perot was having with EDS in Dallas, renting out computer time to other companies, Charles had an idea. On the most basic level, he realized that the data processing center he was paying IBM and Alex to operate for Ward School Bus Company could just as well be spun off into a business of his own, so that instead of paying IBM he would be paying himself. That's when he "sweet-talked" Alex, as Alex puts it, to leave IBM and come to work on this new business. In truth, Alex dearly loves Arkansas and didn't want to live anyplace else on earth—clearly a problem if he remained with IBM. "I thought this was an opportunity to build a career in Arkansas," Alex says. So he threw himself into this new company, Demographics. They would rent time on the data center computers to as many companies as they could sign up, and in the meantime Ward School Bus Company—which Charles and his brother, Steve, had taken over from their parents—would keep them afloat.

Beyond that basic business concept, however, Charles Ward had an idea for linking this new venture to his personal passion—Democratic politics. One of two people from Arkansas on the Democratic National Committee, Charles was also on the DNC's steering committee. He and DNC chairman Robert Strauss were running buddies, flying all over the country trying to help Democratic candidates get out the vote. In forming Demographics, Charles had the grand notion that his new company could become a major national player in computer-generated letters sent out by, or for, Democratic candidates. In his homework phase, he traveled to Tulsa, Oklahoma, to Oral Roberts University. Remember televangelist Oral Roberts? Roberts and his team had pioneered the art of computer letter writing—in his case, as a computer-generated collection plate.

Demographics had been in operation two years when I joined. The plan was for Alex and me to run the business together, as equals. In hindsight it probably wasn't the brightest management decision, but it was the only way forward at the time. I told Charles and Alex that I wouldn't work for Alex, and Alex didn't want to work for me. So Ward started me at the salary Alex was making, and I got 10 percent equity in the company, just as Alex had. Ward would remain CEO, and Alex and I would be senior vice presidents, responsible for building the business.

When I told my boss at IBM that I was leaving, he could hardly believe his ears. He brought in *his* boss to talk to me. I was giving up a brilliant future with IBM, the big boss said—in fact, I'd been identified as someone who might someday rise to the top position in the entire company. Uncharacteristically, he left the door open if I ever wanted to return—IBM usually turned its back on employees who spurned them. In the meantime, his opinion was, "This is insane." It was an assessment echoed by just about everyone I knew, including my parents.

I started at Demographics on January 10, 1972. For the first three months, I lived with Alex while looking for a house. There really wasn't much available, so Jane and I decided to buy property out in the country and build. We found a builder with plans we liked, and moved into a small house in a new subdivision while the builder was finishing the other house.

Jane was happy to move to Conway. Just leaving her life in Fayetteville behind seemed to improve her spirits—clean slate, new chance, starting over. The day we moved into the small house, one of the neighbors was driving by and stopped to welcome us to the neighborhood. In Jane's words: "This girl—her name was Beverly Pascoe—was the most wonderful girl in the world and became one of my dearest friends. She just saved the day." We also joined the country club. So Jane was the new person in town, with new friends in the neighborhood and at the club, and she had the house as a new, consuming project. She was feeling very good about life, and about herself. One indicator of just how much better Jane was feeling: She became pregnant again while we were in that house.

I was feeling hopeful too. After a few months at Demographics, I could see that this was a business with great potential. Besides the service bureau side of the operation, we were already doing political direct mail—in election years we could generate good income helping Democratic candidates reach the right voters. In non-election years, not so good. But I came into the company believing that we could grow both the service bureau side *and* the direct mail side—direct mail was new then, and I saw potential along both political and commercial lines. Thinking back to what I'd learned at IBM—"The Difference is You"—I figured two smart guys like Alex and me could recruit some topnotch talent and really lift this business off the ground. During the meeting to work out the details of my employment, I told Charles Ward that I wanted to make this a $10-million-a-year company—that, I figured, would outdo what my Uncle Ralph generated at Speer Hardware. "That's very ambitious," Ward said. "Right now we're at seven hundred thousand a year."

□ □ □ □ □

BUT A FEW months into the job, Alex and I had settled into a frustrating pattern—being such good friends, we were each trying our damnedest not to offend the other. And to my mind progress was the casualty.

Ninety percent of our interaction was smooth, especially about day-to-day operations. But when it came to new business, new employees, new directions, new anything, we seldom fully agreed.

I never wanted to say, "Alex, you have *got* to do this!" Instead, I'd say, "Alex, what do you think about doing so-and-so?"

"Well, I don't know if we ought to do that right now," he would say. "I think we need to come up with a budget."

"Alex," I'd say, trying not to sound exasperated, "there are only twenty-five people working here, and I know what everybody's working on, and I know what we're paying, and I know every bit of revenue that's coming into this place. I look at our expenses and our financial statements every month. So if I do projections and a budget for the next year, what purpose is that going to serve?"

"Well, you just have to do budgets so you can manage your expenses."

"Fine, we'll do budgets. But I think that's not what we ought to be spending our time on."

That was the tenor of many of our conversations—to my mind, our most *important* conversations. If we agreed on something, we could go ahead and do it; we didn't have to check with Charles Ward on very many decisions. But too often, agreement seemed impossible. Naturally, I saw the situation in car terms—my foot was on the accelerator, his foot was on the brake.

It was a frustrating time for me—and also for Alex, as he would later admit. Fortunately, 1972 was an election year and we were plenty busy with existing work. That year, the Democratic National Committee was still carrying debt from the 1968 loss to Nixon, and chairman Bob Strauss decreed that they had to wipe out the existing debt before the coming presidential election. So they decided to stage a fund-raising telethon on July 8, 1972, the day before the start of the Democratic Nominating Convention in Miami Beach. It was to be a glittering 19-hour TV extravaganza featuring many Hollywood stars; we got involved a couple of months prior to prepare direct-mail pieces both to promote the telethon and to generate seed money to help pay for it. The DNC had various copywriters try their hand at the direct-mail letters, but the ones from Demographics—written by Alex Dietz—always performed best. In this relatively new field of direct-mail marketing, the DNC came to consider us the gold standard. Alex and I both attended the Democratic Convention that summer, my first physical foray into an exciting—but ultimately problematic—world that I would inhabit for several years to come.

Three months later, Jane's fragile good spirits suffered a sad setback. In late October 1972, she and I went with her dad and sister and brother-in-law to Austin, Texas, for the Arkansas-Texas football game, a fierce rivalry that dates back to 1894. We all dressed up in our red and white and turned out to cheer the Razorbacks— *Woooooo, Pig! Sooooiee!* Unfortunately, that day the Hogs lost to the Longhorns 35-15—but, after all, it was only a football game. That night we went to a party as the guests of some Texas people. So there we were, a small, conspicuous island of red-and-white in a vast ocean of Texas orange. We were standing around sipping our drinks and chatting with some of the good sports we'd met that evening, when a couple of men walked past us and one said, in a cracker accent loud enough to make sure we heard him, "I smell *pig* shit—don't you?"

Jane became incensed by the insult. She never could stand criticism, even this indirect kind, and she insisted we leave at once. She was just beside herself, agitated beyond reason. The only thing to do was to thank our hosts and go.

She was still railing when we got back to the hotel room. Within a short time, she suffered a miscarriage; I think her pregnancy was four months along at that point. We rushed her to the hospital, where they performed a D&C. I have no idea if her getting so upset could've precipitated the miscarriage.

I did my best to comfort her; I told her we would try again. But the miscarriage—which happened very near the anniversary of her mother's death—sent her spiraling downward. For a long time she was inconsolable.

□ □ □ □ □

AFTER ABOUT 15 MONTHS at Demographics, I managed to convince Alex that we needed to spend the money to recruit a topnotch core management team—both to handle the work we had and to help land the new work we desperately needed. Our recruiting plan was simple—hire the smartest people we knew, give them a little stock for motivation, and turn them loose.

We started by contacting our old friend from IBM, Rodger Kline. I think it's best to let Rodger and the others tell their own stories of this time. "Charles and I hadn't had any conversations for probably a year after he joined Demographics," Rodger recalls. "Then he started trying to recruit me. At first, I wasn't interested. I was happy with IBM. Then a funny thing happened to me in my IBM career.

"They still had only one salesman in Fayetteville. And our one salesman left IBM because the University of Arkansas had decided to go with a leasing company rather than buy the computer directly from IBM. It was still an IBM computer, but if the client got it from a leasing company instead of directly from IBM, it was considered a tremendous loss inside IBM. It really put the salesman in the doghouse with management, so he quit instead of suffering that abuse. And they forced me into being a salesman.

"What I found out was that I didn't enjoy being a salesman—having to put up with all the politics and stuff that you had to deal with. And so all of a sudden I'd gone from a job where I loved getting up every morning and going to work and putting in long hours and numerous all-nighters trying to fix a technical problem, to a totally different job that I didn't like. I could have moved back to my systems engineering job, and I was *going* to move back. But this episode changed my perspective on the long-term enjoyment of climbing the career ladder in IBM. And that opened my mind to Charles' recruiting pitch.

"I knew that both Charles and Alex were very sharp guys. Even though Alex had been at IBM's Little Rock office and I was in Fayetteville, we went to common meetings and I came to respect him a lot. I knew he was a really good computer guy with his own unique set of skills. He's creative, and also a very creative programmer.

"And for Charles I had the greatest respect—both technically and in terms of his ability to work with customers. He was very good at getting customers to understand that they needed to invest in a bigger computer. So I respected both these guys and bought into their vision—to join them and grow a company and be in charge of our own success."

In May 1973, Rodger joined us in Conway—in a job that ironically involved a lot of selling. "Charles hired me as director of marketing rather than in a technical position," Rodger says, "because he wanted me to be the cash cow that would allow Demographics to go out and do other things to grow. And so I ran the service bureau. I pretty much sold every business in Conway.

"I really enjoyed it—because I was in charge of the programming of it even though I had some programmers who worked for me. I would go out there and find out what the business needed, and then I would make a proposal that we can do these applications for you. We did all the payrolls in Conway. And then we did a lot of management information systems for manufacturing. I would propose it and price it so it would be profitable. And then I'd go back and lay it out for the programmers and give them the concepts of the system and then manage them day-to-day to write the software, test it, and install it."

The next person we brought aboard was my old college pal Jerry Adams. Jerry, the English major, had made the leap from literature to computer programming. "I worked for Ross Perot at the time Charles and Alex approached me," Jerry recalls. "I was a systems engineer at EDS, writing code. I'd gone to law school after Sewanee and just hated it, so I went to work at McDonnell Automation for six months, then did ten months in Naval Officer Candidate School. So I had acquired some programming experience. And I had an aptitude for programming.

"IBM wasn't hiring when I got out of the Navy, so I joined EDS in Dallas. The EDS program I went to was a systems engineering development program—a boot camp that about twenty-five percent of the people washed out of. So it was very good, but I busted my ass for four and a half years. EDS was out of control. There were only six hundred people in the company when I started, and thirty-two hundred when I left—four and a half years later. I had disk drives in my trunk, driving all over Dallas for machine time. If there was machine time open between three and five o'clock somewhere, I was there. I worked a hundred hours a week. It was a great environment to learn technology, and to work for Ross Perot. But you got paid nothing, and there were tough family life issues.

"Charles and I had stayed in touch. He'd been best man in my wedding to Madelyn; unfortunately, I missed his wedding to Jane because I was in OCS. We had always talked about wanting to do something together, which was probably a relatively hollow comment at the time. But then, in January of nineteen seventy-three, Charles and Alex came down to Texas for a motocross race in Fort Worth. They stayed with us, so I got to know Alex. And I went to the race. But while they were there, we talked again about working together. It really was a good time for me because I'd been at EDS for a while. I'd also started a restaurant that wasn't doing very well, so it wasn't a bad thing to run away from.

"They started asking whether I would consider joining them and I said I probably would, and so we kept that conversation going. And then in May nineteen seventy-three, I took some time off to go up to Conway and just explore. I spent a week there, during which I told Alex I'd like to make some calls. I'd like to see what's going on. And I liked it. So I said fine, and went back home and quit. We moved to Conway in June of seventy-three. My first assignment was to join Rodger as part of the service bureau sales team."

Our third hire was Jim Womble, IBMer and my beer-drinking roommate that summer in Houston. "I remember this like it was yesterday," says Jim. "I'd been married for five and a half years but separated for the last year. I'd never really had a goal—something I wouldn't realize for another decade or so. I was just working for IBM in Little Rock, thinking, *It doesn't get any better than this*. Everybody I met was smart. And I thought I was supposed to do what my mother had always told me—be loyal to my employer.

"So I just assumed I was going to march along at IBM, but I didn't know where I was going. I didn't want to move to Cleveland, or Pittsburgh, which you had to do. Every two years, you moved around. Even so, I was still just trying to do the best job I could. I'd been a systems engineer for a while. Then I joined a sales team. The state of Arkansas was my patch.

"My divorce was final on my daughter's birthday—March fourth. And sometime that week, in nineteen seventy-four, Charles and Rodger and Alex called me. They were on the speakerphone in Conway. 'What are you doing?' they said.

"'Nothing,' I said. 'I just got divorced.'

"'Well, you need to come to work up here.'

"'All right,' I said. 'I'll definitely think about that.' The only reason I said that was because I had such respect for those three guys. And I'd heard all *kinds* of stories about Charles Ward.

"The first conversation I had with them, they said, 'We want to be the EDS of political direct mail.' That was the goal. And I'd made a clandestine trip down to

Dallas about two years before to interview with EDS. The recruiters were mostly ex-military guys—those were the kinds of guys Ross Perot hired. So this recruiter had come to Little Rock and called. 'Let's have lunch,' he said. So we did. And during lunch, he said, 'Look, I'm looking for the very best people I can possibly find. And I need to find one or two top people in Little Rock and hire them. Do you know who they are?'

"'Well,' I said, 'you're looking at one of them.'

"'You need to come in,' he said. 'And bring your wife.'

"So I go down there, bringing my then-wife. They took her off somewhere, and they got me in this room and brought in all these different people. Now, I had spent eight years of hard labor, working just unbelievable hours at IBM. But these guys, they go, 'Oh, man, we got cots here. You can work twenty hours.'

"It wasn't that I was afraid of work. I just thought, *This is not for me.* 'Guys,' I said, 'I'm wasting your time,' and I left the interview before it was over. But it was really interesting, and I'm so happy I went down there to talk to them.

"Now Charles and Rodger and Alex wanted to be the EDS of political direct mail. That didn't work out, which in the end was for the best. But, anyhow, I came to work at Demographics in April of seventy-four. My title was general manager, whatever that meant. We did have a number of different operations, such as keypunch, computer operations, letter shop, and so on, and those reported to me."

Our fourth and final hire in this initial round of core management recruiting was as unpredictable as these others were not. First of all, there was no history to speak of. Second, our newest employee was a woman. "So I'm working at IBM on a Sunday," says Jim Womble, "and this young woman walks in. She was— well, now I know she was barely twenty years old and she'd just graduated from the University of Texas with a degree in computer science. Her parents were both professors at UT. She and her husband, who was in medical prosthesis sales or something, had moved to Little Rock to work. Her name was Jennifer Phillips, and she just dropped by that Sunday afternoon and I got to know her. I could tell she was really, *really* smart."

"When I met Jim," says Jennifer, "I was programming the criminal justice highway safety information system for the State of Arkansas—Arkansas was one of the pilot states for that program that linked the prisons and the police departments with the National Crime Information Center. People often ask me about back then, being a woman in a man's profession, but I got a degree in computer science from UT in nineteen seventy and there were only a couple of universities that had undergraduate programs in math and computer science. That gave me a skill set that people were very hungry for, so they kind of overlooked gender. I was the first female programmer the state of Arkansas ever hired.

"I was to help implement that system for two, almost three years, and Jim was with IBM and IBM was the vendor. So I met Jim through developing and installing all those systems.

"After the program ended, I went into the general pool for the State of Arkansas and I hated that. The project had been fun, but the general pool was typical state government. Jim had left IBM the month before and I called him and said I can't stand it in this pool. And he said, 'Why don't you come up here?' So I drove up to Conway and Jim introduced me to Charles and Alex. I never even did a resume, I don't think. Jim knew all my work experience, because I was straight out of college. I started at Demographics in June, nineteen seventy-four."

Jennifer typically plays down the impact of a woman in an all-male management team in those days. But skill set is one thing, aura is something else. In 1974 we guys were in our early 30s—I was 31. Jennifer was an extremely good looking blonde woman of 24. You couldn't help but feel her presence.

Not that she played the female card—far from it. In some ways she was tougher and more manly than the rest of us. She dressed deer herself—on a picnic table just outside her kitchen. Early in her tenure she supervised the computer room, a shock to some of the young programmers who'd never worked for a woman. Trying to run her off, they planted several dead mice in the raised floor where all the computer and printer cables ran, then called her over to see about "a printer problem." The ruse didn't have the desired effect. When they lifted up the floor to check the printer wires, there were all these mice that they'd tried to make look not so dead. "Get those mice out of here," Jennifer said, matter of factly. "Now what's the problem with the printer?"

She was opinionated and argumentative, more than holding her own in meetings; not everyone liked working with her. But she had an impressive ability to compartmentalize things: Work was work, and after work was something else. We'd all go out for drinks, and the argument she'd clung to earlier in the day was left behind—even if her opponent was now sitting next to her. And when we all ate lunch together, she wasn't dainty. "We *wolfed* the food down," says Womble, "and Jennifer would be right in there with us. She was just one of the guys."

Except, of course, she wasn't.

□ □ □ □ □

WITH ALL THIS high-octane talent around us, it was even more imperative that Alex and I be able to make and implement decisions. "A two-headed monster in a Japanese horror flick," says Womble, wryly recalling our strategic management impasse from those days.

In the late spring of 1974, a potential solution to our problem appeared in the flamboyant form of Ghaith Pharaon, a global mover and shaker from Saudi Arabia. Pharaon was fabulously wealthy. At this point he was about 34 years old and had lived a charmed life. His father, a doctor, had been the personal physician for generations of Saudi kings; later Dr. Pharaon was named Saudi's ambassador to France, where young Ghaith attended the best schools in Paris. Coming to the U.S. for college, he received his undergraduate degree from Stanford and an MBA from Harvard. After school, he started his own company, the Saudi Arabian Research and Development Corporation, called by the acronym REDEC. It wasn't long after REDEC's launch that the 1973 OPEC oil embargo tripled the price of oil, sending Saudi Arabia into a building frenzy, meaning that Ghaith Pharaon and REDEC were very much in the right place at the right time.

And now here he was in our little one-story office in Conway, Arkansas. One day he walked in the door with Charles Ward. No, let me rephrase that: Ward walked in the door, Pharaon *blew* through it—his energy was such that he appeared to be a very short and dapper whirlwind. I'll never forget how he sat, both feet on the floor and both hands on his knees, feet and hands just tap, tap, tapping. The guy could not sit still.

He was in Conway because he and Charles Ward were working on a school bus deal together. Pharaon was going to broker a contract with the Saudi government for a thousand school buses from Ward School Bus Company, and Charles Ward was going to pay Pharaon 20 percent of the gross sales price. But while Pharaon was in our office, he wanted to know everything Demographics was doing. "Do you do payroll? Do you do ledgers?" He was like a sponge. So Alex and I walked him through our little operation, showing him our computer room and the variety of services we provided for our clients.

When we got back to our offices, Pharaon said, "All right, we need to put this same thing in Saudi Arabia. We have thousands of workers and not a single computer in the whole kingdom. We'll install the first computers and we can do payroll. I'll connect you with all the banks. We can get all the business we want, and you can run it." And with that, he blew back through the door. He'd been in our office 20 minutes.

Was that for real? Alex and I had to sit and rest following Pharaon's visit. Meanwhile, he was headed to the Little Rock airport where his personal airplane was waiting to whiz him to his next stop. Pharaon was the first person I ever knew to convert a full-size airliner—in his case, a 727—to an executive jet. He also outfitted it with extra fuel tanks so he could fly, for example, from Little Rock to Saudi Arabia with a single stop.

The answer to whether or not this was real was an emphatic yes—not only that, Pharaon wanted it done yesterday. He and Charles Ward worked it out so that both parties would own 50 percent of the operation. Pharaon would provide the building, secure all the contracts and approvals, and we—someone—would run the operation. Right away, he wanted us to give him specs for the building—how many people would we need? What hook-ups? What configuration? And he wanted one of us to come to Saudi Arabia immediately to supervise the setting up of this new computer center.

"Which one of you guys is going?" Charles Ward said. Alex and I just looked at each other.

This was a windfall no matter which prism we viewed it through. One thing we were working on was landing a list processing contract with the AFL-CIO. But new prospects were yet to pay off, and at the same time our political direct mail was in trouble—just-passed changes to campaign finance laws now limited political contributions to $1,000 for individuals and $5,000 for PACs. We still had the telethon and other projects for the Democratic National Committee, but going forward it would be harder for individual candidates to spare the funds to pay for our services. So Ghaith Pharaon and Saudi Arabia would be a much-needed boon to our bottom line.

A Saudi office also offered distinct personal advantages. Whoever went, Alex and I would no longer be butting heads on important long-range matters; we would each have a business to run. From my perspective, we were dangerously close to the exploding point—at least I was. I told Jane that without Saudi Arabia, I would probably have to leave—either that or Charles Ward would have to put me in charge. "Maybe the answer is that *we* go to Saudi Arabia for a year or two," I said. "It'll give us time to figure things out."

The more we talked about it, the better it sounded—and not just because of me. Jane was really struggling with depression. Following the miscarriage in '72, she did become pregnant again, which boosted her spirits for a time. But after our second child, son Rob, was born in November 1973, she started spiraling again. We were in the new house by now, so that building project was over and Jane was feeling empty. Fortunately, she realized she needed help and began seeing a psychiatrist, Chuck Smith, in Little Rock.

Now here, beckoning, was a move to Saudi Arabia—the mother of all projects. As we talked, Jane got excited about it. It seemed to answer all our needs, though of course it wouldn't. Once we were there, reality would take over and we'd be in the same situation we were in now, except worse—we'd be living with our two children in an alien, misogynistic, and authoritarian foreign country. I've already told you how Jane reacted to authority. But the nature of depression is such that the prospect of change—*any* change—outweighs the rational assessment of the likely consequences; for the moment, Saudi Arabia looked like a way out of all our troubles.

The next day I went to the office and told Alex that Jane and I would go. "No," he said, "that's crazy. I'm single, no kids, no encumbrances—I'm the one to go. That's the only thing that makes sense."

In the light of day, I couldn't really argue. Alex lived in a house in a little town called Morgan, between Conway and Little Rock. His buying there had been a strategic personal decision—to put him closer to his very active Little Rock social life. He now had roommates, Jim Womble and Rodger Kline, both of whom were recently divorced. So they were three single guys in a bachelor pad together, while Jane and I had two small children and had just spent a lot of money building a large new house in the country.

On the surface it was a no-brainer.

□ □ □ □ □

ALEX LEFT FOR Jeddah, Saudi Arabia, in late 1974. For months we communicated mostly by telex, because despite all the wealth of Saudi Arabia, many things there didn't work. The distance and time difference added to the complexity of coordination, and the bulk of the difficulty fell on Alex. He had his hands full—making sure the new building had everything it needed; setting up a complete data center; training computer operators that we had to hire internationally, from Conway; making presentations to banks and construction companies about computerizing their payroll. Even buying the computers was hard—we had to order them from IBM Europe.

I went over at least a couple of times in the first year of the operation. On one trip, I spent a couple of weeks with Alex and Charles Ward making calls, so I felt that I had a pretty good sense of the situation. Our new building was situated in proximity to the research and construction arms of Ghaith Pharaon's other ventures, and Alex lived in a condo in a gated compound in that general area. Ghaith himself had a fabulous complex on the Red Sea, with 20-foot walls behind which all sorts of debauchery took place. He often threw lavish parties, at which Alex was a regular—as were Ghaith's senior staff and other connected people in town. It's very hard to gain admittance to Saudi Arabia, so almost every outsider in Jeddah was working on a joint venture with some Saudi company. I was invited to one of Ghaith's parties: chamber music, great food, beautiful people, and so much liquor that it looked like they'd brought it in by tractor trailer. And this is a country that bars the importing of alcohol.

While it was my impression that Alex was now a quasi-member of the REDEC "family," he was also cut off from most natural human interaction. He had almost no communication with the outside world; he had no wife—he was the sole single person in our Jeddah office; and there were no women for him to date. It was impossible, let alone dangerous, to meet local women; and in Saudi Arabia, single women from outside can't come into the country without the king's permission.

The only single woman he had any contact with was Ghaith Pharaon's executive assistant, a woman named Mary. I met her. She was half Egyptian and half Greek, a beautiful combination. She'd been married when she arrived in Saudi Arabia, but she and her husband had divorced. By then she'd become essential to the smooth operation of Ghaith's office, and since he knew the king he was able to obtain special dispensation for Mary to remain in Jeddah.

She lived in a huge condo in a compound two blocks from Alex. And the way he later explained events to Charles Ward and me, Mary approached him one day with a request for friendship. It went something like this: "Look, I'm here by myself, you're here by yourself. Ghaith has his family, and he's often gone and sometimes I can't go with him. So here I sit in this big condo and there you sit in yours. I'd like to have some company sometimes—a friend, that's all I'm talking about. This is nothing else."

Who can blame Alex for thinking it was a good idea?

□ □ □ □ □

MEANWHILE, BACK IN Conway, we were struggling. We'd brought in all these hotshots to help build the business, but it was extremely slow going. We had political work that came and went as the candidates won or lost, and we were spending an inordinate amount of time on 125 service bureau clients, some of whom were paying us as little as $15 a month. Our big client, the school bus company, seemed always to be in financial trouble; our most profitable client, a land developer called Diamondhead that for years had sent monthly computer-generated letters offering free vacations to potential retirees, had just abandoned their direct mail campaign due to the mid-'70s recession. Our best client, gone overnight. This was no way to build a railroad. Eventually, we would confront all these issues head on, but not yet; for the moment we seemed to be just feeling our way forward.

And not much felt right. One day Charles Ward said to me, "You need to go meet with Jerry Brown in California." I can't recall exactly when this was—I don't think Brown was governor yet; maybe he was still California Secretary of State. I can't even recall the reason for the meeting, except that it involved data—a mailing list—that Brown had access to and we might want. So I flew out there and sat down with him, just the two of us. He was a mere kid, just five years older than me. What I do remember is that the meeting felt fishy.

Another time I found myself in late-night motel-room meetings with representatives of the Kennedy political machine—there was something we might do for them and they were trying to figure out how to pay us; I got the feeling that a paper trail was a problem. And then there was the time that we were approached about buying the Massachusetts master voter registration list, which I think is illegal to even have. Stay in it long enough and political work will just start feeling *wrong*.

Even our computer work for the AFL-CIO was becoming problematic; unions presented their own difficulties. But what we were doing for them was groundbreaking, and I had a sense that this could be a pattern for our future. The man we were working with, John Perkins, headed up the union's Committee for Political Education, commonly known as COPE, and he was a forward thinker—I still think of him as the Big Daddy of Political Big Data. In the mid-1970s, the AFL-CIO didn't know much about the people in its individual member unions—the Brotherhood of Electrical Workers, say—beyond their names and home addresses. They didn't even know their phone numbers. Perkins wanted us to help him change that. He wanted to know everything there was to know about those individual members, including if they were Democrats or Republicans. Armed with that information, he could begin to mobilize this vast membership in support of causes—and political candidates—that COPE deemed friendly to labor.

The way it worked, COPE hired people to go out to critical voting districts and compile voting information. Back then, voting records were usually buried away in individual courthouses, so it took a massive manpower effort to *mine* this data and bring it together in one place. That was step one. Step two was for us to buy a white-page telephone list from a company called Metro Mail and match the union membership rolls to the voting data. Step three was for COPE to set up phone banks to start calling these union members, to find out where they stood on a particular issue, and whether or not they needed assistance getting to the polls.

It wasn't rocket science. But what it was, way back in 1975, was the beginnings of the ground game that allowed Obama and the Democrats to win presidential elections some three decades later. Perkins was absolutely the father of that. It was also the first stirrings of the data-gathering skill and large scale name-and-address processing that would one day put our small company on the world map. As with Sam Walton before him, from John Perkins I learned a vital lesson in the power of data—that if compiled and acted upon, it can change the world.

☐ ☐ ☐ ☐ ☐

THE FIRST I heard about our Middle East problem was in a telex that Alex sent to Charles Ward and me. He and Mary had become serious, he said, and Ghaith Pharaon was upset about it—so upset that he'd decreed that they stop seeing each other. As I came to understand the sequence of events, Alex and Mary had hidden their relationship from Ghaith, but they felt guilty about it so they finally decided to go to Ghaith and spill the beans; the beans apparently included the fact that Alex had asked Mary to marry him.

The meeting with Ghaith had not gone well. All that nervous energy he'd displayed here in Conway? It was like his nerve endings were lit fuses connecting to a cache of explosives deep inside him. Now it went off big time. Alex was stunned; Mary probably wasn't. Because Mary wasn't just Pharaon's executive assistant; she was also his mistress—something I wouldn't learn until much later. Another crucial element to this saga is that Mary apparently had, at some point, told Ghaith that she didn't want to be a mistress forever and had demanded that he marry her. That was impossible, Ghaith had said—if he married an expat, he'd be banished from the presence of the King.

These events happened just prior to Ghaith's annual Mediterranean cruise for his clients and customers. As majority owner of Ward School Bus Company and Demographics, Charles Ward was invited on the cruise, along with his wife. So were Alex and Mary, though not together. Charles told me that he and Alex were extremely nervous about what might happen on the cruise—would Alex find himself thrown overboard in the middle of the night? They pretty much held their breath as they boarded the ship.

But early in the cruise, perhaps at the opening ceremony, Ghaith started speaking in the big ballroom and proceeded to announce that Mary and Alex were getting married. Everybody gave them a big hand. And Ghaith, Charles said, was all smiles. "Oh, I'm so glad," he gushed. "I'm so *happy* for you."

So it appeared that he'd changed his mind. But after they docked in Saudi Arabia, Ghaith called Alex and Mary in. "You will not even speak to each other unless it's purely about business," he said. "What I am saying is, you cannot even *talk* to each other. Is that clear, is that understood?"

Fast forward to the inevitable. When Alex refused to terminate the relationship, Ghaith revoked his Saudi sponsorship and forced both Alex and Mary to leave the country. They quickly packed bags and fled in the dead of night, bound for her father's home in Athens, Greece.

That was on a weekend. On Monday morning Arkansas time, Alex phoned Charles Ward and told him that he and Mary had been thrown out of Saudi Arabia. At which point Charles began frantically searching for me.

My family and I were on vacation at Hilton Head Resort in South Carolina. We went there every year with extended family, and Jane loved it. She seemed to relax there among familiar faces. The only battles she and I had at Hilton Head were across a tennis net. She was a very good, very competitive tennis player.

But on the day Charles was trying to reach me, I'd left my vacation for a couple of days to fly to Washington for a meeting with COPE's John Perkins. I remember walking into John's office and he said, "Charles Ward is desperately trying to reach you." So I ducked into another office and called Charles back. He was beside himself—breathlessly spilling out this crazy story about Alex, who was now exiled in Athens. The bottom line here is that we had some $100,000 invested in this Saudi deal, which was suddenly looking very shaky. To complicate matters, Charles and Ghaith were working on another school bus deal for Egypt, so there was a lot at stake. Charles wanted me to fly straight home from Washington—leaving, for the moment, my unsuspecting family lolling on the beach at Hilton Head.

Soon after my plane touched down in Little Rock, I met Charles at his apartment there and we managed to get Alex on the line. He explained the situation, and we hatched a plan: This was Monday evening—I would fly Tuesday morning to Athens, where I would debrief Alex and find out the extent of the damage; from Athens, I would try to go to Jeddah—I had no visa—to inspect the operation there; meanwhile, Charles Ward would urge Ghaith to meet us both in London the following weekend. So I had five days to get from Little Rock to Athens and do my business there, then to Jeddah to do more business, and finally to London for what might be a shoot-out with Ghaith.

"I thought he was going to get killed," Jane says today, reflecting on how she felt after I phoned her in Hilton Head and told her what the rest of my week looked like.

It was a long, lonely flight. I remember sipping my Jack Daniel's and thinking about Alex—all those crazy good times we'd had together. Tears came to my eyes.

I wasn't sure what was about to happen, but I did know that this whole debacle didn't bode well for him.

Wednesday morning, when I got off the plane in Athens, Alex wasn't there to meet me; only Mary was. "Where's Alex?" I said.

"Out buying a car," she said. Mary was driving a rental.

So for the first couple of hours, Mary had me all to herself. Clearly, she had set this up so she could grill me—it was like I was on the witness stand and she was a prosecutor; a very, very aggressive prosecutor. She wanted to know everything Charles Ward was thinking, everything I was thinking, what we planned to do about Alex and the Saudi meltdown. Finally, at my hotel, she dismissed her exhausted witness, suggesting that I take a nap—after which, she and Alex would come and pick me up. She had insisted that Alex buy a car, she said, so they could take me on a tour of Athens.

I slept for several hours. When at long last I saw Alex, he seemed unsettled— naturally so, considering. I was ready to get on with the debriefing, but they couldn't be dissuaded from their sightseeing plan; it was as though they wanted to delay the unpleasant talk as long as possible. The truth is, I wasn't angry; all I wanted to do was find out the extent of our trouble—and, for Alex, to take some of the pressure off the situation. Instead, we spent most of the rest of the day touring the city and even the countryside, stopping occasionally to get a bite to eat in simple little Greek restaurants. Finally I asked Alex what he was going to do.

"Stay in Europe with Mary," he said. "Find an IT job and work here."

Cool, I thought. *Of course you don't have a European work visa.*

"I know this is a huge embarrassment," he said, picking at his plate with his fork. "And I know I have to leave the company. Mary doesn't want to live in the U.S., she wants to stay in Europe. So that's what I'm going to do. Stay here with her. Somewhere in Europe." It all sounded nuts to me, but I understood that Alex was under tremendous pressure.

That was Wednesday. On Thursday, I talked with Alex in more detail. Then, sometime during that day, Mary phoned me at my hotel to say that Ghaith was on his way to Athens and wanted to meet with me Friday morning. He didn't want to see Alex.

The breakfast meeting with Ghaith, arranged by Mary, was at the restaurant in my hotel; she had pulled strings to get us a large table in a dining room that wasn't being used at the moment. Ghaith first talked with Mary, just the two of them. Then it was my turn. I'd been curious to see how this would go—loose cannon or studied calm? It was the latter. Speaking like the Harvard MBA he was, Ghaith affected a serious, businesslike manner. "I am so sorry about all this," he began. "I had *such* high hopes that this business would do well, but Alex has totally failed in his duties, and I had to remove him."

"I see," I said.

"I just wasn't comfortable with him leading the company any longer, and I had to act because it was damaging the chance for the partnership to be successful."

"Mmm-humm."

He then said he wanted me to go to Jeddah immediately to shore up the staff. "You'll need a visa," he said, "and I'll work it out with the government. Someone will meet you at the airport with the papers. I'll get you on a plane tonight."

That evening I boarded an airliner for the first leg of my trip to Saudi Arabia—without an entry visa. Would I be taken hostage? Would my hands be cut off? Would I ever see my family again? I changed planes in Cairo, where there'd recently been "an incident"—the airport was full of grim-looking soldiers carrying machine guns. I was glad to leave Cairo, but very apprehensive about what the airline called my "final destination."

We landed in Jeddah around midnight. Sure enough, the immigration people knew nothing about me. "You come to Saudi Arabia with no visa?" They were incredulous. I told them someone was to meet me with the papers, but I could tell they were wondering what kind of scam this loony American was trying to pull.

They detained me for a very long half-hour—then a man I had met before, an expat working with one of Ghaith's companies, showed up with the papers. He was ashen-faced, as nervous as I was. He explained that he'd had trouble getting through security to come to immigration. The immigration people studied the documents as I watched their faces for hints at my fate; they didn't seem to be happy. Then, finally, they stamped the paper and motioned me to basically get out of their sight. Relieved to be free, the expat and I walked out into the balmy night air and he drove me to a hotel.

On Saturday, I met with the service bureau staff. They were nervous about talking, but they knew the truth—not just about what had happened, but also about Ghaith's hair-trigger temper. The effect of it had trickled down to them. I told them Ghaith had said that Alex was incompetent. "That's bullshit," one of the computer operators said. It was clear to me that they liked and admired Alex. "He was under unimaginable pressure," another said. At that moment I really felt for Alex. What a mess. We talked much of the day about their various projects and what we needed to do going forward. The next morning, Sunday, I caught a very early flight to London.

I arrived at my hotel about 20 minutes before Charles Ward and I were to meet with Ghaith. I didn't have time to change clothes or freshen up, but I did manage a quick powwow with Charles. "What's your assessment?" he said.

"This deal is fucked," I said. "It's going to create nothing but heartache. We've got to get out of it. I suggest we tell Ghaith that we'll support a transition management of the service bureau. After that, we'll walk away, forfeiting all monies we've paid in. Just take the high road. Demographics is screwed, but maybe this way your Egyptian bus deal can be saved. There's no other way—Ghaith has all the leverage. And you, Charles, have too much at stake on the school bus side."

And that, in somewhat less candid terms, is what I told Ghaith at our meeting—that Ghaith had a good opportunity with the service bureau but we couldn't support it without Alex; in essence, we had gotten in over our head and would do the honorable thing—help with the transition and then turn everything over to Ghaith, forgoing our equity in the deal. Ghaith seemed very pleased by that outcome.

Months later, safely back in Arkansas, I learned three things about this whole sad saga that I hadn't known before. One, Ghaith had told Charles before our London meeting that any future dealings between Charles and REDEC would be over if Ghaith *ever* heard that Charles had hired Alex Dietz back for anything. Two, Ghaith eventually married Mary; in Saudi Arabia, having multiple wives is legally permissible. And three, the king of Saudi Arabia later approached Ghaith at a large function and slapped him on the cheek in front of everyone. "You have disgraced us all," the king reportedly said. And to show the depth of his displeasure, he forbade Ghaith from leaving the country for five years. Little Ghaith, tantrum thrower, placed in time out.

Far left: Speer Hardware Co. in Fort Smith, Arkansas—last outpost of civilization before the wild frontier.

Left: My grandfather, Ralph Speer Sr., ran it for a time.

Below: My grandmother, Betty Black Speer. We kids called her "Woggie."

Below, clockwise from left: My uncle, Ralph Speer Jr., who took over the hardware store in 1955. His sister, my mother, Betty Speer Morgan. My father, Charles Donald Morgan, whose life at Speer Hardware was made miserable by Uncle Ralph. Melanie Holt Speer, Uncle Ralph's wife, tried to make up for her husband's rudeness.

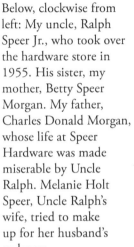

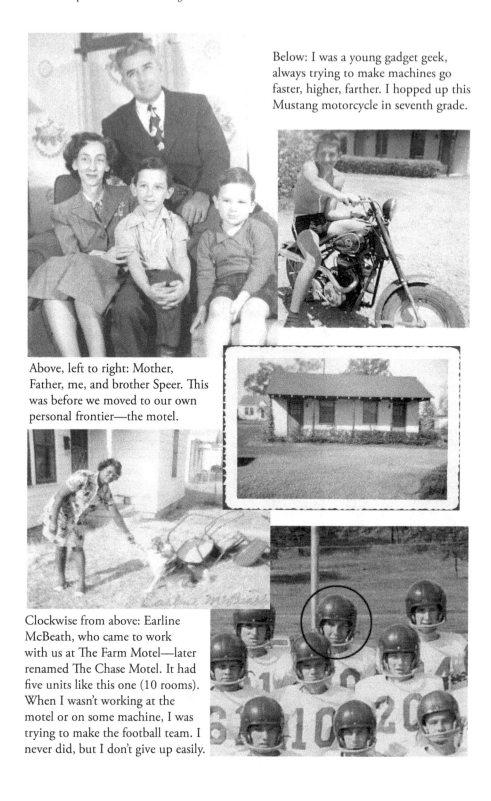

Below: I was a young gadget geek, always trying to make machines go faster, higher, farther. I hopped up this Mustang motorcycle in seventh grade.

Above, left to right: Mother, Father, me, and brother Speer. This was before we moved to our own personal frontier—the motel.

Clockwise from above: Earline McBeath, who came to work with us at The Farm Motel—later renamed The Chase Motel. It had five units like this one (10 rooms). When I wasn't working at the motel or on some machine, I was trying to make the football team. I never did, but I don't give up easily.

Left: My dream car, a Jaguar E Type, a wreck I found, bought, and rebuilt in 1965 in Houston, during a summer job with Humble Oil. The next year I started my career with IBM.

Above: Jane Dills and I married in August 1966 at the home of her parents, Lucille and Bob Dills.

Top left: Jane and I pack the Jag for our honeymoon.

Right: At the Dills' home in 1967.

Above: With Father and baby Carrie, born in September 1967, at a motocross race— my new passion.

Above: Christmas 1968 in the living room of the motel home. That mantel was where Mother's prize dish sat, until I shot it off with a rubber dart.

Left: At IBM, the hardware geek fell in love with software. In both 1969 and 1970, I was named Outstanding IBM Systems Engineer in the state of Arkansas.

Above: My IBM/motocross pal Alex Dietz in Mad Max mode. Alex and I would go on to play huge roles in each other's lives.

Left: I continued to reach new heights in motocross, winning many races.

Right: Our son, Rob, was born in November 1973. Here we are on the day of his christening—Mother, me holding Rob, Father, young Carrie, Jane and her father, Bob Dills.

Left: In 1972, I left IBM to join Alex Dietz at a small service bureau called Demographics, where we provided computer services to other companies. We specialized in mailing list processing. Today, the data contained in this whole room of disc platters could be held on a single memory stick.

Above: To grow the company, we started hiring the smartest people we knew, like Rodger Kline of IBM and my college pal Jerry Adams, an alum of Ross Perot's EDS.

Above: Jerry Adams talks with Demographics owner Charles Ward and his wife, Sharon.

Right: Me, Jim Womble (another hire from IBM), and Alex Dietz. Clearly, it was the '70s.

Left: In 1974, the fabulously wealthy Ghaith Pharaon—leg up, talking with Charles Ward at left—wanted to start a branch of Demographics in Saudi Arabia. Alex Dietz, in sunglasses below, went over to head it up.

Above: The deal was complicated (an understatement) by Alex's relationship with Pharaon's executive assistant/mistress, Mary, above with Ghaith.

Right: I arrive at the office in Jeddah, with driver, to see if the situation could be salvaged.

In 1978, I finally fulfilled my longstanding ambition to race cars. Above, my Datsun was what's known in racing circles as a "shit box," a car with a volunteer crew and only my engineering know-how to tweak the old engine and chassis. Compare this to the car (below) driven by Paul Newman and Bob Sharp—all top of the line. Still, I made it to the National Championships my first year. At right, Bob Ingenito, friend and colleague, and his wife, Lyn, at the track watching me run.

Growing Up: Clockwise from top left, Carrie, 14, leaves for boarding school to avoid conflict with her mother and, to a lesser extent, me. The original Demographics team in 1985 after we went public under the name CCX. My indispensable executive assistant, Sharon Tackett (still with me today), stands next to last in front row, right. Next to her in white dress is Jennifer Barrett. Rob, 12, loved all sports. Even at age 9, he wanted to follow me into motocross.

Below: Me with my damaged car at Daytona in the early '80s. In this race I lost the rear deck lid and finished with no wing—but I did finish.

From Little Data to Big Data: Left, our company's first computer, 1973.

Below, data was contained on magnetic tape.

Below center: How tape cartridges were stored.

Bottom: Acxiom's grid computing system circa 2002, essentially a private "cloud."

From the original white-roofed Demographics HQ in the center, by the late '80s CCX was on a building spree. I told the architect I wanted something that would "knock the socks off any New Yorker who visited," and he delivered.

Clockwise from above: Members of the Arkansas Business Council, a group known as "The Good Suit Club." Next to me is Charles Murphy Sr., of Murphy Oil; to Murphy's left is Don Tyson, of Tyson Foods. At the lectern are Sam Walton and then-Governor Bill Clinton. Right: In their later years my parents started a little list business of their own and I gave them space in our building. Bottom: Jane and I built this big house outside of town in 1986. It burned in 1991.

Log Cabin Democrat

6

DO OR DIE

1 0 0 1 0 1 0 0 1 0 1 1 0 0 1 0 1 0 0 0 1 0 0 1 0 1 1 0 0 1 0 1 0 1 1 0 0 1 1

ALEX STAYED IN Europe about a year. Then he came home to Arkansas, took a job managing the data processing for a Little Rock bank, got married, and became father to two children. I did track him down a few months after the Saudi episode and offered to buy his stock in Demographics; he agreed to sell. After that was consummated, we didn't see or speak to each other for maybe three years. I missed him as a friend, and I missed him as a colleague. I was sorry about what had happened to him. But I can't say I wasn't relieved to be able to finally run the company my way. I assumed the title of president; Rodger Kline and Jim Womble became executive vice-presidents.

By this time—approximately spring 1975 to spring 1976—several things were coming to a head, both at work and at home. We were very busy—Jerry was working with Senator Lloyd Bentsen of Texas on his 1976 re-election bid; Rodger was overseeing the service bureau business; and Jim, Jennifer, and I were handling the COPE account, which included writing computer programs. And now there was a complicated new wrinkle in our dealings with the AFL-CIO—the union's board had decided that they couldn't trust such sensitive work to be done in a little shop in Conway, Arkansas; they wanted us to start doing our data processing in their secure Washington headquarters.

I think we all recognized that we were just treading water—and barely keeping our heads above it. "Payroll was exciting," Jerry Adams recalls. "Ward School Bus was not a very good payer and they were our biggest customer. So we were always in contact with their CFO saying, 'You know, we need to make payroll.' Those early days were very galvanizing—there's nothing like having a common enemy like payroll." Once, I was even forced to borrow money from Bob Dills, Jane's dad, in order to pay our people.

With all this daily stress, it was hard to think beyond the moment. That's why, in the mid-'70s, I initiated a series of executive retreats at the Red Apple Inn, about an hour away in Heber Springs, Arkansas, on beautiful Greers Ferry Lake—the resort where Jane and I had taken our truncated honeymoon. Three times a year, we would meet for two days amid soothing woods and water. I would prepare an agenda and we would address those specific subjects.

It was somewhere in here that we had our come-to-Jesus meeting. The question on the table was, "What do we want to be when we grow up?" A very spirited discussion followed, and the consensus was that, as soon as we finished up this AFL-CIO work, I needed to grab my briefcase and fly to New York and, trading on our newfound talent at processing large name-and-address lists, drum up some commercial data-processing business. That—what today we call marketing databases—would be our chosen direction. We also agreed not to solicit any more political work; if something really great came our way, we might take it. But we weren't going to keep beating those sordid bushes looking for it.

It was a solid plan, and we all felt better having made it.

But life on the home front remained unpredictable, as it had for some time. There were many components to this unpredictability, all of which can be filed under the general heading of "Family."

By 1974, my parents had sold Morgan Supply Company in Fort Smith and moved to Conway to be near us and their grandchildren. It was nice to have them close by, and we saw them at least once a week and on holidays. But I could tell that Father still clung to the dream of being in business with me—soon after they moved to Conway, he floated the idea of opening a Pella Window business together, a dream I had to dash. I was busy enough trying to build Demographics. As it turned out, he and Mother ended up buying a little list business, selling names and addresses, so suddenly we were in the same line of work again. Accordingly, I arranged for them to use an office in our building, and for the next decade or so they operated out of there with a succession of lap dogs, which they insisted were integral to their work. The first dog was named Dixie, and she didn't bark. What she did was go to the bathroom in the corridor, where my parents allowed her to stretch her legs when she got restless. I naturally received some complaints about that and tried to reason with Mother and Father, who always promised to do better but never did. When Dixie died, they replaced her with a pair of dogs named CeCe and Sage.

My parents—Mother with her dogs and her denied narcolepsy, and Father, the eternal salesman, with his twinkling blue eyes and black-framed glasses beneath a shock of pure white hair—became a beloved if slightly wacky presence around the office. There were many stories about them. Later on, once we'd become a successful and influential company, a campaign staffer for an Arkansas gubernatorial candidate phoned our office and asked for "Mr. Morgan." The call was mistakenly routed to Father, who heartily accepted the proffered invitation to a fancy fundraiser at the Conway Country Club. He went and had a big time, all these solicitous people coming up to shake his hand. I can't recall if he wrote the candidate a check.

My parents' presence in Conway also impacted my home life. Jane had often accused me of "living in the clouds" because I was always doing things like losing my keys and forgetting my wallet. At home, I could be sitting in the middle of our den with the TV blaring and noisy children playing and all sorts of other distractions going on and I'd be lost in whatever I was reading or doing. "Come in, Dad! Come in, Dad!" Carrie and Rob would say, as though I were in outer space. In fact, I was usually concentrating on some project; to me, this was *focus,* one of my great strengths. But once Mother and Father moved to Conway, Jane began thinking maybe I had inherited what she saw as my "obliviousness" from my mother.

As I've mentioned, Jane was very depressed following Rob's birth. About four months later she had a hysterectomy. "So after my hysterectomy," says

Jane, "I came home from the hospital and Betty came out to cook dinner for us. Rob was four months old and I was in my bedroom, of course, and all of a sudden I hear Rob screaming at the top of his lungs and he doesn't stop. Finally I get up to see what the problem is, and there's Rob in the den by himself in his little infant thing screaming his head off. Well, I look all around and can't find Betty anywhere. Then I look through the window and there she is, outside happily picking wild flowers. I'm not being critical; it's funny now—that was just Betty."

Three weeks after Jane's surgery, I came up with an idea that I thought might help both of us. Demographics' bookkeeper had become ill, and Jane had done bookkeeping for her father's concrete company, Arkhola. So I asked if she would step in.

She did, and seemed to enjoy it. The whole experience seemed to boost her self-image. She came to the office every day and stayed until she had to pick Carrie up at school around 3:30. During this period Rob was at home with my mother. "While I was at Demographics I became very well acquainted with the employees," Jane recalls. "I just had a ball with them. One of them, and I wish I could remember who it was, said I was 'the Morgan with feelings.' I loved that."

Our regular bookkeeper's illness seemed to come and go—she would feel better and return to work, then have a relapse and need to take off again. Jane seemed so happy being part of the team that I asked if she'd come to work permanently. But this was one step too far—she set an impossible condition. "I'll do it if you and I both come home at five o'clock," she said. How could I do that when there was so much work to do—when Rodger and Jerry and Jennifer and Jim and everybody else were working such crazy hours? Demographics was still basically a start-up, and start-ups require both Herculean effort and a very flexible clock.

So this short experiment ultimately turned out badly, though not to everyone. "Jim, Rodger, and I had a great fear that Jane would come into the company," says Jerry Adams. "Jane has always loved Madelyn and me, and we loved her—she was incredibly kind to us from the beginning. She helped Madelyn arrange our kitchen when we moved to Conway—rolled up her sleeves and unpacked boxes and put things away. We ate KFC with Charles and Jane three nights a week in the early days of the company. But Jane is very opinionated. It's like, 'I'm gonna back my car over you.' If she didn't like somebody, they were doomed."

Following Jane's brief career at Demographics, we settled into our usual home life. I'm gratified to learn that Carrie, who was 8 in 1975, recalls some happy times during her growing-up years. In the hazy way of memory, all these fleeting images Carrie remembers run together—our family's regular Sunday pizza night…Jane and me standing at the kitchen island fixing supper together…a house full of kids much of the time…me out in the garage rebuilding a wrecked 1974 Mercedes…Jane and I playing take-no-prisoners tennis matches, which she—an Arkansas state champion at age 17—usually won…the whole family driving over after supper to check the progress on whatever house we might be building or renovating at the moment…on the drive, my hand covering Jane's on the front seat of the car.

But there were also times when Jane didn't get out of bed…when she blew smoke in my face if I complained about her smoking…when she was drinking to excess. "No *wonder* we went to marriage counseling," says Jane today. "I was depressed, everything was wrong, I felt like I couldn't do anything right—but I've always been a perfectionist. I had to admit at the time, but haven't admitted since—I did a lot of drinking when I was going through that depression leading up to my diagnosis."

In late 1975, Jane and I planned a little getaway with Jerry and Madelyn Adams to the Grand Hotel in Point Clear, Alabama. But just days before we were to leave, I got a call at work from Chuck Smith, Jane's psychiatrist in Little Rock. "I've had to put Jane in Three Northwest," he said. That was the psychiatric ward at St. Vincent Infirmary Medical Center.

"What? I'll be right down." I knew things were bad, but *this* bad? I was totally blindsided.

"No, Charles," Chuck said. "Don't come. You can't see her."

"How long will she be there?"

"At least two weeks," he said. "And you can't see her for a week, and then only briefly. I'll let you know when you can come."

SIX MONTHS LATER: June 1976, that overheated summer of Tall Ships, patriotic celebrations, and enough red, white, and blue bunting to stretch from sea to shining sea. All of it was in honor of America's Bicentennial, and we were right in the center of it—the nation's capital—forced to do our AFL-CIO work out of the union's headquarters in Washington, D.C. I wouldn't say we were in a celebratory mood, however.

The business situation for Demographics was becoming dire—we could see a tunnel coming, but not much light. We had the service bureau, which was limping along, and we had the political work that we planned to quit after Senator Bentsen's re-election campaign, so that would be over in November; in the meantime, Jerry's frequent—and necessary—travel was draining away a lot of our available cash. Even our ace in the hole, Ward School Bus Company, was in increasingly serious trouble.

The AFL-CIO work was coming to an end, too—it would be over with the November election. The only bright spot in the picture was that the AFL-CIO had proposed that if we could rewrite the Brotherhood of Electrical Workers program that was on our IBM computers and get it up and running on the Brotherhood's non-compatible system—a Univac—they would buy that software from us for a pretty good chunk of change. I've forgotten exactly how much it was, but it amounted to significant and much-needed funding. We had 60 days to get the job done—much beyond that and it would be too late for this data to help with the election.

Fortunately, even in his threatened state, Charles Ward was profligate enough to maintain a two-bedroom apartment in Washington, overlooking the infamous Watergate apartments. So that's where I usually found myself amid the galas of that Bicentennial summer. I'd basically built the database of the Brotherhood of Electrical Workers with Jennifer Phillips' help, so it made sense that she and I would be the ones to go there and get the job done.

And what a job it was. Usually, we could only get access to the Brotherhood's computer after midnight and on weekends. I knew nothing about a Univac, so sometimes we got help from one of their computer operators. Mostly, though, it was just Jennifer and me—I was rewriting software while she was figuring out the administrative plan, outlining everything we needed to do. It was a high-stress time, working whenever the computers were available and going at it until we were brain dead. And the clockless aspect of the schedule sometimes made the world feel upside down—we would emerge, dazed and blinking, from the quiet of the Brotherhood's data center and there would be a buzzing city getting started on its day.

One night when I was just exhausted, I poured myself a Jack Daniel's and stood on the apartment balcony looking over the lit-up city. My mind was unsettled, roving from subject to subject—I was certainly wrestling with some aspect of the current job that I was having trouble with, and the company's looming cash-flow crunch refused to stay tucked away in its pigeonhole. We had solid plans and some good leads, but we just couldn't quite seem to capitalize on them. I sometimes felt like a man pushing rope uphill.

Home was also much on my mind. Jane had remained in the psychiatric hospital for the full two weeks. Part of it was pleasant, she later said—finally she had a chance to get back to her needlepoint. She also enjoyed talking with the other patients and hearing their stories. But it turned out that she was very ill—during this time Chuck Smith had diagnosed her as bipolar. Reluctantly, he had started her on lithium, which my daughter, Carrie, now calls "the magic secret sauce, the Big Girl drug." During Jane's hospitalization, I'd had no clue how to be both father and mother to my children—especially to Carrie, who at age 9 was young enough to be afraid her mother was gone forever, and old enough to be aware of just how ill equipped I was. "He didn't have any tools," recalls Carrie today. "I mean, he could provide food, but he was just lost."

Jane would have to be on lithium *forever*—either that "or you're crazy," as Jane says. Chuck Smith was very hopeful that the drug would level her off, but it had only been a few months now and that was yet to be seen. All I knew for certain was that Jane and I were coming up on our 10th anniversary and I sometimes dreaded going home for fear of who I might find waiting for me there. Chuck had also strongly urged the two of us to attend group therapy sessions, so I'd been driving twice a week to Little Rock, where Jane and I shared our problems with a group of issue-ridden fellow professionals.

Sipping my whiskey on that Washington balcony, I felt a presence behind me. I turned around. There stood Jennifer, backlit in a negligee. "What the fuck are you *doing*?" I said. "Everything in my life is going crazy."

I was tired, I hated my life, and I wasn't home. Leading her to the bedroom, I rationalized it as "just one of those deals." From then on there was at least something to look forward to in our grueling schedule.

My relationship with Jennifer would go on for four years—but never in Arkansas. We were very circumspect. Even when traveling on business, we wouldn't do stupid things to make sure we were in the same city at the same time, or were flying on the same plane. There had to be an unassailable logic behind any joint plans. That care may sound like extreme cunning, but it didn't feel that way to me. Certainly we didn't want to be found out—too many people would've been hurt by it. But this, at least to me, was more a physical relationship than a romantic one. When we could be together, we were glad to do it. Otherwise, we continued on with our lives.

□ □ □ □ □

THE AMERICAN BIBLE Society was our first database marketing prospect in New York. I wouldn't say it was exactly what we were hoping for, but it was a start. A manufacturer's rep I'd contacted had gotten us in the door, and now it was up to us to see what we could make of it.

Located in Manhattan, ABS had a long and distinguished history, having been founded in 1816 to work with individual donors and various charities—both in the U.S. and abroad—to put Bibles in the hands of people who might otherwise never have one. Among the American stalwarts who'd participated in ABS's growth were John Jay, John Quincy Adams, Francis Scott Key, James Fenimore Cooper, Rutherford B. Hayes, and Benjamin Harrison.

We weren't ready for anything international, so our goal was to convince ABS to let us build a database of their previous U.S. donors for the purpose of future prospecting. Bernice Grossman, the woman who oversaw the Society's direct marketing, was very funny—she defined herself as the American Bible Society's "token Jew." They already had outside contractors doing their direct-marketing work, she said, but we convinced Bernice—and her boss—that we could do it better in Conway, Arkansas. We finally got her to come down to look over our operation, and I'll never forget how astounded she was. At the time, our little one-story building sat in a pasture otherwise occupied by grazing cattle. This native

New Yorker couldn't believe her eyes. Talking to her boss from my office phone, Bernice peered out my window and said, "Oh, my God, Jim, I'm looking at *cows*. I've never been this close to a cow before."

We'd been working with ABS for a few months when I came across an even bigger opportunity—a company called Direct Media, run by a displaced Texan named Dave Florence. If I had to name one client as the cornerstone of the company we became, it would be Direct Media, whose headquarters was in Port Chester, New York, up in Westchester County.

Dave Florence had worked for Dun & Bradstreet, the big credit data firm, so he had a firm grounding in both business and data. And what he'd done with that firm grounding was to become a business pioneer—the very first person to come up with the concept of a business-to-business database, an idea that had made Dave a legend in the direct-mail industry. Direct Media did both list brokerage and list management. Simply put, a list broker acts as a go-between, an agent, between someone who wants to launch a direct-marketing campaign and the various list owners whose lists will provide the leads for that campaign. A list manager compiles and maintains various lists, renting them to direct marketers who want to target people on those lists.

But Dave's genius was to focus on business to business. Let's say you're a plumbing supply manufacturer in Missouri and you want to reach plumbers throughout a certain region of the U.S. You come to Dave and say, "What I'd really like is all the left-handed plumbers in Little Rock and North Little Rock."

Dave would say, "Even if I could do that, there'd only be three of them. But what I *can* give you is all the plumbers, plumbing contractors, and plumbing supply houses in Little Rock and North Little Rock."

"Fine," you say, "send it on."

That would be Dave working as a list broker. On the other side of his shop, someone in the list management operation might have the bright idea to compile a list of all the plumbers in Little Rock and North Little Rock. But then who're they going to sell that list to? "I know just the guy!" the list manager in charge would say, and they contact that plumbing supply manufacturer in Missouri.

Now here's where it gets sticky—there are all kinds of plumbers out there. Some, as indicated by the magazines they subscribe to, are commercial plumbers; others—again as indicated by other data matched to their names—are residential plumbers; still others are plumbing contractors. And there are all kinds of lists for all these kinds of plumbers.

"Why don't we put them all together?" said Dave Florence. "If we put these lists together, we have a much better list resource. Even though the same plumber might be on several different lists, on each list you find out something different about these guys that could help you target better—one list might be of people who've bought a lot of pipe, for example. Typically, multiple lists add to the overall picture of the people you're trying to reach."

So now Dave had a pretty powerful product for direct mailing. At the time I met him, his business was flourishing.

But there was one giant flaw in Dave's operation, and I saw the effects of it within minutes after walking through Direct Media's door. I wasn't there to meet Dave; that came later. My appointment was with Bob Foehl, the most senior of Dave's managers. Bob was busy when I arrived, so I was escorted to a waiting area outside his office. On the way, I passed through a very large room—maybe 50 by 50 feet—lined with dozens of desks, and at those desks were people shrieking at one another: "Jerry! Goddammit, reverse my order! We got it all screwed up!" They were running around the room, pounding on desks, pulling their hair. The air was a blizzard of paper, the floor like snow—paper was *everywhere*. It made me think of a demented stock exchange.

"Yes," said Bob Foehl when I finally got to meet with him, "this place is so screwed up it's a nightmare."

The problem was that even though computers had put Direct Media's massive amount of list data on magnetic tape, the process to extract that data was totally manual. They would get hundreds of orders a day, and they had this data at two or three different service bureaus—their telephone list was at one place, their business database was at another, and their management lists were at yet another. So if Joe's Plumbing Supply at 111 Main Street in North Little Rock, Arkansas, wanted to do a 2,000-piece mailing to people on one of those lists, some human had to tell some other human exactly which names to take from the computer tape and put on the labels, according to the specifications of the order—it could be the names of particular kinds of plumbers, or plumbers in a certain Zip Code. So now somebody had to figure out how to write those specs—for each of the service bureaus involved—so they isolated exactly what Joe's Plumbing wanted to buy.

Then those instructions had to be couriered out, generally once a day, to those service bureaus, which in turn would give instructions to their own people in order to convert those original instructions to simple little computer programs to do the selection, put the names on labels, and deliver the labels to a letter shop. The process entailed a zillion manual steps, took nearly two weeks, and they hardly ever got anything right. The result was that nightmare room at Direct Media.

Oh, what an opportunity for a good computer system!

"This is solvable with computers," I told Bob Foehl, "and I've got some ideas." At that point I was bullshitting all the way, making it up as I went; my main idea was to land their business. "We've done a lot of large-scale list processing with the AFL-CIO," I said. "We have a lot of expertise in list processing, and we've seen similar problems."

"What do you mean?"

"Well," I said, "give me a little information so I can be sure I have a clear understanding of the problem. Then I'll come back to you with some proposed solutions."

On the airplane back to Arkansas, I reflected on the information I'd collected, the people I'd talked with, their chaotic process as they'd explained it to me. *I think I know how to do this*, I thought. We could create an automated list order fulfillment system. These guys at Direct Media would need a terminal in their office that would talk directly to our computers in Arkansas. List specifications would be entered in Port Chester; in our computer center, out would come the requested selection—everything totally automated. That was the general idea, anyway. But "Structured Query Language," or SQL, didn't exist at the time, so our job was to *build* an SQL-like system that could also produce mailing labels. It was a daunting challenge, but I was confident we could figure it out.

□ □ □ □ □

AND SO BEGAN our do-or-die stand. Even though I believed in us, there were times over the next six months when I wasn't sure which—do or die—would win out in the end.

Back in Conway, I got together with Jim and Jennifer and laid out the Direct Media problem. Over the next week or so, we worked out the broad strokes of what we christened the List Order Fulfillment System, or LOFS. This was basically the idea I'd mulled on the airplane back from New York, with a few elegant flourishes—elegant on the surface, that is; the whole concept was still wafer thin.

A couple of weeks later Jim Womble and I flew up to present it to Bob Foehl. "Here's what I think is the solution to your problem," I said, and proceeded to give my pitch about LOFS. Bob was skeptical, to say the least. It was clear to him that we'd failed to grasp the complexity of Direct Media's problem; not only that, we obviously lacked a thorough understanding of the list business. The good news was that Bob was willing to take the time to help us sort it all out. Over the next hour or two, the three of talked through all the nuances, until Jim and I felt we had a better handle on the issues we needed to solve.

There were probably a couple of meetings after that, each one confirming our progress over the meeting before. But by now I was getting antsy about Dave Florence. So far I'd had very little face time with the guy who would ultimately say go or no-go. From our few scattershot conversations, I could tell he thought we were chasing a pipe dream. On the other hand, this problem was killing them. So Dave was content for us to keep plugging away, as long as it didn't cost him anything.

But I needed to move things along, so I told Bob and Dave that we were putting together an early prototype system that we'd like to demonstrate for them. We couldn't do it New York, though; they would have to come to Arkansas to see it. And to make that easier, we would fly them down and back on our—Charles Ward's—corporate jet. None of this crowd had ever been on a private jet, and that appeared to be of some interest. Otherwise, they'd have had to fly from LaGuardia to Atlanta or Memphis and change planes and do it all again on the return trip. These crusty New Yorkers would never do that—to go to *Arkansas?* As it turned out, Dave Florence decided to pass on the trip anyway.

But Bob Foehl and another senior manager came, along with the woman who managed their list processing. We picked them up and flew them to Little Rock, then drove 45 minutes south to Pine Bluff, where we had a remote terminal we were using for another project. For presentation purposes, this remote terminal was to simulate a terminal in Direct Media's office in Port Chester, which would be connected to our terminal in Conway. We showed them how, with such a connection, the list owner could eliminate all those middlemen, the service bureaus. Everything would be in the list owner's hands. We would write a program making it easy for someone in the list owner's office to enter their request on their computer, and our computer in Conway would retrieve the data, put the correct names on labels, and send the labels to our own letter shop. Instead of a two-week process, the turnaround time would be three or four days—and eventually overnight.

Our presentation was mostly smoke and mirrors; we'd done the front-end design work, but behind that was essentially an empty stage. They were impressed, though—they *hoped* it was true. They peppered us with questions, and through the subsequent give and take we were able to plug several holes. By the end of our session, this thing was starting to have real substance. It was also going to be a bear to program.

Following the presentation, we drove up to Conway to show them our computer center, where we would receive their request. Then we toured our letter shop. After that, we whisked them back to Little Rock, where they boarded Charles Ward's well-stocked private jet for the trip back to New York.

We'd been working on this project for about two months now—I'd spent probably half that time on it myself, including many weekends. With our other work, we were stretched too thin but couldn't afford to take on more people. The AFL-CIO had paid us for our software, but we still had to provide some support—essentially additional work now. In the lonely income column, all we had was a monthly pittance from American Bible Society. I remember sitting on the edge of the bed one morning and telling Jane, "If we don't land this project, we're done. We're bankrupt."

After making the necessary changes to our concept, Jim, Jennifer, and I headed back to New York for another try. And this time, I pulled out every trick I could think of. Charles Ward, bless him, owned a palatial condo across 1st Avenue from the U.N. Building, overlooking the East River. We would stage the presentation there. And to give the presentation, I placed my bet on Jennifer; not just scary smart but also young and sexy, she might nudge the dial in the right direction. I know, horrors—I'm the first person ever to use sex to sell something.

Bob Foehl and several senior managers attended that meeting, but that wasn't all. Dave Florence showed up too, along with a consultant named Bob Ingenito. Dave even turned on his hearing aid. I didn't know until then that he wore one, so this was a revelation. In months to come, we gauged Dave's interest by whether or not he switched on his hearing aid.

After that presentation, Bob and some of the others were over the hump—they were ready to spring. "But Dave," Bob said, giving me that wincing look. "He still thinks we're wasting our time."

Our group was staying in the city, but the next day I took the train back up to Port Chester to see Dave. He seemed gloomy, I guess because we now had Bob on our side; Dave was in that lonely spot where bosses often find themselves—having to make the tough decision even when his team is blowing the other direction.

"*Dave*," I said, and as his name escaped my lips I hoped it didn't sound like a whine—because inside, I felt myself close to begging. "Look, I'll give you an *exclusive* on this program."

He peered at me from the depths of his funk. "Don't be stupid, Charles," he said. I could tell he felt a little better. "Why would you give me an exclusive? What does that do for you *or* me? You'd be trying to advertise this system through a single client, and I'd be paying for the whole thing. How stupid would *I* be?"

"Well, I just want you to do it," I said, lamely.

"Don't ever offer anybody an exclusive," he said. "It's not good for you and it's not good for them. Don't be stupid, Charles." Dave was maybe a decade older than I was—an experienced guy in a very tough business.

"Okay, Dave," I said, trying to salvage my dignity, "I won't be stupid."

With the stupidity issue settled, I went at him from other angles, never retreating. Whenever he knocked me down on one point, I bounced back like an inflatable boxing toy.

Finally he'd had it. "All right, goddammit!" he said, rising surprisingly from his desk. "All *right*! This fucking thing isn't going to work, *but just go do it*!

□ □ □ □ □

MONTHS OF HARD labor awaited us, and it was going to be 99.9 percent on our own dime. Dave Florence made quite clear that he "wasn't going to pay for this damn thing until it works." We did agree on a rate-per-thousand labels once the program was operational, but there was no contract at the outset and there wouldn't be one between us for 20 years. It was all done on a handshake. Dave did grudgingly agree to pay us a piddling amount along the way to help defray certain development expenses, but any real money would come only when we were up and running. I estimated that to be in four to six months, and I dearly hoped for four.

By now it was early fall of 1976. Back then we were like *Mission: Impossible*—we necessarily shifted people around according to the immediate needs of the company. In fact, later when we could afford to hire all the people we needed, I tended to hold to that modular philosophy—it keeps employees, and the enterprise itself, from becoming stale. So I put together an ad hoc team of programmers—Jim, Jennifer, Jerry Adams, and a couple of topnotch staff programmers, a woman named Sue Kennedy and a man named George Balogh. George stood out among our programmers because he'd been a history major who had aced the computer aptitude test that we'd stolen from IBM. You can't judge by externals who's going to be a great programmer.

For the next few months, the LOFS team was holed up like techie monks, breathing, eating, and sometimes sleeping the seemingly endless litany of 1's and 0's that make up the digital language. I personally was writing code 50 hours a week and running the company 20 hours. And I was still taking off most of two afternoons a week to go to Little Rock for group therapy with Jane. By now I was driving down in my second XKE, green like the first one. At least I could speed out some of the cobwebs on my way to group.

It was clear, after more than six months on lithium, that Jane was better. It had taken great effort for Chuck to get her lithium levels right, but once they were set, she was much calmer, much less prone to impromptu rages. She wasn't supposed to drink anymore, but she still poured herself two or three glasses of wine in the evenings.

Considering the pressure on me at work, at some point I suggested that since she was doing so well maybe we could stop going to group—or at least *I* could stop. In the old days Jane would've spewed vitriol my way for a week. Now her anger took a more reserved form. "Charles had always told me that if I got my shit together, everything would be all right," Jane recalls. "So now I told him that I *had* my shit together, and he could either go back with me to group or he could be gone when I got home. He went back with me to group."

Ultimatums seemed to be in the air that fall. When LOFS was about 90 days from finished, I was told we absolutely had to have a dedicated computer for the project—or else. It just stood to reason: This was to be our breakthrough project, our first venture as supposed grown-ups. If not now, when?

But Demographics had no money and I personally had no savings. Ward School Bus was bleeding money. So I went to the bank, First National of Conway, and explained our situation to the bank's chairman. Thank goodness for small towns. This man liked us; more importantly, he believed in us. He'd lent us money in the past, completely unbankable loans, based on his belief that—as he now told me again—"We like what you guys are doing. You're going to make it." So he accepted my pledge of the Ward School Bus account as collateral—an account he and everybody else in town *knew* was worthless—and lent us funds for the new computer. One more hurdle cleared.

But as 1976 faded into 1977, I faced the fact that the moment I had dreaded—had tried my best to stave off—was upon us: We would soon be out of money. Between payroll and the debt on the new computer, we would be in a negative cash-flow position until we started generating income from the LOFS project. And there was nothing I could cut, nobody I could lay off—everyone was working 60 hours a week and we needed all their projects just to stay where we were. And I thought I'd known the meaning of the word *dire* before.

Then a brilliant, if radical, idea came to me—what if we executives take 50 percent salary cuts? That was the starting point; from there I worked out a formula for eventually making them whole again, and then some.

When the crew showed up for my impromptu meeting, my first words were, "I see no choice but to cut everyone's salary in half." That, I promise you, is a real attention getter. Now there was silence in the room, all eyes and ears trained on me. I explained the circumstances that had brought me to that decision; then I went on say that if this scheme kept the company afloat long enough for us to start making money, I would pay them back *double* what they had given up. In other words, if someone earned $3,000 a month and we cut that to $1,500, when this was over I would pay that person $3,000 for every $1,500 he had forfeited during the three- or four-month period I expected this belt-tightening to last.

Once the shock subsided, most of the executives went along with this emergency measure without serious qualms—they believed that much in the potential of LOFS. But no matter how fervent their faith in our project, it was their ability to survive for months on half salary that determined their response.

The single guys, Jim and Rodger, could cut corners and get by. Jennifer's husband made good money, so it was fine by her. It was hardest on Jerry Adams. He and Madelyn had two kids, a sizable mortgage, and no other source of income—Jerry was *very* concerned. But he also had $5,000 in savings, and in the end he decided to take the risk.

So with Jim, Rodger, Jennifer, Jerry, me, and a couple of others taking 50 percent cuts in salary, we gained $10,000 a month, bringing us to cash flow neutral. That's how close we were cutting it. Four months later everyone was back to full pay.

□ □ □ □ □

SUCCESS WOULD EVENTUALLY make us very unpopular among our competitors in the New York area. When LOFS was finished and we were processing names and addresses from the manufacturing Yellow Pages for Direct Media's business-to-business clients, and printing their mailing labels in record time, the word soon got around. "This system was revolutionary," says Jim Womble. "It was by far the most advanced data mining system of its time. Charles had probably designed it in four minutes or something—the high-level concept, I mean."

LOFS was really the first "online" order system. So people in New York could sit at their terminals, and in the high-level language we developed they could basically say, "Give me all of the electrical supply stores in northern Minnesota or in these Zip Codes in northern Minnesota and address it to the purchasing manager." And we translated that into instructions and ran this big program against all these myriad lists that we'd built into a tape database, pulled off the 250,000 names and addresses, printed them, and sent the labels to the client's letter shop. There the catalogs would be printed, and then they would run through this conveyer, where the labels we had prepared would be glued on.

"To put this in perspective," says Womble, "that's what Amazon.com does today. When you get on Amazon's website, and it goes, 'Hey, thanks for coming back. You know, we saw you read this book. You want to read this other one?' What we developed for those purchasing managers receiving those catalogs in the 1970s was the very same thing for that era."

So now we had a powerful, proven product to sell, one that in years to come would disrupt New York's comfortable dominance of the market database world.

7

FINDING
THE ZONE

100101001011001010001001011001010110011

HOW MANY TIMES had I sat in Charles Ward's office begging him to hire someone to take over the day-to-day operations at the bus company. From Charles, I learned that just having good ideas and the ability to put them into action isn't enough to ensure success. To be successful, companies have to be operated in an effective manner every day. Excellent companies generally have excellent execution. The company that Charles' parents had turned over to him and his brother was headed for bankruptcy because of poor operations.

To give Charles his due, it wasn't all his fault. "His father, Dave Ward, was an old blacksmith guy," says Rodger Kline, who managed our Ward School Bus account. "Dave was still in the business and he didn't much like those new-fangled ideas. Dave and Bertha Ward, Charles' mother, still had a big presence at the school bus company in those days, and so you had the son trying to implement new stuff and you had the mother and father who were skeptical about what we were doing with computers."

It was even messier than that, if possible. Even after Dave Ward dropped dead of a heart attack, they were making dumb decisions just to get them to next week. In the end they started doing stuff that was borderline illegal. So I knew they weren't going to make it. They'd been in trouble since I joined—since *before* I joined. This had been a multi-year pattern. Charles' dad was a terrible business guy. Charles and Steve were terrible business guys. They had a sister who was a shrink *and* a lunatic. They all owned stock in the big company but the mother still had controlling interest. Charles was by far the strongest personality, but he didn't have control. They literally had family fights in the hallway over issues. It was just dysfunctional as hell. They had a good CFO, Royce Cullum, who kept them above water for a very long time. But even he couldn't overcome their abysmal business practices forever.

Sometimes I would get so frustrated that I would go to Charles' office, close the door, and level with him in a way that no one else did. "Charles, you are a brilliant son of bitch," I said. "I've seen you come up with a lot of great ideas. But I've also seen you do the dumbest shit in the world. And I can honestly tell you, Charles, you've done more stupid stuff and let people do more stupid stuff than I can even imagine. This business has got no prayer unless you find somebody to run it...."

He could've thrown me out of his office. He could've fired me. Instead, he knew I was saying these things out of love for him. "Help me," he said, and I did try to help him hire a young go-getter who ran one of the other manufacturing plants in town. In the end, though, this brilliant manufacturing manager got scared off because Ward's financial position was so dismal.

The insane things people will do to try to put off the inevitable one more week are really bizarre. They get crazy. And it becomes a group insanity because everybody knows that if we don't do something today we can't make payroll. So, in Ward's case, they lied about how many buses they'd finished because they had a finance arm in Kansas City who had to pay them as soon as a bus was ready. I used to joke that they would roll buses off the line without engines and say they were finished. Ward's credit was so bad they had to pay cash in advance for anything they bought, so they couldn't pay for parts until the very last minute. Of course they'd pay way too much for them, and they had to emergency ship them, flying in parts by airplane. That alone tripled the cost. They would roll "finished" buses off the line and put them in a holding place they called "the bus hospital," where you could usually find 300 buses waiting for mirrors, waiting for bumpers, waiting for drive line components.

And yet Charles was so addicted to his high living that once, when he came to my house, he refused the Scotch I offered him because it wasn't Chivas Regal.

My final effort on Charles' behalf was to design a "throughput" system for their school bus production line. Updated daily, this computer system basically told them what level of production they needed to achieve in order to be profitable. What they absolutely couldn't continue doing was running buses back and forth between the production line and the bus hospital—that was just digging the hole deeper. They were doing crazy things like finishing a bus except for five parts, and then when they received three of those parts they would move the bus back to the line and install those parts, then move the bus back out to the hospital. Later they would have to move the bus to the line *again* to install the remaining two parts. What I tried to make Charles understand was that every time they took a bus out of the bus hospital and put it back on the line, the labor cost on that bus rose dramatically, reducing their profit. Charles was interested, at least intellectually, and I feel sure he understood the importance of what I was telling him. Maybe he was already defeated by then. Anyway, the throughput system never got implemented.

□ □ □ □ □

THE INEXORABLE UNRAVELING of Ward School Bus Company was only one of the strains we were feeling in the fall of 1977. Even with LOFS generating impressive, documentable benefits for Direct Media, allowing us to make payroll, we were still just limping along. This was primarily due to the fact that Ward School Bus owed us accounts receivable in the amount of some $200,000. Would we *ever* see that money?

In any case, it was high time to go out and find another customer with a challenge just as great as Direct Media's was. And it was our friends at Direct Media who pointed us in the right direction. "If you think we got problems," said Bob Foehl, "you ought to see American Management Association. They've got it a lot worse than we do."

AMA, one of Direct Media's top clients, staged hundreds of seminars each month on all aspects of management. The Association was headquartered in an eight-story building in Manhattan, where on any given day there might be 30 seminars in progress; they also had remote locations in Atlanta and Chicago. But they held seminars all over the country, and they marketed these seminars to doctors, lawyers, corporations, institutions—any entity, be it an organization or an individual, with an interest in managing its business better.

Here, though, was AMA's big problem—how do they find attendees? It does no good to send a blanket mailer to IBM saying, "Hey, we've got a specialty seminar coming up on new trends in remote computer terminals" and maybe three people out of IBM's 50,000 employees are interested. What they needed to do was to identify specific targets.

AMA knew that, but knowing and executing are two different things. Their idea was to target potential seminar attendees by drawing from the subscription lists of various business publications. It was sound thinking—somebody who subscribes to a specialized publication about desktop electronics could be a perfect candidate for the right specialized seminar. But there were many obstacles in AMA's path, especially the usual suspects—list brokers, list managers, and the traditionally backward-looking service bureaus. These were the people handling the lists of the individual business publications. True to form, most of the process remained manual—all chaos, all the time.

The American Management Association was potentially a *huge* piece of business for us—each of their hundreds of monthly seminars was like a small client in and of itself. Jim Womble headed up our sales effort. "AMA was the first end-user we'd ever called on," says Jim. "We'd been working with the brokers and the middle- men between the mailers and the publishers. But now we were working with a mailer, and it was my deal. I'll never forget—I had to put a proposal together, and I'm flying up there, and I got my beer consumption exactly to the magic level, and I started dreaming up this terminology. One that I came up with was 'Geo-Function Analysis.'

"What it meant was a matrix. Take Atlanta—that's the geography, and let's say the function was secretaries. So you go to your database and say, 'Give me all the secretaries in the northern part of Atlanta who work for medical institutions. Because I'm going to put on a seminar.' So instead of designing a class and then just hoping somebody will come to it, they mine the database and, 'Wow, there are fifteen thousand secretaries in northern Atlanta who might want to come to a class, and we only need thirty of them.' AMA's business just went out the roof when we started working with them."

Of course it wasn't as easy as that. First we had to convince the powers at AMA to hire us. As it turned out, both Jim and I had identified the real power there. It wasn't the CEO, and it wasn't the VP of marketing; it was a whip-cracking tyrant of an Italian woman who lived in Harlem and just scared the shit out of everybody she worked with. Cathy Rapuano was her name, and she ran the list department, which meant she took the necessary information about upcoming seminars from the Association's event planners and turned that into mailing lists. This entailed severe and ongoing browbeating of the list brokers and service bureaus until they got her orders right.

Our strategy was to fly as many of AMA's key people to Arkansas on Charles Ward's jet as we could get to come. With LOFS up and running, at least this time we had something to show them that wasn't made up—it was real, and they could see it in action. As I recall, the CEO declined our invitation, but several of AMA's top execs did fly down, including Cathy. I made a point of sitting next to her on the flight to Arkansas, chatting her up and telling her that we would really treat her right—that we would make her a hero.

It worked. No matter what anyone else thought or said after our LOFS demonstration, she decreed that AMA was going with Demographics, and that was that. Even after we had problems getting some of the top New York business publishers to let us put their lists in our database—McGraw Hill, one of the biggest, refused permission for a very long time—Cathy Rapuano championed us, and we made sure she got everything she needed.

But growth inevitably presents problems, and landing AMA brought about its share. The existing LOFS software was about 75 percent workable for AMA, so we had to spend considerable time revising the program according to the Association's specific needs. More serious was the fact that we couldn't afford a computer with the processing capacity—enough speed and tape drives—to handle AMA's vast data requirements; nobody but the U.S. government was able to buy a computer that big in those days. Instead we had to improvise, the way I had improvised back at IBM when I was assigned to make the slow printer run faster.

Now I had to insert my mind deep inside the software to gain a microsecond here, a microsecond there. While our competitors were writing programs in high-level computer language, we got down and dirty in machine language, achieving advances the hard, slow way.

For me it was an exhilarating time, since I love to be lost in the intricacies of solving a particular problem. But it was also frustrating because of the nay-saying and hand-wringing among some of the people around me. "We'll *never* be able to afford a computer big enough," they said, "so this is just a waste of time." I could practically hear the click-click-click of their worry beads.

"Quit worrying about it," I told them. "Computers will eventually come down in price."

"But not *enough*," they whined.

When I really thought about that scene later, I found several reasons to be concerned. Ironically, through participation in Chuck Smith's group therapy sessions with Jane, I had started paying attention to human nature—both others' and my own. Before group, I'd thought that if I just hired very good people and got them working together in the right direction, everything would turn out fine. But now, as I felt the company starting to catch fire under me, I was having second thoughts about that.

These were the first crude stirrings of my heightened awareness as a leader and a manager, an intellectual process that would only intensify in the coming years. For now, though, I was starting to see things around me with fresh eyes. Take my top managers—after several years of working with them, I realized I could predict how each would react to any proposed new project. Rodger would proclaim, with knee-jerk certainty, that we couldn't afford it. Jennifer would pick it apart, finding only fault, telling you your project was *dirt*. Jim would be over the moon, packing his briefcase to start selling, liking the project even better than I did. Jerry would follow the prevailing mood, washing merrily along with the flow.

But when it came to predictability, my most serious concern was me. All of my life I'd had my head stuck away somewhere dark and private—under a car hood, inside a computer—where I could be alone with the problems I lived to solve. And given the slightest justification, I gravitated to that comfortable place still: *We got to get this fulfillment software operational if I have to work around the clock… Strategically, this software is the most important thing I have to do….*

I realized I had tunnel vision, that my tendency was to let vital parts of running the company slide while I was off on my private coding missions. In such moments of stark self-awareness, Charles Ward's failures as a manager frightened me for myself.

This led to other epiphanies. One was that in an organization, structure matters; I would need to give that considerable attention going forward. Another was that I needed protection. There would be macro and micro aspects to that epiphany—I had to have a top accounting person; later, once we went public, I would need an excellent lawyer to make sure we stayed out of trouble with the SEC. I could even foresee needing a personal attorney. I always told my people, "I don't ever want to find myself under oath in a court of law and having to wiggle the truth to stay out of jail because we did something stupid."

Right now, though, I realized I required protection on a more basic level. I needed someone I trusted on the administrative side, someone to cover for me, someone to make sure I got good information, someone to see to it that I did what I needed to do when I needed to do it.

At the time—early 1978—Sharon Tackett had been at Demographics for about a year and a half. She'd joined the company at age 19, starting as a receptionist. But she'd had formal secretarial training, and as soon as possible we transferred her to the executive office to handle administrative work for Rodger, Jim, and me. "But everybody understood that Charles was my primary responsibility," Sharon says.

Now I set out to strengthen my bond with Sharon. The first thing I did was to take her aside and tell her, candidly, what I needed from her. I ended that conversation by saying, "I want you to remember that when someone is trying to get in touch with me, the first person they're likely to talk to is you. If a customer calls, if a banker calls—I don't care who it is, I am you. If you're snippy, if you're not helpful, they're going to transfer that to me. I don't care who it is."

She handled that magnificently. Many years later, I heard her chatting away with someone on the phone. Finally she said, "Bill's on the line."

"Bill who?" I mouthed.

"The *President of the United States*, Charles," she said.

As I write these words, Sharon and I have worked together for 37 years. And if I've learned one thing in all these decades, it's this: Whenever she says she needs to talk with me, I drop everything and listen.

□ □ □ □ □

I ARRIVED AT one additional insight about myself during this period: I was unbalanced, too much business, no personal fulfillment, no fun. Jane was better, but home still lacked warmth. I'd just turned 35 and everything felt out of kilter. I needed an escape of some kind, and the word that kept coming to me was *racing*. All my life I had been dreaming about it, talking about it, planning for it. But I had never needed it more than I needed it now.

In the spring of 1978 I started trying to figure out a time that I could get away from work to attend a week-long course at the Bondurant School of High Performance Driving in northern California. When I told Jane about it, she actually seemed excited. "I had signed up for this," she says today, as though she had been waiting for it to happen. Maybe she remembered the early days of our marriage, when she and Carrie would go with me on motocross weekends. Maybe she saw a benefit in racing—a chance to bring the family closer—that I didn't yet see.

Just as I thought I'd found a window of time to escape through, Charles Ward called me. "Can you come over?" he said. "I need to talk to you. There's some stuff I need to tell you." His tone didn't make me expect good news.

Sure enough, when we were in his office behind closed doors, he said, "We're not going to make it, Charles. I know we're not going to make it. But you guys *are* going to make it, and you're going to make it big, I think."

He went on to say that he didn't want Demographics to get tangled up in Ward School Bus's inevitable bankruptcy, so he had concocted an elaborate plan to ensure that we sidestepped the bus company's legal problems. His lawyers had been working on the details, but here were the high points: One, Charles would trade most of his bus company stock to wipe out the debt Ward School Bus owed Demographics; two, he would retain about 10 percent of his Ward stock, which he wanted for the protection of himself and his family, and which he would probably turn over to his father-in-law—with a buy-back clause—to repay money the bus company had borrowed; three, Charles' brother would also divest himself of his stock, turning it over to us. Thirty-five years later, I can't recall the intricate legal maneuverings that would accomplish that transfer. But I remember Charles's words of warning as though they were spoken yesterday. "If we don't do this," he said, "you *are* going to get sucked into this bankruptcy. If *we* still own Ward School Bus stock, it will be sold to the highest bidder. And since we own a controlling interest of Demographics, you guys will lose control of the business."

Finally there was this. "I want you, Charles, to end up with control of this company. I want you *personally* to end up with all of the stock. I trust your judgment. I don't want anybody looking over your shoulder. I want you to run this thing."

At that point I owned 30 percent of Demographics—the 10 percent I'd been given at signing, the 10 percent I'd bought from Alex, and another 10 percent I'd bought from an early investor, George Jernigan, and for which I had outbid both Rodger and Jim in a sealed bidding. The remaining stock in the hands of the Wards amounted to seven percent for Charles' wife, Sharon, and the 10 percent Charles intended to keep for himself and his family. All the rest of Charles' and Steve's stock—50 percent—they wanted to place in my hands.

"Thank you, Charles," I said. "And yes, I'll run the company. I'll be in control. But I want the people who're helping me make us a success to get a bunch of this stock."

"I think it's a mistake," he said. "You need to talk to Jane right away. There's a six-month statute of limitations, after which this arrangement can't be reversed. So we need to know the details and do this transaction *immediately*. And then, no matter what, we have to keep Ward School Bus going for another six months. Until the statute of limitations has passed."

Jane was violently opposed to my sharing the stock, prompting the kind of raucous fight we hadn't had since before she'd started the lithium. I tried to reason with her. "Look," I said, "I have partners. If I take all that stock, Jim and Rodger and Jerry and Jennifer are going to resent the hell out of it, and I need them to be committed heart and soul to this company."

Jane couldn't believe I was so stupid.

The arrangement I finally worked out with a dubious Charles Ward was that I would keep 51 percent of the stock and distribute the balance—29 percent—to the others on very favorable terms. As part of that agreement, I would also receive a proxy from each of my managers allowing me to vote their stock—essentially giving me 90 percent control of the company. They were happy, I was happy, and that's how we left it for the next few years.

I've never regretted the decision to share that stock. It's a good thing I did share it, because later on I would again have to ask my management team to accept a temporary pay cut. Imagine how that would've played if they'd been working 24/7 and I'd been making all the money. Generosity, I have found, generally pays generous dividends.

□ □ □ □ □

THE JETLINER LIFTED off and rose through the autumn clouds to the bright blue sky above. Then it banked slightly, heading west. I was bound for San Francisco, to attend a conference of the Direct Marketing Association. But after that, I was going to tack on a week of driving school.

Looking down on those heavy clouds, that thick gray buffer between me and my ground-level complications, I sipped a Jack Daniel's and ruminated on all I was leaving behind—if only for scarcely more than a week. Already, I felt a sense of restored sanity. I promised myself that this was the start of a new way of living.

In time we crossed the mountains, rugged and beautiful through wisps of white clouds. That challenging terrain made me think of Charles Ward, struggling to hold his broken company together for a strategic few months more. In our talks about his impending bankruptcy, there'd been moments when I'd heard the echo of characters in a stock cowboy movie. *I can't make it, Charlie, but you go on. Leave me behind and save yourself.*

Soon the plane was making its descent into San Francisco. In a matter of minutes I was in a taxi speeding into the city. In a couple of days, I would cross the Golden Gate Bridge to Marin County, on my way to a hotel near Sears Point Race Track. There I would finally come face to face with the reality of a dream I'd carried for decades.

Bob Bondurant grew up riding motorcycles on the dirt tracks around his hometown of Los Angeles. Then he moved up to sports cars, driving Corvettes and winning 30 of the 32 races he entered. Recruited by race team owner Carroll Shelby, Bondurant next drove Shelby cars in Grand Prix races, partnering with Dan Gurney to win their class at the 24 Hours of Le Mans in 1964; he won that race again the next year with partner Jo Schlesser. After that he drove at Daytona, then for Ferrari at Watkins Glen and the Monaco Grand Prix. In 1967 he was racing flat out in the Can Am series when a steering arm on his McLaren broke and he flipped eight times, breaking bones throughout his body. He did walk again, counter to doctors' expectations, but his racing career was done. So the next year, 1968, he started his driving schools. They quickly gained the reputation of being *the* place to learn, whether you drove a race car or a getaway car. I was soon to discover that, for me, the two were one and the same.

There were 10 of us in the class, including a racing celebrity—Don "The Snake" Prudhomme, a champion drag racer. At 37 years old, he was already a legend. But drag racing—a violent, screaming burst of speed on a straight quarter-mile, then an abrupt stop aided by a rear-end parachute—is very different from running in a pack on crowded, winding Grand Prix courses, or even balls-to-the-wall competition on an oval NASCAR track. Prudhomme was interested in making the move to a different kind of racing, and I was impressed that he too had chosen the Bondurant school.

The first day was all classwork. The instructor drew diagrams on the blackboard—"Here's how you get through the corner," and he dashed off an arrow indicating the proper angle. He talked about brake turns and skid recoveries, and then: "Here's how you heel and toe." Heel and toe, a technique for downshifting using your left foot for the clutch and your right foot for both the gas and the brake, is very hard to master. On the second day, when they took us out to the track to do skid pad exercises—driving through cones, and seeing how fast we could push the car in a large defined circle while keeping all tires within the circle's circumference—that was difficult enough; when we added the heel and toe, the combination took hard to a whole new level. I felt despondent. *Maybe I don't have a facility for racing*, I thought.

On the night of that second day, three of us went to the hotel bar for a beer. We were a quiet group, everybody afraid to ask how the others were doing—the last thing you wanted to hear was somebody say he thought driving school was easy. So we talked half-heartedly about everything else—*any*thing else—when driving school was all that was on our minds.

Then Don Prudhomme walked into the bar. He looked like his mother had just died. "Hey, guys," he said. "Can I sit with you?"

"Sure!" we said. "Good to see you." He'd been kind of standoffish up till now.

He ordered a beer, then looked at us and shook his head. "You know, I'm really depressed," he said. "I can't do this. Are you guys doing okay?"

"No!" we said in unison, almost coming out of our chairs—so relieved were we to expose our fears to the healing air. "We're the same way, man."

"Oh, thank God," said Prudhomme. "I was about to go kill myself. I'm supposed to be this big-time drag racer, and I feel like a klutz out there."

After that, we kept no secrets from one another. We relaxed and started enjoying the week. We were buddies, joking and laughing, focused on mastering our lessons instead of worrying about how someone else was doing with them. It was a much better way to spend the time.

Don Prudhomme and I became friends, at least for the rest of that week. We would knock back a few beers in the evenings, sometimes joined by the other guys, sometimes not. We talked a lot about cars and engines. On the evening before our final day, Prudhomme said, "Man, I'm really feeling good about this now."

"Me too," I said. "What a difference from the beginning of the week."

"You know what?" he said. "I'd like you to ride with me tomorrow. I'd like to show you how I'm doing."

"Great," I said. "I want you to ride with me too."

We checked with the instructor, who was okay with our riding together. So the next morning we suited up and I buckled into the passenger seat of Prudhomme's car. He scared the living shit out of me. He was a maniac, just on the edge of control—when he wasn't beyond it. I thought we were going to crash four times in the two laps we did. After it was over and I finally planted my feet back on the track, it occurred to me: *Don Prudhomme makes my old friend Sammy Phillips look like a driving instructor.*

I'm sure Prudhomme was unimpressed when he drove with me. My lap times weren't as fast as his, but I remained in control all the way. It made me think of something Jane once told someone about my driving: "Charles wants to be in control of the driving like he wants to be in control of everything else. But about the driving, I'd rather have him in control than anybody I can think of."

□ □ □ □ □

ON THE FLIGHT home, I realized how little I had thought about the office that week. Racing can do that for you—free your mind, take you out of yourself, transport you to what seems like another dimension. It's that mentally intense, as I knew from my years in motocross.

When I was really in the zone in a motocross race, I knew on one level that I was riding that motorcycle. But at the same time I didn't feel that I was really doing the racing. I was *observing* the racing and giving myself instructions from afar. So it wasn't like, *I want to go over this jump and I'll land over there or speed up here.* It was more like I'd left my body and was managing the process at a higher level. It sounds crazy, but I got good enough at motorcycle racing in some of the big races that I was riding far above what I should have been doing. But I was completely in the zone.

I was deep in the zone the day I ripped my ligament. Normally when you see a football player tear a ligament, he immediately falls to the ground and writhes in pain. But I finished the race on one leg and never stopped. My mind was so detached from my body that I didn't feel pain. Yes, I knew it had happened. I knew I had ripped my ligament. But I didn't stop. I still finished in the top half of the field on one leg.

In time I would learn that, for the most part, car racing isn't quite as intense as motocross—even though you're going much faster. Maybe it's the nakedness, the physical vulnerability in motorcycle racing that greatly increases the intensity. But car racing *is* intense, and the zone transfers from the bike seat to the cockpit. When you're really successful in car racing, you're almost totally unaware of the coming corner—and you're not aware of the next one at all. You're not thinking, *I'm going to go to there and brake.* You're just doing it from somewhere outside yourself. Instead of driving the car, you start feeling it: *I feel the car slide. I feel the front end doing this. I feel the car getting looser.* It's like you're aware of what the car's doing, but you're not thinking about what you're doing to drive it.

This kind of intensity can benefit your work life. Once I started racing regularly, I would generally leave Thursday to go racing and come home Sunday night late, or maybe even Monday. This pattern continued through periods of the very highest stress in my life, both at home and at work. But after leaving the racetrack and returning home I would say to myself, *Now what do I need to be thinking about for tomorrow?* And I couldn't remember. Even my most difficult problems were so out of my mind that I had to reorient myself. And almost always when that happened, I started realizing that the problem I'd left behind on Thursday looked vastly different on Monday after a race weekend. I just had a different perspective on it somehow. I'd cleared my mind to the point that I could look at it from other angles. And many times it turned out that *this* was really the answer, not *that*.

Jane embraced my racing in ways I couldn't have imagined. Sure enough, she viewed it as a family activity, and she bought us a comfortable RV to travel in—she bought several over the years, as a matter of fact. She also footed the bill for race expenses in my early racing days, which included paying for my first race car. In my Bondurant course, we'd driven front-engine rear-drive sedans, and I liked them. So my initial plan was to buy a Datsun and race in Sports Car Club of America (SCCA) C Production amateur class. To give you an idea of what that means, it's the car and class that Paul Newman was racing in those days.

We, however, were in a whole other league from Paul Newman. I would race with him numerous times over the years, and his was always a top-drawer operation—the best, most powerful cars, the most experienced race crew behind him. I had an all-volunteer crew. And after the cost of the car itself, our first full year ran us about $14,000; every year after that it increased by some $10,000. Even so, that was very cheap in the world of automobile racing. A set of tires was $600, and I would try to run all race weekend on one set; I probably bought 10 sets the whole year, which meant $6,000 of my annual budget went to tires. The rest went to travel—a major expense—and parts. Because we couldn't afford to *buy* a racing engine, we fell back on my engineering know-how to tweak it to racing level.

So I drove what's known in racing circles as a "shit box." But I found that I loved the kind of racing our team was forced to do—the hands-on, engineering-oriented detail work, figuring out as we went what the car needed. As we gained a bit more budget we didn't just go racing; we also went *testing*. For as much as two days prior to a race we would work through a whole range of setup options for the car—shock absorber settings, suspension settings, spring, brakes, sway bar rates, ride height, rake in the car, all these things. And I really got into analyzing the data and trying to make the car better, always better. The overall pleasure of racing for me was virtually half on the engineering side and half on the driving side. Later on, I would actually design and build a car that I raced all over America.

As Jane hoped, racing marked a new phase of our family life. I raced a little in the remainder of 1978, then competed the full season in 1979. Most of the races were in the summer, so the kids went, too. When I started, Rob was just a little guy of 5, running with his pals on their Big Wheels—I could never have predicted the degree to which *he* would take to cars and racing. Carrie, 11 going on 16, complete with lip gloss, was rapidly approaching that age when her parents and little brother were the last people on earth she wanted to be cooped up with in a motor home over a long weekend. But she was a good sport about it, especially if Alex Toth, our affable crew chief, was along as a buffer.

"We had some adventures," says Jane. "Once during SCCA days we took that motor home up California's Pacific Coast Highway, and, be it poor planning or whatever, we were literally on the edge of the earth with not only an eight-ton motor home but a race car in tow on a nine-ton trailer. I looked at Charles, who was driving, and his lips were blue—I mean *blue*—as he tried to get us through there without falling off. All the blood and oxygen had left his lips. The rear view mirror was scraping a cliff on the right. Rob was sitting in my lap crying. And in the back of the motor home, Carrie and Alex Toth were playing gin rummy, oblivious to everything, including the scenery.

"Another time, Charles and Alex and I were stranded on a mountaintop in Tennessee, at night, while Alex repaired the motor home engine with a fork. All the tools were in another vehicle with the rest of the crew."

When I started racing the full season in 1979, my immediate goal was to qualify for the national championships in Atlanta. That meant I had to log thousands of miles on racetracks. In our Southwest Division, many of those tracks were in Texas—Texas World Speedway held two or three races a year, and there was another track at an old airport in Dallas where I raced occasionally. Another big track was Hallett Motor Speedway in Oklahoma, which staged maybe three races a season. I hit them all, family in tow—Jane sometimes even served as my timer. We went to a few other racetracks too, because I was determined to get enough points to qualify for the Nationals my first year.

Which I did. So in the fall of 1979 I made my first trip as a driver to the fabled race course Road Atlanta, a world-class, two-and-a-half-mile track with 12 turns. It's a track that will forever be a looming presence in my family's life, for reasons that will eventually become abundantly clear.

Datsun was a big sponsor back then. They promoted their cars through racing, so they'd set up a Datsun tent where all the Datsun drivers could mingle. Paul Newman was there that first year, along with Bob Litzinger and other big-name drivers I hadn't raced against but had surely heard about. It was a heady experience for a relatively new guy like me to be there alongside the best in the SCCA.

There were probably 36 cars in C production there, and they were really nice ones—it was that year at Road Atlanta that I got my first look at Newman's car and crew. But I drove what I drove, and I never forgot that it was my shit box car and my volunteer crew that had gotten me to the national championships. So on the first practice run, on Thursday, I pulled onto the track intending to give it everything we had. On that first lap I was at the fastest place on the racetrack, a complicated section where you went down a big hill and then up a hill and underneath a bridge. Even in our Datsun, I was probably doing 140 going downhill.

When I got to the bottom and put on my brakes, I saw that somebody's engine had dumped motor oil all over the track. It had just happened, I guess, and I was one of the first guys through. So the car started spinning, and I lost control heading for the bridge, which was coming up fast. It was my first experience of knowing that this was really going to hurt. But it turned out that the seat harness in the Datsun was good enough so that I escaped with a sore neck and some bruises from the belts. I was lucky. The car wasn't so lucky. I hit a tire barrier and it tore up some bodywork, and also busted the suspension. We had parts to buy and many hours of repair work to do before race day.

I missed all the practices. So when qualifying day came, there I was, brand new at Road Atlanta with maybe eight laps on the racetrack under my belt, and now I had to go qualify with a shit box car. I remember going into turn one, a high-speed right-hander uphill—it's very difficult, a pretty famous turn in racing. You go down the front straightaway staying at the brakes, then you go through sort of a semi-bank turn into a climbing turn at 100 miles an hour. As I was going into the turn, Paul Newman passed me on the outside, which you generally don't do. But I was going so slow that Newman just came through outside everyone; then *vrrooom,* and he disappeared over the hill. It was very depressing. I qualified dead last.

Long story short, I started the race at the back of the pack, but somehow I managed to finish 18th or 19th out of 32. Some of the other guys broke down, some of them crashed. I don't know if I out-drove or out-raced very many of them, but I didn't feel too bad about the way my first championship race turned out. I felt that I was starting to get the hang of it. I was getting better. I could do this.

A THEORY
OF TIME

100101001011001010001001011001010110011

IN BUSINESS, AS in life, seemingly small events often turn out to be catalysts for unexpected things. So it was with a telephone call I received from Dave Florence one day in 1979. I was at Hilton Head, four days into our annual family vacation.

"Charles," Dave said, "I'm selling the compiling business and I want you to buy it." Dave's compiling operation, an ambitious undertaking whose eventual goal was to create a master database of businesses from the Yellow Pages of 4,350 phone books across the country, was the linchpin of our work with Direct Media. But his partners had laid down the law—the compiling was too expensive and way too much trouble, and Dave had three choices: continue it himself, sell it, or shut it down.

"Dave," I said, suddenly feeling ill, "we don't have the money to buy it." With AMA now up and running, Direct Media's list work was no longer our lone golden goose. But we sure didn't want to see it waddle away.

"You're not listening to me, Charles," he said. "You've got to buy it or you'll lose it." He'd already talked to one of the major compilers in the country, National Business Lists, who'd been consistently undercut on price by Dave. They wanted to buy his compiling business and shut it down. If he didn't sell it to them, he would sell it to Dun & Bradstreet.

Next thing I knew I was putting on long pants and a blazer and flying to New York, where my attorney met me. We negotiated with Dave on Friday, Saturday, and Sunday, and on Monday we had a deal—a very, very favorable deal. Dave Florence *wanted* us to have this, and a big chunk of money in hand wasn't the point with him. Basically we didn't have to pay Dave anything upfront. We could just make payments out of the earnings.

So we moved the compiling and computer staff to Arkansas, a huge undertaking that added 50 people to our payroll in a single stroke. The sales team remained in New York. At the time we took over, the compiling business was being run by Bob Ingenito, a brilliant consultant and strategist who'd often worked with Dave. We'd gotten to know Bob a little during the few months he'd been trying to straighten out Dave's compiling operation, and we were impressed with him and his ideas. In short order, we named Bob our New York Head of Sales, basing our office in Harrison, New York, where Bob lived. As we were soon to discover, Bob Ingenito was a force of nature, New York Italian version, not to mention a wise and compelling philosopher. Both aspects became very important to me. And this, specifically, is what I mean when I say that seemingly small events can become catalysts to unexpected things.

Before Bob Ingenito came aboard, our forays into the sharp-elbowed world of New York consumer list brokers and managers had been hit-and-miss. This was a tough, tough bunch for whom business was blood sport. Trust was distrusted. "We brought some of these New York guys down," recalls Jerry Adams, "and they thought we were putting on an act because we were genuinely nice." But most of these hard-edged businessmen knew where to draw the line. Several times when I phoned a firm for an appointment, I was asked, "Are you associated with the Monskys?" What? I didn't know what they were talking about. But after weeks of trying to get my foot in the door at Woodruff-Stevens, then the largest consumer list manager-brokers in the world, I finally found out. This time Stan Woodruff himself picked up the phone. "Charles," he said, "you got to change your fucking company name. Whenever I hear that Demographics is waiting to see me, I get a bad taste in my mouth. Change it to anything, I don't care. If you don't, people won't ship data to you. They'll think you're those Monsky guys."

"Those Monsky guys" were a notorious pair of brothers who ran a company called Demographic Systems, and who were known to steal data from the people they did business with. They were just crooked as hell, and CEO Marvin Monsky eventually did time. Seeing no future in being mistaken for the Monskys, in late 1979 we took Stan's advice and quickly changed our name—to Conway Communications Exchange, which we shortened, in conversation, to CCX.

Woodruff-Stevens was comprised of five equal partners, but Stan Woodruff was the most equal, having been elected "Chairman and CEO" by the others—probably because Stan had the strongest personality. A couple of the other partners were drunks, and if you tried to talk with them after their three-martini lunch, you were out of luck. It was a very screwed-up office.

We did do some work with them, however, and it was perfectly fine, except that Stan never stopped pushing. One day all the partners and I were sitting in Stan's huge office and he was really grandstanding, just putting on a show. "Do you realize, Charles, that you haven't got a chance in this town without me," he said, strutting around the room. "If you don't do work for us on our terms, you're dead in this town. We're the biggest guys on the block!" Then he delivered a five-minute monologue about why I had to sign an *exclusive* contract with Woodruff-Stevens for consumer lists, using LOFS; he would deign to let us continue doing business lists for Direct Media. Basically, though, Stan expected us to become his personal service bureau.

I listened for a while, recalling what Dave Florence had told me about giving exclusivity to anyone. Then, in an exaggerated drawl, I said, "Gee, Stan. You *know* I'm just a poor dumb country boy from Arkansas. I don't know shit, so I guess I've *got* to do what you say because you're such a big, important man in *New York City*." His partners almost fell out of their chairs laughing. For years they must've been waiting for somebody to pop Stan's balloon. Stan wasn't a bad guy, just a little pompous. We actually became friendly once he understood that we would work with him on our terms, not his. But the whole time I dealt with Woodruff-Stevens, some of the partners kept trying to get me to move to New York and run their company; they wanted to fire Stan, they said.

"Life's *way* too short for that," I told them.

□ □ □ □ □

WHICH BRINGS ME back to Bob Ingenito. Once we joined forces with him, Jim Womble and I started spending great amounts of time in New York making calls with Bob. He knew everybody and could get us in anywhere. "It was like taking candy from a baby," recalls Jim, who actually moved to Harrison, New York, for a while to work with Bob. "We were closing deals right and left, knocking off all these list brokers and managers. One managed the *Fortune Magazine* list, another the list of *Life* subscribers, and we were selling them on LOFS, our revolutionary List Order Fulfillment System, boom, boom, boom, boom."

While I certainly appreciated Bob's business acumen and his contributions to our bottom line, it was his personal side that made the most lasting impression on me. He had his own agenda, doing anything and everything he wanted to do. And he made no excuses to anybody about it.

One of Bob's hands was deformed at birth—he probably had two fingers on that hand. He grew up in the Bronx, a bright kid and a good student, but his formal education topped out after a few months in college. Then, as he explained it to me, there came a point in his life when he was at a crossroads—join the Mafia, or go into legitimate business. He chose the latter. But he still knew many people who'd made the opposite choice. One night we were in a restaurant and this big guy stopped by the table. "Hey, Bobby, how you doin'," he said, and they gave each other a bear hug.

"He's a made man," Bob said when the guy left.

Bob's second wife, Lyn-Miriam, was a former Rockette, and they had a crazy, stormy, passionate relationship. When I started going up to Harrison to work with Bob, there were no reasonably priced hotels in the area. "Come stay with us," Bob and Lyn said, so for at least five nights a month I bunked in with Bob, Lyn, and their two daughters. They had a beautiful two-story home in a very nice neighborhood in Harrison—not that we were there all the time. Bob also kept an apartment in Manhattan, and his usual routine was to spend most of the week in the city and come home on weekends. When I was visiting, sometimes we would have clients to entertain, and sometimes we'd have dinner with Bob's friends. Other times, it would just be the two of us, hanging out in Manhattan. It was on such a night that I first heard Bob espouse his philosophy of life.

He had—still has—a theory that life is about choices of time, and your life is defined by who you choose to be with and what you choose to spend your time doing. "*I'm* going to choose how I use my time," he said. "I'm not going to let other people choose that for me. I'm not going to be driven by my business, driven by my family, so that I have no choice of time. I will spend my time, which is the most precious thing I have, in the ways I choose." Recognizing that some people, such as spouses, might bridle at such a philosophy, Bob had a ready response. "I choose to still be with you," he said. "I choose to spend time with you. If I don't spend *enough* time with you, you have to understand that there are other things in my life that I'm going to spend time on."

As a man trying to balance the conflicting time pressures in my life, I was mesmerized. It's not like Bob wasn't aware of business obligations—he was, and is, driven to spend considerable time on business. He's one of those guys who's always got a business idea. He's a born entrepreneur. Everybody at our company liked him because he had good ideas, worked hard, and was totally honest. I feel sure he never even lied to Lyn. But knowing Bob, she knew that if she pressed him on something, she might not like the truth.

A peculiar facet of Bob's personality was that he refused to carry a key to his own house. "Somebody better be waiting there for me when I come home," he said, "no matter where I've been." Even though this amounted to wanting it both ways, the double standard seemed to work for him—until one night when we took a late train back from Manhattan. It was probably 10 p.m. and the door was locked. Bob couldn't believe it. He began *pounding* on the door.

Lyn opened it, and Bob blustered in with me behind him. Suddenly Lyn hauled off and punched Bob in the gut. I could hear the air whoosh out of him as he curled into a ball and dropped to the floor. "You son of a bitch," Lyn said. "I *told* you I was cooking dinner for you and Charles, and you no-showed, you inconsiderate asshole!" I quickly excused myself and headed off to bed. Lying there in the dark, I concluded that Bob's take on time was like many ideas—neat in theory, messy in practice.

And yet I felt besieged with problems for which Bob's theory of time held great appeal. At work, our swelling employment ranks put a premium on my fragile management skills when in fact I preferred to spend my time writing code and doing research and development—after all, isn't that the job of a leader, pointing the way to the future? Ironically, Bob's salesmanship was bringing in so much additional business that we needed to hire even *more* people, eating up a greater percentage of my time and attention. And where in the world were we going to put all these people? When we moved Dave Florence's compiling operation to Arkansas, we built a little metal building behind our original building. Then we built another metal building, and after that we started adding trailers for additional offices. Now, when we brought potential customers down to visit CCX, it was like they were visiting a junkyard. I needed to make a plan and deal with that, and *soon*.

Then when I went home after work—as I now did every evening for family dinner at 6, per Jane's decree—the contrast was shocking. It was a quiet house—which has its benefits—but I began to sense something disturbing in the silence. It seemed, increasingly, that Jane didn't want more. Given the choice, she preferred to sit and read a book, and the only people she appeared interested in seeing were the black couple who lived on our property and helped us around the place. She even began resisting our occasional country club dinners with friends. I worried that we were growing in separate directions.

The best times I remember from those days were when the evening was over and the kids were quiet and I had finished any work I was doing. Jane and I would then go back to the bedroom and read, and I would have a Jack Daniel's nightcap, maybe two, and she might have another couple glasses of wine. I would even smoke a few cigarettes, despite my loathing of Jane's heavy smoking; by this time in the day, she was well into her second pack. But we would read—novels, biographies, history. We liked the same books, and she tore through them much faster than I did—naturally, since she spent most of her day reading. Those were good moments. But were they enough to build a life on?

Whenever I thought of that, I inevitably drifted back to Bob Ingenito's theory of time.

THE RACETRACK WAS where I felt most comfortably myself. By 1980, I decided I wanted to branch out, to compete in more than one big race a year and to try my skills against drivers outside the SCCA's southwest division. The race I decided on was a "double national," which drivers from all over the country can enter. They call it a double national because you get double points toward a national championship.

As it turned out, the country's biggest double national was on Memorial Day 1980 at Paul Newman's home track in Lime Rock, Connecticut. It was perfect—I could work with Ingenito in New York, then shoot over to Connecticut for practice and competition. All that spring my excitement grew—I was going to attack Paul Newman, Bob Litzinger, and all the other big dogs from that region on their own turf.

When race week arrived, I went to Lime Rock on Tuesday for practice day. The drill was that you paid the track $200 and you could run all day long. There were probably 15 cars testing, but the only two in C Production Class were Paul Newman and me. Since I'd never been on that track before and he practically lived there, I wasn't shocked to see him pass me several times during the morning runs. But I also don't like to lose, so I found myself trying to fight off a funk. This race was a new level of self-testing for me. When 30 cars roared off the starting line on race day, I sure didn't want to be at the back of the pack.

Sometime around midday I noticed Newman sitting in his car on pit lane. His crew was working on his car, as my crew was working on mine. So I decided to take the initiative and go introduce myself. When I got up to his window I leaned down and told him who I was. Then I said, "You can probably tell I'm struggling a little bit with this racetrack. Have you got any pointers?" He still had on his helmet, so at first I hadn't seen much of his face. Now he turned to look at me. His eyes were so blue they were scary.

"Charles," he said, "the secret to this racetrack is brakes." A beat. "Quit using them."

I knew instantly what he meant—I was over-slowing for the corners. I thanked him for his good advice and went back to my car with new resolve. That afternoon, I applied his tip to my practice laps and clocked much faster times. And on Friday, qualifying day, I didn't bring up the rear. Against a truly national set of drivers, many the best in their regions, I qualified 10th—well in the top half of the field. *Man*, I thought, *I'm making some serious progress here.*

But on race day, I surprised even myself. I finished third, behind Paul Newman and Bob Litzinger. The three of us stood on the post-race podium to receive our trophies. *How the hell did this happen?* Unlike me, most of the other drivers had professional cars, lots of money behind them. Some crashed and some broke down, but not everybody did. And still I finished third. Standing on that podium, I was having a hard time interpreting the data. All I knew was that this race felt like a turning point.

Looking back now on that wonderful moment, I'm struck by how applicable it seems, in retrospect, to my life beyond the racetrack—if, in fact, there ever was such a thing. I'd been racing against one or another foe—time, money, self-image, Uncle Ralph—since boyhood, and any edge I'd gained had always come as a result of intense focus, strategic tweaking, and a refusal to quit. If I wanted to push the thought even further, this little company that had been such a part of me for the past eight years had much in common with my race car. Both had started out as shit boxes propelled by grandiose dreams, competing against more moneyed opponents through talent, ingenuity, diligence, and heart. There had been lots of scrappy races in the hinterlands, and a fair number of spin-outs and crashes. But today I believe that when I stood on that podium at Lime Rock in May 1980 and felt I had reached a turning point, I was intuiting something bigger, broader, deeper. For the 1980s would be our company's pivotal decade, positioning us for a success that would surprise even us.

□ □ □ □ □

THE PRODIGAL SON—Alex Dietz—came home in 1980. Actually, I had brought Alex in as a consultant in 1979 to write code for some of that new business we were generating under Bob Ingenito's leadership. "After I worked a little while as a consultant," recalls Alex, "Charles said, 'You need to come back.' And I was happy to because I didn't enjoy working at the bank. I was so used to a lot of personal freedom and creativity in the way I ran things, and everything at the bank was very regimented. So I came back at the beginning of nineteen eighty, staying until I retired. Charles put my date of employment back to nineteen seventy, making me the longest-serving employee. I really appreciated that."

Also in 1980, after a multi-generational stewardship linking the age of the blacksmith to the age of the computer programmer, Ward School Bus Company finally reached the end of the road. That July, the company filed for bankruptcy. Its owners were $21.5 million in debt. We at CCX held our collective breath during Ward's legal proceedings, but we never heard a thing—Charles Ward had planned the turnover perfectly, and Royce Cullum had kept the bus company afloat until about two days after the statute of limitations on the stock turnover had expired. Once it was all done, a new bus company bought Ward, and we continued to do our service bureau business for them.

As for Charles Ward, he and his son went into the list business. I saw him from time to time, and helped him financially on multiple occasions. He'd been so good to us—to *me*—that I wanted to do whatever I could for him. But, financially at least, his story didn't end happily. Charles and Sharon divorced and he remarried, meaning Charles was cut off from the CCX stock that he'd so carefully put in Sharon's father's name. As far as I know, he never profited at all from that effort.

Finally, 1980 was the year I ended the relationship with Jennifer. She and I were flying back from a business trip together and she turned to me and said her marriage was lousy and she hoped I would divorce Jane and we could get together. "I know you're miserable," she said.

While I admired the courage it had taken for her to say those words, I knew it wouldn't work. "Look, Jennifer," I said, "I've got kids and I'm worried about them. There's no exit for me that feels good as long as my kids are young. But beyond that, you and I aren't compatible for the long haul. We like each other and we work very well together professionally. But we've done that too long for me not to know that if we lived in the same house, we wouldn't make it."

It was an awkward, painful moment for both Jennifer and me. But the next day at the office, we were business as usual. "I'm proud of both of us," Jennifer says today. "It could've been disastrous. But I'm proud of the way we got past all that without it ever really affecting our working relationship." I am too. Fortunately, while there had been some speculation in the office, very few people *really* knew about our relationship. Bob Ingenito did, and so did Jim Womble, who walked in on us in a New York hotel room I was sharing with Jim. Stupid me—why hadn't we gone to Jennifer's room? But that was pretty much the extent of those who had, in Womble's words, "empirical knowledge" of the relationship. And I wouldn't be telling about it here if it hadn't later doubled back to bite me.

One challenge much on my mind in these years—probably *the* most important challenge facing me—was how to manage this fast-growing business to greatest effect. One time I surprised the management team by bringing in Chuck Smith, my wife's therapist, to conduct a group therapy session on us. But group therapy wouldn't suffice long term. My gut told me that my main job as president was to set the agenda and to make sure our managers were on the same page going forward.

Because it was almost impossible to see the big picture in the office, I decided that my best way of accomplishing this goal was through our executive retreats at the Red Apple Inn, whose blessed isolation I valued now more than ever. "In the company we gave a thing called the Birkman test," says Jerry Adams. "We gave it to everybody, and it was very important because it wasn't right or wrong, it just told you who you were, and how you made decisions. We used it, for example, if we were going to reconstitute a team. We could run a report and say, we're going to put these ten people together, and here are some things you need to be aware of in your inner relations. The Birkman had a measurement called the structure score, and the more structured you were—eighty-nine, ninety, one hundred percent—that's how disciplined you were. Charles' structure score is three. That's good to know. It means if you go to him with five items to discuss, don't count on getting to all five of them."

Well, at least I *knew* I needed these getaways. Sometimes I had to almost hogtie some of my people to pull them away from what they thought were their "more pressing" concerns. We tend to get caught up in the everyday unless we're forced to rise above it.

One strategic issue we were confronting during this period was how to deal with the immense computer challenges facing us as a result of all this new work, there simply being no computer large enough to handle it all. Another topic of some urgency was what to do about a new building, which we desperately needed. We also addressed shorter-term tactical issues, such as reorganization of executive assignments.

But beyond the practical solutions that we arrived at as a team, it was the intangibles that I especially prized. During the days, we worked in a meeting room, beginning late morning. Then about 6 p.m. we repaired to the bar, where remnants of earlier business conversations might now mingle with lighter topics. Eventually we would have dinner together in a private dining room. I called these retreats "planning meetings," but my main purpose wasn't to create plans; it was to create a common understanding of where we were going. I wanted our team to emerge from each meeting with a firm commitment to our joint goals—where we wanted to be in a month, a year, five years, a decade.

I was also especially leery of office politics, which I had seen cripple even large companies like IBM. I made sure everyone knew exactly how I felt on that score, so if someone had an issue, here—right now—was the forum for airing it. We had some lively discussions, I can tell you. And again, I was able to observe how different managers responded to different situations.

As usual, Jennifer was the spark plug of these discussions. Jennifer would get right in your face and tell you how wrong you were. She wouldn't come out and say you were a dick head, but that's the message you got. Jerry Adams couldn't deal very well with Jennifer because Jerry didn't like conflict. Actually, Alex and Jerry both had quite a bit of trouble with Jennifer. Jim and Rodger and Bob Ingenito got along with her okay. It's not like they would go out to dinner with her—but they'd rather go to dinner with her than deal with her in a business setting.

So here we had conflict—absolutely. But I wouldn't call it politics. Politics wasn't allowed.

□ □ □ □ □

BY 1982, WE WERE well down the path to building a new headquarters facility. With help from the City of Conway and the State of Arkansas, not to mention our bank, we hired an architect from Albuquerque—Jim Miller, a nice guy I'd met and raced against in C Production competition—to design a three-story building for us. I told him I wanted it to knock the socks off any New Yorker who walked into it, and Jim responded with a huge atrium and a subtle taste of the Southwest. The architect's renderings were magnificent—so magnificent that they made us stupid. We were so proud of them that we posted them on the bulletin board so all the employees could be proud of them too. And up in the left hand corner there was an area labeled "Executive Spa."

I still had a whole lot to learn.

We broke ground for the new headquarters in September 1982. Meanwhile, we were continuing to break ground in other ways, too. From the very earliest iteration of our company, we'd been forced to work smarter than our competition. Ingenuity had often stood in for cash. Take computers, for example. In the early-to mid-'70s, the newest IBM mainframes would've been prohibitive for us to buy. Fortunately for us, the man running our computer operation was Rodger Kline, who dearly loves to pinch a penny. "So what we started doing," says Rodger, "is going to the next generation back. Because the name of the game in computers, for IBM, was to come out with a newer, faster model and obsolete the old model. By the time a machine was two generations behind, it would be very inexpensive.

"But the way IBM obsoleted these older computers was, they charged more for maintenance—they made it too expensive. Maintenance might be $30,000 a month and the software might be $30,000 a month. We solved that problem by hiring the IBM field engineers who repaired and maintained the computers. We knew these guys from our days at IBM. So when they retired from IBM, we'd put them on our staff. None of them were full-time and they didn't want to be.

"As for the software problem, we solved that by using operating systems that weren't IBM mainstream—they were either third-party operating systems or the free version of IBM's VM operating system. IBM didn't like that and did everything they could to discourage it. But for us, these operating systems were a fraction of the cost of the IBM MVS, IBM's top-of-the-line operating system. So with this strategy, we were able to install in our data center many big IBM mainframes that had been the top of the line, say four, five, six, seven, eight years ago—back when they were $25 million computers."

We all recognized Rodger as a master of the art of buying used computers right. So now we handed him the problem of accommodating the massive amounts of data being generated by our new business stream. "As we were growing in the direct mail industry, we always needed more and faster computers," says Rodger. "This culminated in the best purchase I ever made. Eight or nine years before, the IBM 3084 had been top of the line, a $20 million computer. I bought ten of them for $100,000. And by this time, we'd also started buying extra computers for their parts."

It was brilliant, the data center becoming Rodger's zombie computer lab, totally self-contained—a steady blast of industrial-strength air conditioning to keep the machines breathing, plenty of technicians to monitor the vital signs, and shelves of spare parts in case an arm or a leg fell off.

And this was just the beginning—we were about to need Rodger's operation more than ever. One day in 1982, I got a call from a man named Hank Ponder, who asked if we had an opportunity for him. Originally from Arkansas, Hank had been working for a major competitor of ours operating out of Denver. But he was fed up with his boss, Phil Wiland, whom Hank considered a self-righteous religious zealot who drove around with a cross on his van, a cross on his mirror, and a Bible on his console—one of those guys who loved to screw people in business when he wasn't in church. When Hank came by the office to see us, I had a sense of someone who'd reached a Bob Ingenito point in life—he wasn't spending another day working for someone who made him miserable.

So we hired Hank, who turned out to be our team's resident rebel, for both good and ill. "Those of us who lived through the birthing process, or soon after it, seemed to drink the Kool-Aid pretty well," says Jerry Adams. "Hank came in as a transaction guy, and his philosophy seemed to be to hell with that. If this doesn't work out, I'll do something else."

What Hank brought to the table—besides a gift for brutal candor—was deep experience in business-to-consumer direct marketing, because in his former job he'd been working with several large banks. Now he started calling on some of those contacts on our behalf.

Early in 1983 Hank landed us our first job for Citibank. It was a small piece of business, which we handled to the bank's satisfaction. So they gave us another little job to do. This was all very exciting. Because not only did the big national banks and their ubiquitous credit cards play to our unique list fulfillment strengths, the banks also regularly marketed their services to millions upon millions of people. These first little jobs for Citibank were no less than a toehold in Big Data before the term "Big Data" was even big.

But there was a problem, Hank said. None of these big banks had ever heard of us. "Who the hell are these guys in—where, *Arkansas*?" they would say to him.

"We like you, Hank, and we like what you're doing. But we're going to have to do some more financial due diligence...." The unspoken, as Hank read the standard response, was that we needed to significantly raise our profile. I totally agreed with him.

That spring I noticed that the IPO market seemed especially hot, and in a meeting with my advisors I floated the idea of going public. Even though a lot of guys in the list industry were chronic slow payers, we were doing okay financially at the time—we were definitely profitable, enabling us to build up a little cash and secure some lines of credit. But for a decade we'd been operating like paupers, doing our work under a constant cloud of money worry. "If we went public, we could get some investment in this business," I said. "That would give us credibility."

Everybody liked the idea, and soon we were talking with investment bankers in Houston about going public. I was clueless about investment bankers in those days—so much so that I didn't even know that Stephens, Inc., right there in Little Rock, did this kind of work. Then I got a phone call from Mike Smith, one of Stephens' top people, asking why we hadn't come to them. That's when I learned that Stephens was touted in those days as "the biggest investment bank outside New York." I also received a not-so-subtle call from Bob Dills, my father-in-law, who was a close friend of Stephens co-founder Witt Stephens. With $7 million in revenue in 1982, CCX—we went public as CCX Network, Inc.—was just a minnow in the Stephens pond. But they liked where we were heading, and besides, home state pride was at stake. In choosing Stephens, I decided I'd rather have a friend in Arkansas than somebody I didn't know in Houston. More to the point, why trade a Houston stranger for a powerful enemy at home?

"The market's hot, but we think it's starting to cool off," Stephens said. "If we're going to do this, we'd better do it fast." And so, amid the swelter of an Arkansas summer, the intense work of going public got underway.

□ □ □ □ □

"HE CHECKED OUT," says my daughter Carrie today, speaking of me in the context of her own turmoil as a young teenager in the early '80s.

Even while I was wrestling with problems at the office, plus trying to take us public, I made a point of being present at all of Carrie's dance recitals and at ball games where she was a cheerleader. Later I went to all of Rob's football games, too.

I thought I was being a good dad. When Rob was in junior high, I built him a motocross track and took him to races—not a zillion times, but maybe five to eight times. We even did a number of race events together. But just as, at work, I was struggling to understand the complexities of the human animal, at home the challenges approached the Ph.D level. Was there a software program to explain all this?

"I started having a lot of adolescent emotional problems," Carrie says. "At fourteen, I started drinking and smoking pot. He really didn't know what to do with me. He didn't know how to affirm me, and I didn't know how to ask for it."

"One time," recalls Sharon Tackett, "Charles and Jane were away at a race and my husband and I were to stay at their house with the kids. It was before we had children. And I was still at work and my husband was at our farm out of town. He was supposed to come in and pick Carrie up for cheerleading at a football game, but there was a wreck on the highway and he got stuck in traffic. So Carrie, who had no driver's license, took her mother's Porsche and drove herself to the game. She didn't show up at home until close to midnight. And I was supposed to be responsible."

Carrie was one of those kids who're so smart that they can't be stimulated, so Jane had taken her to see Chuck Smith as early as Carrie's fourth-grade year. Now, in early 1983, Chuck suggested she go away to boarding school, an idea Carrie seized upon with all of her considerable will. "Even at fourteen, I knew I needed to get out of there," Carrie says. "I mean, our house wasn't a walk-on-eggshells house. Nobody was in any kind of addictive behavior. I didn't feel any tension. Mom would have headaches and be in bed a lot, and that scared me as a child; now that I look back on it, she may have been depressed."

Then there was me. "The combination," says Carrie, "of the engineer, which is the meticulous, quantitative, logical, sensible side of his personality, combined with all the IQ points, combined with parents who sent him to school by himself at three and to New York at seventeen. Through the years I've become reconciled that his inability to acknowledge feelings and his tendency to put emotions behind him was because when he was little he had to be so big. Then there was the work ethic—what did you accomplish today, and did you do it by yourself?"

While I believe that each of us has the right to our memories, I also know that memory is seldom perfect. Many things can influence it—even distort it. Today Carrie sometimes ascribes motives to me that never even crossed my mind. My recollection is that Carrie and I had a fundamentally good relationship. I never fought with her, or with Rob, the way Jane did. When the kids got hurt or something, Jane was always there for the wounded. But every time there was a problem, I was there for them, too. If they needed to call me, they didn't have any trouble reaching me. Sharon knew to get me out of *any* meeting if one of my children was on the phone.

The thing I remember, in the house we lived in before building the big house in the country, was that Carrie and Jane were going at each other day in and day out. They fought twice as much as Jane and I did. Jane, who bridled at the very word *authority* when she was growing up, now expected her children to snap to whenever she gave an order. Many of Jane's and my arguments were precipitated by her insistence that I side with her in whatever squabble she was having with Carrie or Rob, and often I didn't—because I thought Jane was being unreasonable. She would *scream* at Carrie for little things, like the fact that Carrie's shoelaces weren't tied.

Remembering the fights between Carrie and Jane, Rob—who was then in elementary school—says, "If I saw it coming, I would try to get away from it. I would kind of go into my own little world."

Carrie wanted to go to boarding school because she and her mother couldn't live in the same house together. So when Carrie said, "I got to get out of here," Jane said, "Thank goodness." But despite the sparks between them, they also shared a closeness based on their mutual problems. "When I started drinking at fourteen," says Carrie, "my mom said to me—after explaining for years what her illness was, and how to cope, and talk, and have therapy—she said, 'You got the gene, and let me tell you what happened to your grandfather.' My mother's dad was an alcoholic who quit drinking in 1938 and remained sober nearly half a century; he was also bipolar, which unfortunately wasn't diagnosed until he was in his sixties. But he was a mentor, helping countless young men get sober in Fort Smith.

"Mom did that too, about mental illness. People in Conway would come to her and ask her about depression. She would see the yard man's cousin or the black basketball player at the college. She was an open door, putting a face on mental illness for many people, because she didn't fit the stereotype. She was very open about being bipolar. She didn't apologize for it. So she talked to me a lot, about anger and other issues. She was my rock."

But getting Carrie ready for boarding school was extremely stressful for Jane. The school we selected was in western Massachusetts, and I volunteered to take Carrie up there before the start of school in September. "It was a teary good-bye," she recalls of the day she was finally on her own, and indeed it was. But our house was also calmer once Carrie and her mother had half the United States between them. "Yeah," says Rob, laughing. "If anything, it got more normal."

Carrie's leaving coincided with the run-up to our public offering, which meant I was more than swamped at the office. Going public is a fulltime job itself, and you've got to run the company while you're doing it. Our first major hurdle was getting the "red herring" written. A preliminary prospectus filed with the Securities & Exchange Commission, this tells about the company and is used to solicit expressions of interest in the issue. It's called a red herring because of the bold disclaimer in red on the cover of the thing stating that this is a preliminary document and much of the information in it could change. But all that potentially changeable information is a bear to prepare, and we literally spent months on it, going back and forth, rewriting, checking with Stephens, and rewriting again. The young guys I had assigned to prepare it never could get it right, so I finally gave the job to Alex Dietz, who wrote it to the satisfaction of all the accountants. Then we had to distribute the document and allow people time to digest it. I think we finished that part of the process around Thanksgiving of 1983.

Almost at the same time, we received a 20-page financial document from Citibank. Hank Ponder had some big things cooking with Citi, but they wouldn't give us more business until they conducted a complete financial review. A team of Citibank auditors was set to arrive in Conway once we returned the completed 20-page document.

Fortunately, the timing saved us. We sent their blank document back with our red herring attached, along with a note saying that we were in the middle of an IPO and were legally prohibited from making financial disclosures other than those in the attached preliminary prospectus. We never heard another word about it from Citibank; instead, they started giving us business. Even our *march* toward becoming a public company seemed credibility enough for them.

The last step prior to IPO was a brief road show, which entailed my having a couple of meetings in Boston and a couple in New York, along with Stephens making a few phone calls. The IPO took place in mid-December. We sold 20 percent of the outstanding stock at $12 a share, and one day I turned around and found myself worth more than I'd ever dreamed of. I was 40 years old.

"Growing up," recalls Carrie, who came home that Christmas, "I didn't know a salary number, I didn't know how much a car cost. If there was money stress, they didn't offload that on me. I knew we were taken care of and we had what we needed and it was not our dinner-table conversation to talk about how much money Daddy made or anything like that.

"But I do remember, during that Christmas break, driving to Memphis to go back-to-school shopping with Mom. Somewhere on I-40, I said to her, 'I'm so afraid that my going to boarding school is putting you guys out.' I'd seen on some form that tuition was ten thousand dollars, and I felt very guilty.

"She looked over at me and smiled. 'Honey,' she said, your dad has just gone through what we call an initial public offering.' And she told me a number of twelve million dollars. Today that number still seems unreal.

"When she told me that, I was so relieved. *Ah,* I remember thinking, *I'm okay.* I didn't have to feel guilty. *We* were okay."

Part Three

BIG DATA

9

LIKE A WEED

100101001011001010001001011001010110011

AFTER THE IPO, while I no longer owned 51 percent of the company, I still had board and stock control through my senior managers' proxies. Control is a double-edged sword. So is going public. But in that incomparably intoxicating time following our NASDAQ debut, I felt like a man who had conquered the world.

To add to the high, we were actually starting to make big money. Between 1982 and 1991, our annual revenue would grow from $7 million to some $90 million—the vast majority of this from giant national banks like Citi. And that was just the beginning. "Hank Ponder basically built his own subsidiary focused on the banks," says Jim Womble. "He was a real loner, wanted to control everything, and he was bringing in the revenue. For Citi, we bought their own computers for them, their own programmers. Then in the late eighties we got the Chase account, and *boom*."

Today we hear the term "Big Data" all around us, and I want to clarify what we're talking about. The term Big Data generally refers to extremely large masses of *unstructured* and *partially structured* data that typically has some kind of content that can be used for marketing, or for business decision-making, or even—as you saw in the prologue of this book—for tracking bad guys. I'll talk more about unstructured data in succeeding chapters, because unstructured data only started becoming a factor in the late 1990s, and very much so in the 2000s.

Back in the '70s and '80s, though, we didn't even use the term Big Data. We talked about "massive databases" or "huge data problems" or something like that. And even if we had used the term Big Data, it would've referred to something much different from what we mean by that term today. The data then was different both in volume and form. First, there just wasn't as much data available. We didn't record what came into a call center, and business wasn't done by email; it was done by phone and letter, and we didn't have any way of translating it.

Second, it was also largely *structured* data. To put that in perspective, an Excel spreadsheet contains structured data. It's organized into rows and columns of information comprised of financial data, inventory data, sales data, accounts receivable data, and various and sundry other transactional data. Traditionally, a lot of data in corporations has been structured data. And when Acxiom was getting started with the banks, most of the data was structured credit bureau data.

The big banks were marketing credit cards, which would become the basis of our great success. But it wouldn't all happen overnight—in fact, it would take us some 15 years to give the banks everything they wanted to achieve. Because in the early '80s, their voracious vision of the power of data surpassed all capabilities of the time. Computers had to get faster and cheaper. And even with our literally *acres* of computers, we had to embark on a long-range program of building the tools to reach their goals. From the start, we had their end game as a concept, and we could slowly add to it. But along the way, we had to develop new techniques for managing unprecedented volumes of data, combining that data, updating that data, cleaning that data, maintaining that data. Those techniques and processes just didn't exist on this scale in the early '80s. So there was a huge amount to be *invented* to realize the big banks' dream.

What the banks envisioned was the pulling together of all the data from the three national credit bureaus. But not just once—they wanted the monthly snapshot for every single person in this country with a credit history, and they wanted each person's monthly snapshot to go back five years. So we were talking about 200 million credit records times 60 months of credit data, and that was just the *credit* files. They also wanted years' and years' worth of transactional data on their some 50 million credit card customers.

All of this would go into a massive database, ultimately resulting in thousands of data elements for every household in the United States. The simplest of this information answered such questions as: How long have you lived in your house? What's the value of your home? What are the characteristics of your neighborhood? Is there evidence of automobiles being owned? How many licensed drivers are there in the home? What's your ethnicity? Not all of that data came from credit bureaus—we would take a census overlay for your area and even your block. We also collected data from telephone directories: How long has this person been listed at that address? We could trace you back year after year after year.

But inaccurate data is useless data—it's even *harmful* data where these big banks and their credit cards are concerned. So when the three credit bureaus conflict with one another, which is all the time, how do we determine which is the correct information? And when we pull names from the telephone directories, how can we be sure that the J. Doe at 111 Main Street in Little Rock is the Jonathan Doe who'd lived there two years before and had good credit, and not the Jay Doe who'd once gone bankrupt?

The answer to that last question took many years to come up with, as you'll later see. But in general, getting it right—as right as possible, in any case—was crucial to the banks, because they were in the business of extending credit to people they didn't know. As it turns out, lots of people manipulate their credit history, and if the bank doesn't spot the fraud before offering such people a premium credit product with a high credit limit, it can cost the bank dearly. Banks being banks, they know *exactly* how much it costs for each wrong call—something like $500, as I remember. Multiply that by the millions of people they were targeting with their credit cards, and, as the old joke goes, pretty soon you're talking real money.

To a bank, it's not who'll respond to a credit-based credit card offer; it's who will give the bank the greatest value after credit loss over the lifetime of the relationship. Part of it has to do with response rates. If I send out 1,000 pre-approved credit offers, how many people are going to respond and say yep, I want to fill out an application? The next question is, what percentage of those people will ultimately accept the offer? Then, how many of the ones who accept are actually going to be profitable customers?

That's defined in a lot of ways. Personally, I'm a terrible customer of Citibank because I pay all my bills every month and keep no balances. I don't use that 18 percent interest rate, which is a bitch to them—they don't like it one bit. So I'm not profitable to the banks issuing me credit cards. Another question banks need to answer is how many of their customers are going to end up with bad credit and walk away from a $10,000 balance due without paying? And here's another question—is this applicant one of those guys who takes a teaser interest rate, keeps his card for 12 months, and then switches to another bank's card?

So the banks study the credit scores, pore over the response rates, and run all this data through their extensive analytics—the ultimate point being to answer a couple more key questions. One: What is this applicant's expected lifetime value to us? And two: How accurately can we predict how much money this applicant is going to make or lose for the bank if he says yes? Citibank had 100 people in Long Island City, New York, trying to answer those questions—trying to create models and create mail tape specifications based on the data we gave them. It stands to reason that for a bank to create accurate models, they have to have accurate data.

So accuracy of information is what it's all about. And that's the reason we had so much success with the banks—our whole business strategy was directed toward building computing systems, and software, and tools to allow our customers to create these models on these huge data assets. A model built on faulty data is junk—garbage in, garbage out. We had a computer strategy the banks needed, a software strategy they needed, and even our organizational strategy was directed toward working with Citibank, say, to find out exactly what they needed. For us, the bank work wasn't just some add-on; it was what we *did*. We might not have been able to achieve the banks' whole goal immediately, but even by the mid- to late-'80s we could get to step one—then to step two, step three, and beyond—faster and with more accuracy than anyone else, and at a lower cost. And we kept getting better and better. The banks tried occasionally to get other people to do it, so as to test us, but we were the guys who produced the best quality data—allowing them to create models that were highly predictive. So we dominated this industry.

We dominated because, thanks to our unique computer strategy, we could process Big Data. Nobody else could.

□ □ □ □ □

WE DIDN'T KNOW much about boards of directors in those days. Before we went public, our important management decisions were generally made by a loose cadre of senior executives, with me having the final say. But now that we had stockholders, we had to codify our corporate decision-making process. That meant a CCX board of directors, which would be comprised of a few top inside people who would share the duties of company oversight with several well-respected, independent business leaders from outside the firm.

On our initial board, our insiders were Rodger, Jim, Bob Ingenito, and me. From outside, there was Walter Smiley, founder of Systematics, a company that produced data processing software for smaller banks (it was eventually acquired by Fidelity); Mike Smith, from Stephens, Inc., who had taken us public; and Larry Powers, a business associate of Bob Ingenito's. Our meetings were professional, but also cordial and collegial, befitting a "family" company—which is what CCX still felt like to me.

As the forward-looking head of the family—my relationship to time was always dynamic, since I toiled in the present but a portion of my brain lived five years in the future—it had always been my job to create company agendas aimed at achieving future goals. Now I had to take them to the board.

All these rapid-fire company changes had really pressured our infrastructure, and I don't mean just the hard, organizational, having-enough-office-space kind—though there was certainly some of that. But so much new business, so fast, created internal, emotional stresses as well. Having always believed that recruiting was the lifeblood of any organization, I was now approving new hires willy-nilly. I don't mean we were being sloppy. When Womble needed help with an urgent new project, I'd say, "Go to the college and hire a couple of those bright young grads that we've wanted to recruit." Like IBM, we always tried to hire the best and the brightest available. But it was happening with disquieting frequency, and each new hire made the already slippery concept of *structure* just that much harder to get my hands around.

For half a decade now I'd been wrestling with questions of leadership. Around the time we went public, I read Tom Peters' and Robert Waterman's book *In Search of Excellence* and, like executives all over America, was taken by a deceptively simple concept they talked about in their book—"management by walking around." The back story was that Peters and his McKinsey & Co. colleague Bob Waterman had been so stultified by the mind-numbing bureaucracy of the banks they'd been studying for their research that they'd taken a side trip to Palo Alto to visit Hewlett-Packard. There, they heard about "management by wandering around," a refreshing and longstanding HP philosophy dating back to founders William Hewlett and David Packard. In the broadest sense, it meant cutting through corporate bureaucracy. But what captured the imaginations of executives like me was the *so*-non-MBA notion of actually getting out of your office and walking around and talking one-on-one with your people. That way, you'd know firsthand what was going on in your company.

I already had an "open-door policy," but it wasn't the same thing. If any employee wanted to discuss something with me, they'd peer through the glass and see me consumed with a desk full of the minutia of running a company. *Whoa, daunting. Sure doesn't look like a good time to pop in and bare my soul to the boss.*

Such were some of the issues I'd been mulling when, during a board meeting very soon after we went public, I proposed that Bob Ingenito become president of CCX. The way I pitched it, Bob could mostly manage the day-to-day business of the company from New York, even as he continued spearheading our sales effort. What I didn't tell the board was that when I had first talked with Bob about the idea of his becoming president, I told him he'd have to move to Arkansas. He vehemently rejected that notion, citing his home in Harrison, his family's deep roots there, his other businesses. But at the same time he had urged me to give him a chance to show that he could be an effective commuter-president. Finally I relented, because with Bob running the day-to-day company, I, as CEO, would be free to devote my energies to research and development, which was vital to our continued success; to working on new software programs for our increasing focus on banking databases; and, of course, to managing by walking around. I guess it was a testament to my strong hold on this company that the board approved such a plan—a plan about which even I'd had misgivings.

I also proposed, at another early meeting, that CCX become a sponsor of my car racing. After two or three years of financial support, Jane had finally told me she couldn't afford it anymore and that we needed to find another way to pay for it. "No problem," I had said—and this was at least a year before the subject of going public had even been talked about. Now, though, here we were, and the proposal was on the boardroom table. I had no trouble arguing the case—still don't. Automobile racing is a major spectator sport in this country, and for fans to see our high-tech company's logo emblazoned on a sleek, *very* high-tech race car—to me it makes perfect sense. I also had a higher racing profile by then, having turned professional in 1981 following my trophy finish at Lime Rock. Also, I was driving a much better car—a prototype racer built in England. Unlike the Datsun I'd been racing up till then, prototypes are pure racetrack cars, aerodynamically designed to go fast. I would drive prototypes from 1983 until 1992, when I would, for the first time, design and build my own race car.

When Jane had given me the news about needing other means of paying for racing, I'd gone out and recruited a few sponsors, and after the IPO I paid for quite a bit of it myself. But I wanted CCX to sponsor me, too. I wanted my racing to become a point of company pride. I could already imagine our bringing customers and their kids to the racetrack for a day of excitement—"courtesy of CCX."

The proposal passed, and for nearly two decades our company name appeared on cars I drove. And for nearly two decades someone was trying to talk me out of it. One way or another, Rodger Kline was usually behind it. A man with a well-honed internal financial governor, Rodger appeared to feel positively *violated* by our investing in auto racing. Jim Womble used to try to get him to look at the bigger picture. "'Look, Rodger,' I would say," recalls Jim. "'This is definitely not your concept of what we should be spending money on. It's probably not mine. But give Charles credit for all the right decisions he's made. If this one's not exactly right, so what?'"

Jerry Adams tells a funny story that's emblematic of the efforts to undercut our racing sponsorship over the years. "When I ran corporate marketing," Jerry says, "we were spending dollars on NASCAR racing that I didn't think we had. So I made three runs at Charles to talk him out of putting money into the NASCAR stuff, and I was 0 for three. I was also 0 for thirty-four years telling Charles anything he didn't want to hear. It almost became a spectator thing. The last time I let it be known that I was going to talk with Charles about getting out of NASCAR, it was like there were bleachers set up outside Charles' office. Like there was a betting pool, and it was all against me.

"So I had the meeting and came out, and everybody was waiting. And even though Charles said no, I felt like I could bring it up to him. If I hadn't had the root system I have with Charles, there probably would've been moments over all those years that I could've been asked to leave the company. My way of judging when to stop pressing was to watch for his ears to get red."

Another longstanding debate concerned our corporate airplane, which I recommended to the board a couple of years after we'd approved the racing sponsorship. "I was the resident skeptic the first time the board agreed that we could get an airplane," says Rodger Kline. "I abstained from voting and caught a bunch of hell over that. Not directly from Charles, though he gave me one of those looks. But Walter Smiley's company had an airplane and Walter swore by it. 'If you don't vote for an airplane,' Walter told me in that meeting, 'you're retarding the growth of the company.' So I shut up about it. But I remained skeptical over the years as we continued to upgrade—to get bigger and bigger airplanes, faster and faster jets."

□ □ □ □ □

IN BOTH MY business and personal life, I tend to remember the second half of the 1980s as kind of a train wreck—if you'll pardon a serial car-crash survivor his mixed metaphor. The good news is that the train-wreck years would lead to smarter, happier times, on both fronts.

The first time I remember thinking that way was in 1986. I was in Atlanta again, lying flat on my back in a hospital bed, the trauma unit, and boy was I pissed. I wanted to go back to the racetrack but the doctors wouldn't let me. They needed to "observe" me, they said. They had me hooked up to a catheter, which was bad enough. But I was starving and they said I couldn't eat a thing for 24 hours. "Are you kidding me?" I was really mad now. To make matters worse, somebody was always opening the door to my room and looking in. "What is this," I said to the nurse, "Grand fucking Central Station?"

I wished Jane were there to help me. She and Carrie had come with me to Atlanta, but for once, instead of going to the race, they'd gone shopping—Carrie needed new clothes for college in the fall. So it would be hours before they got back to the hotel room and heard what had happened.

Once again the scene was Road Atlanta, site of my bad crash in 1979. This time—Memorial Day weekend, 1986—I was driving my English-made prototype with the CCX logo painted on it, and I was going as hard as I could during qualifying. Suddenly, as I reached the very same place on the track where I'd crashed before, my brake line snapped. I was at the bottom of a hill going about 165 when it broke, and I came all the way up the hill and at the top there was a slit in the earth with a bridge over it; I first hit the same tire wall I had hit before, then hit the bridge in the air at about 70 miles an hour; the car ricocheted over and down the hill, coming to a stop about 100 yards away. I'd crashed so hard that everybody assumed I was dead.

I was dazed, and probably had a minor concussion, but I was conscious. I sat for a few seconds collecting my faculties, then people were all around me. They asked where I hurt, and I said I felt some pain in my lower back. "Don't move!" one said. "We're going to cut you out!"

I didn't think I was hurt—nothing looked broken from the outside—but the officials insisted on checking for internal injuries, so they rushed me to the hospital by medevac helicopter. Right away, the doctors X-rayed my lower back; then they put in the catheter and wouldn't let me eat anything. So there I lay, stomach growling, the door opening every few minutes, people peering in. It was damned irritating.

A million things went through my mind that day, and I started realizing that the wreck metaphor extended beyond my immediate surroundings. CCX was making a lot of money, but I had made some bad decisions. For one, Bob Ingenito wasn't panning out in his new leadership role. Less than three years into the job and he'd turned out to be more helter-skelter than I was—or maybe it was just the impossible logistics that I'd ultimately ignored when I appointed him president. "I would fly to Arkansas every other week, arriving Monday morning and returning to New York after work Wednesday," recalls Bob. "It was pretty rough—but I didn't realize it was rough. In those days you traveled a lot, worked a lot. We were young."

But important things weren't getting done, and a lot of people were confused. "I was new then," recalls Cindy Childers, who would later become indispensable in helping me address deficiencies in the company's structure. "I was in the accounting department, which was on the executive floor. All I knew was that we had this president, his name was Bob Ingenito, we never heard from him, and we saw him once in a blue moon. Nice guy, though."

I consider myself the most generous of leaders. I hire good people, give them a mission, and turn them loose on it. I'm even happy to help them get back on course a few times if they stray. But there comes a point. "Charles will give you all the rope you need," says Rodger Kline, "but eventually, if he reaches the conclusion that you're not doing your job, it's all over. Once he loses faith in you, forget it. I've counseled any number of people about that. I can see the path these people are on, but Charles is so easy to get along with that they weren't taking seriously that they needed to improve their performance. When they didn't listen to me, the inevitable happened."

Another knock on my hospital door. Then someone peeped in and, just as quickly, ducked back out. Infuriating.

Acquisitions were another thorny problem. In that case, it was like we were trying to live up to some vague outside idea of what a successful, fast-growing (like a *weed*) company ought to be doing, instead of focusing on what we do really well. What the hell were we thinking, buying a letter shop and a fulfillment center? It was one of those deals that looked okay on paper, as long as you squinted your eyes real hard. The truth is, we let the banks pressure us to become a turnkey business—printing, handling, and distributing their direct mail pieces. Nightmare after nightmare.

Then one day Alex Dietz walked into my office and tossed an article on my desk. It was all about how companies need to concentrate on their core competencies. Alex and I looked at each other and said, "Right." We were good at computers and IT technologies, but terrible at operational logistics. So we jettisoned the letter shop and fulfillment center and figured out other ways to service our bank clients. Rule One: No more work that involves trucks and sheds. On the learned-our-lesson side of the ledger, we acquired a computer company in England—Southwark Computer Services, Ltd., in London. So now we adjusted our scope to an international market.

At home, there were wrecks in progress and a doozy on the horizon. Jane seemed to have settled into a pattern of good years and bad years. During the good years, I would think, *She's back*—this *is the girl I married.* But during the bad years, it was like living with a volatile stranger. We'd be riding in the car together and she might say something like, "That sure is an ugly gray sky. I think it's going to rain." And the sky would be clear and blue. If I told her it was clear and blue, she would just go off on me, calling me a liar. The simplest things could spark fierce attacks—such was the breadth of our disconnect.

Jane was relatively happy at the moment, since she had a new project—we were building a huge new house in West Conway, 120 acres of land in all. But I could already predict that her mood would soon change 180 degrees, probably within the year. Bob Dills, in very poor health, had told Jane that he planned to leave more of his estate to Jane's sister than he did to Jane, explaining that it was because we were in better shape financially than Nancy and Ewell were. I had tried to make her see the justice in that, from her father's point of view. But Jane—who didn't quite believe it was actually going to happen—would, I knew, take it as an elemental and very personal betrayal.

The door to my hospital room opened *again,* then slammed shut. "What in the *hell* is going on here?" I asked the nurse. I was just about to yank the catheter and storm out.

About that time—literally about that time—a woman opened the door and she and several other women looked in. "*That's* not Paul Newman," the first woman said, and there was a hint of disdain in her voice. Immediately it was clear. Paul Newman had driven at Road Atlanta that day too, and the rumor around the hospital was that *Newman* had crashed and was in the trauma unit. There must've been 50 people making the trek to trauma to catch a glimpse of the famous movie star.

Even in my crankiness, I had to chuckle. I still think of that as The Day I Was Paul Newman.

□ □ □ □ □

BOB INGENITO LEFT the company in early 1987. "Charles phoned me on a Sunday afternoon," Bob recalls. "The company was growing, the board wanted a fulltime president. He was talking to someone else about the job. 'You'll get a nice severance, plus a consulting deal,' Charles said. 'Of course you'll keep your stock, and I'll get you an option program. That's it. What do you think?'

"'Charles,' I said, 'it's Sunday, I'm home with my family. I don't know what to think. I just wonder why you didn't talk to me about this before. That's it. I'll talk to you when I get down there.'

"I don't know how he felt that week, but I toughed it out, I just toughed it out. Then when I got to Arkansas, he picked me up at the airport. The other guy hadn't taken the job. 'We can't go back,' I said. 'I know,' he said. So I said good-bye to everybody and left. Somehow, though, Charles and I kept up a communication."

Even though the Ingenito experiment hadn't worked out, I still believed that my most vital role was to focus on R & D. That meant I needed to find another president, and this time I wanted a proven manager. Once again, I turned to IBM. It wasn't a perfect company—what company was?—but there were enough things right about it that it remained a kind of template for us at CCX.

After discussions with my senior leadership, the man I chose was Phil Carter, a fellow Arkansan who had risen through the ranks at IBM and was now somewhere in the Northeast running a small division. He had some 500 people reporting to him. I didn't know Phil personally—he was several years younger than I—but all of us had heard of him. Phil's early claim to fame, the achievement that put him on that ladder to success, was that he had personally convinced Dillard's Department Stores to switch to IBM from whatever they'd been using. He was a very impressive guy, and somehow I persuaded him to leave IBM and come run CCX day to day.

I felt really good about having Phil on board. He was the polar opposite of Bob Ingenito: Where Bob was absent, Phil had his hands on everything; where Bob was unengaged, Phil was engaged up to his eyeballs. Phil apparently loved every part of running a business that I loathed—paperwork, organization charts, regular meetings, detailed employee reviews. "Charles' idea of a review," recalls Jerry Adams, "was to phone me and say, 'Hey, you're doing great.' And then hang up." Phil Carter was going to take a lot of what I considered drudgery out of my life. The way I viewed my role was, I would keep finance and computer operations and programming, while Phil handled general operations and marketing. I could now concentrate on new business, on acquisitions, and of course on R & D.

And I stayed intimately involved with our customers like Citibank. You let those relationships slide at your peril.

It was a very fluid time in the company. Headcounts were increasing so fast that sometimes I could walk down a corridor and not know half the people I met. From 25 employees when I joined the company, we now had maybe 400 working there—not counting our associates in England. The hiring pace got quicker once we landed the Chase account. And what were we doing with all these people? One indication is that we were printing probably 20 boxes of business cards a day, to accommodate people who'd just been promoted from manager to director to vice-president to senior vice-president. That was a telling fact I didn't focus on until much later.

In May 1988, my vision of mixing racing and clients finally became a reality. That year I was racing again at Lime Rock, Connecticut, so we set up a hospitality tent and invited a bunch of Citibank people up for the day. They brought their kids, who got to have their pictures made sitting in the race car. To my mind, the day was an unqualified success—and proof that investing in racing could be tantamount to investing in client goodwill.

But the truth is, goodwill seemed a rare commodity at Citibank. They'd been our client for a little more than five years, and they were paying us very well. But that desirable piece of business came with an increasingly high dignity tax. Citibank had apparently become used to mistreating its suppliers. They were arrogant and demanding. The more business they gave us, the more imperious they were. They would call out of the blue, for example, and say, "We need this project out, and we need it *now*. And we insist that you cancel all your work for other clients until this is done." We'd started doing work for several smaller banks, and Citi had grumbled some about that. But it was when we landed the Chase account that they really went over the edge.

One day I got a call from a Citibank executive, Jeannine Farhi. She didn't control our business from a daily operational standpoint, but all the people who did reported to her. Jeannine was very diplomatic. She said she'd told her guys that she "wanted to meet with Charles," so of course I said I would be happy to see her. She also said she'd prefer that the two of us meet alone, nobody else in the room. Fine with me, I said.

Jeannine turned out to be very attractive, probably in her late 30s, but she had progressed up the Citibank ladder quite nicely. She clearly had something on the ball. I had arranged to meet her over in the production facility instead of in my office. She didn't waste much time with small talk. "Your company has become more and more important to us," she said, "and we know that you're working for some other banks. That's a potential concern for us, so one of the reasons I didn't want anybody else in the room is I'm telling you, you're going to have to resign from Chase Bank and these other banks if you want to keep doing business with Citibank. We've made that decision and I regret that we have to ask you to do this. But we know we're giving you twice, three times as much business as Chase is right now, and we know that all your other business from all these other guys can't be as big as you're doing with us. So if you want to keep our half, then I'm going to have to ask you to resign from all these other accounts. We'll be reasonable—we'll give you enough time to finish what you're doing."

I didn't say anything for a long moment. The mind is a wonderful computer—once again, I saw Dave Florence saying, "Don't be stupid." But in another instant I flashed on a face from high school—the face of a bully who'd pushed me around until the day I had just had enough. I hauled off and gave him a huge black eye, and that changed everything. From then on, he wanted to be my best friend.

"I understand, Jeannine," I finally said. "So what you're going to need is several tractor trailers, probably three or four."

She looked baffled. "I'm sorry, Charles, I'm not following you."

"Well," I said, "we have three or four tractor-trailer loads of magnetic tapes and other media that you're going to need to pick up. Because we're going to cease work—immediately—not for the other guys, but for you. And if you're going to finish these projects, and if you're interested in getting new ones started, you'd better have all your old backup data and everything so that there's no serious interruption to your work."

I noticed her mouth was now hanging open.

"Our guys can help you all load this stuff, or maybe even find you some trucks, if you want us to do that. Unless you do climate control, there might be some data lost. But with climate control it may take a while to transport that much data...."

"Uh, Charles," she said, "maybe we need to talk about this some more. Why would you say this to me—we give you all this business!"

"Jeannine," I said, "Citibank is the worst fucking business partner anybody could ever have. You demand this, you demand that. We never know what you're going to ask us to do, we don't know how much computer capacity you're going to require, you don't give us any planning data. You just say, 'We're starting a new project, it's going to be this size, it's got to be completed on this date.' No matter what else we've got in the house. We don't know if you're going to keep giving us business for six months, twelve months, we don't know if you're going to be here in a year. You guys just throw shit over the wall and start telling us to jump. I'm not living this way anymore, and neither are our guys. This is a blessing in disguise. We're generating a very important new source of revenue for Citibank, but it's killing us and it's not even fun. And if you guys want us to keep working with you, not only are we going to do work for these other banks, but *you're* going to have to be a better partner."

"Charles," she said, "I had no idea."

"Well, you're not in it every day, so you don't see it. But it's hell working for you."

"Obviously, we've got some soul-searching to do. Forget what I said. I'll be back to you."

No wonder she backed off: Many years later I would learn that our work for *Chase* at this time was bringing that bank a profit of $500 million—against their payment to us of $25 million a year. We were doing *twice* that amount of business with Citibank, and Jeannine was putting it all at risk. I had no idea how much power I really did have over them.

Jeannine got back to me quickly, requesting that we schedule a CCX-Citibank planning meeting. All these top executives wanted to fly in to discuss what I'd told Jeannine. We did have that meeting, and it went well. We explained that we could do a much better job for them if we'd have regular executive planning sessions and briefings. Because then they would understand what "state of the art" is, and what we were able to do for them. In that way, they would become better at executing their business *through us*. "A bad partner can only get bad results from their vendors," I told them. "If you just throw something over the wall and say do this, you're not going to get a great result."

After that meeting we started gaining access not just to executives at Jeannine's level, but also to their bosses, to people in other areas of technology, and finally to the executive who owned Citi's credit card operation worldwide. We became an important "global partner" of Citibank. There was also a bit of trickle-down throughout the banking industry. Before, most other banks of the era were no better at vendor relations than Citi had been. Now, when Citibank executives left for other banks, they often took this new attitude with them. And all because we'd been forced to force a change in Citi's corporate culture.

□ □ □ □ □

I CAN'T RECALL exactly when I started getting the picture. It was late '80s at the soonest, maybe even the early '90s. I like a looseness of spirit in an office, even when we're very busy, as we certainly were during this time frame I'm talking about.

There was a lot of coming and going starting in the late 1980s. Jerry and Madelyn Adams had moved to New York so Jerry could take charge of our business for *Guideposts*. Then the man who'd run our London subsidiary had a heart attack, and I asked Jennifer to go to England and take over until he was well enough to work; she was there nine months. Everybody was going every which way. "There was a period," recalls Jim Womble, "when Charles and I might not be in the same office but once a month."

I was traveling plenty myself. By this time, I was on the board of the Direct Marketing Association, so some of my trips were to DMA board meetings— meetings that were surprisingly contentious and, to me, very eye opening. Before the '80s, I'd rarely heard anyone voice privacy issues regarding the massive amounts of data that we, and others, were collecting on millions of Americans. The words *privacy* and *data* were yet to become inextricably linked in the public mind.

Not so, however, in the narrower mindset of the Direct Marketing Association. In these meetings, some board members talked about privacy as though it were an obstacle to be busted up and kicked out of the way. I got in a huge fight with one woman who complained that privacy was nothing but a cost center that hurt the DMA's efforts. We were actually screaming at each other, she and I. She stood her ground, filibustering like a demented senator—"We've just got to fight it, to nullify *any* gains in privacy, whether through the congress or the press. We've got to make these privacy guys look like *crooks*. Our answer to privacy is to *stamp it out!*" As a businessman who knew that trust was one of our company's biggest assets, I brought that crazy message home and started pondering how we needed to counteract it.

So it was a busy time, the late '80s. To top it off, we had to change the name of the company again. I hated it, but there was another company listed on NASDAQ, or maybe it was the American Stock Exchange, whose symbol was so close to ours that many investors were becoming confused. But what made this a big problem was that this other company—something to do with copper—didn't appear to be very stable, and Phil Carter really wanted us to change our company name. And I really, *really* didn't.

"Charles was not in favor of it initially," recalls Alex Dietz. "He liked CCX, the name that we went public with. I mean, this other thing was more of a nuisance than anything else. And if it had been up to Charles, we'd probably still be CCX today. But Phil was very keen on the idea of changing our name. So this was in 1989, and we went through one of those deals where we hired a firm that generated weird names like Unisys and stuff like that.

"Finally, one of the local advertising agencies that was working with us came up with 'Acxiom,' which had the 'CX' in it. That was what won Charles over, because he wasn't about to leave the CX behind. A-c-x-i-o-m is not a real word, of course, but it was a unique way of spelling the word *axiom*, which *is* a real word. The definition of an axiom is 'a self-evident truth.' So it worked."

The juxtaposition of what comes next may make it sound as though I had it in for Phil Carter over the name change, which was certainly not the case. I love the name Acxiom—an elegant solution to our problem—and am glad, in hindsight, that he pushed us to change it. We were expanding globally, and CCX—Conway Communications Exchange—was sounding increasingly provincial.

I will say, though, that prior to the name change, most of my interactions with Phil had involved just the two of us alone. Now I got to see him more in small-group settings, and I began picking up some disturbing signals. You remember my saying I liked a certain looseness of spirit in the workplace? Watching other people, especially our associates, interacting with Phil, I could see that they were anything but loose. In fact, some of them seemed downright terrified.

So I began gently probing. And one of my methods was to devise a managerial experiment.

First, a little background. Long before I even thought of pushing a confrontation with Phil Carter, I was aware that we were having trouble executing. The problems seemed to be company-wide, and I didn't know what the root problem was. So in my reading I had learned about "Quality Circles," a Japanese business concept—very trendy at the time—whereby you have groups working as equals within a company to study problems and come up with solutions. "Phil," I had said, "look at this," and I gave him a bunch of literature on Quality Circles. "We ought to test this here. You ought to organize it." Nothing ever happened. So I devised my little managerial experiment also as a kind of Quality Circle test.

I had been working very hard to hire smart kids from various universities, hoping that they would take off and do some cool stuff—fresh eyes, the audacity of youth, all that. So we had a lot of young people in the ranks. And I had a software project that we really needed—this wasn't a made-up assignment—but that I'd been having trouble getting done. So one day I came up with the bright idea of handing it off to a team of these young associates—people who'd been with us a year, a year-and-a-half.

I picked the three I thought were best, two women and a man, and sat them down in my office. "I want you all to work for me on a CEO-sponsored project," I said, "to help me solve a serious problem." I went on to explain that we needed to get this software built, and we needed a team to build it, test it, and make sure it was correctly implemented. "And instead of putting this in the regular organization, I wanted you guys to work on it as a short-term project to help me help Phil Carter, our president, get this done."

So I laid out the problem for them and gave them some ideas about how to approach it. "Now," I said, "I want you all to take the next two or three weeks, interview people, study the problem, and then come up with a suggested solution— along with some idea of the resources and the particular people we'll need to get this project completed."

Three weeks later they were back to give me the presentation. The team said they had *three* options for solving the problem, and they proceeded to explain all three. I listened politely, and when they finished, I said, "I was really hoping you'd give me *one* option that you felt strongly about."

"Any of the three is fine with us," they said. "Whatever you'd like."

Now these were all real smart people. So after we discussed their three options and I gave them feedback on each one, I said, "I want you to go back and decide firmly *which* of the three you're going to recommend. Then I want you to do what I first said—give me not only what you think we need in terms of resources, but tell me who would be the two or three best people in the company to assign to this project."

Next time they came back they'd picked one option, but they were really, really weak on specificity. And they had no names to give me. I was irked. "I gave you a very specific charge," I said. "To tell me who in the organization you think can do this."

"Well, we talked with a whole lot of people, and we're not sure."

"Okay, guys," I said. "Third time—I want you to come back in another week. And I want some names."

Soon, Phil Carter showed up in my office. These young associates were really upset, he said, "because you want them to make recommendations and they're afraid they're going to make somebody mad." He went on to explain that because we were growing so fast, good people were in short supply. So if this team of young people made recommendations that ended up taking some manager's critical resource away, there would be retribution against them.

And I thought we were a no-politics company.

So I summoned the team again and asked them about what Phil had told me. They basically said I didn't understand "the culture around here." *You do something like that and you're going to be in hot water. And we all want to have a long career around here, and we don't want to get somebody mad at us. It's going to cause us personally a big problem if we do what you say we should do. We're too afraid to do it in this culture.*

Talk about a red flag.

Now I started seriously researching my own company. I discovered that Phil Carter had laid down the law to people not to go to me with *any* recommendation—about *anything*—that he hadn't previously approved. That, I found to my dismay, was common knowledge throughout the organization. And the more I dug, the worse it got. When Phil had arrived, he'd told everyone (except me) something to the effect that he expected three things—the third of which was "respect me." That had intimidated many associates into submission, but Hank Ponder—who left the company because of Phil—was incensed by it. "You don't demand respect," Hank had groused to Womble. "You *earn* it."

But while Hank had taken action, he wasn't the only one put off by Carter's buttoned-up, process-oriented, command-and-control persona. "People were scared of him," says Cindy Childers. "He just wasn't a warm and fuzzy man." There was a lot of friction in the organization. There wasn't a lot of joy.

By the early '90s we had maybe 700 employees. We had an operation in the UK. We also had a big outsourcing deal in Chicago. Another of my disturbing discoveries was that Phil Carter was clearly trying to control things in all these places at a *very* micro level. This helped explain why the organization wasn't working very well, why things weren't getting done, why we were having trouble executing and achieving particular development goals—a bottleneck at the top.

We were also building up many, many levels of management, because we were hiring so many people and making those we'd just hired work for the people who were already there. By the early '90s we had 13 layers of management in the organization and fewer than 1,000 employees—hence the ridiculous number of business cards we were printing daily.

It had been good for me to concentrate on R & D, on new software—I knew that was true; my work there had benefited us in the marketplace. But in the process, I had allowed myself to become blindsided, letting down my company and my people in a larger way. Acxiom was broken and needed fixing.

And this time, no more outside presidents. I had to figure it out for myself.

10

GREEN
FIELDS

1001010010110010100010010110010101100 1 1

IN 1991 OUR house burned down. That was also the year I fired Phil Carter. So Jane was rebuilding the house as I was rebuilding the business. It was a very stressful time for both of us.

Springtime in Arkansas is beautiful but treacherous—we live in a part of the country where violent storms are a fact of life. It was April and I was racing in Atlanta; Jane was with me, and so was Carrie, who now lived in Atlanta. Rob, a junior in high school, hadn't been able to get away.

"It was a big house out in the country," says Jane. "We'd been in it for five years when it got struck by lightning. It was the middle of the night. Rob was supposed to be there but he didn't pay any attention to his curfew, so he was in town with his girlfriend. But a friend of ours, who was separated from his wife and was in the process of getting a divorce, was there. His name was Bill and he was staying with us. And Bill knew immediately what had happened. He managed to get the cars out, and then drove to the house of a fireman we knew, Curtis. But Curtis was on duty and his wife wouldn't let Bill in.

"He finally talked her into calling her husband at the fire station, and so they got people out there—two or three volunteer fire departments and the Conway fire department. But the house was burned. The attic was completely burned off. The second floor was burned to the studs. The first floor was basically destroyed by smoke and water.

"We were in Atlanta at the race, and we couldn't get back because the line of thunderstorms stretched from Canada to the Gulf. You could not get around that sucker. So we sat in Atlanta until three o'clock that afternoon, twelve hours. Finally we got around it.

"It was not a fun time. We were in a rent house for eight months while they rebuilt it."

□ □ □ □ □

AFTER MANY WEEKS of quiet research and analysis, I concluded that we weren't going to "fix" Phil Carter. What probably sealed it was when Sharon came into my office, shut the door, and told me how mean Phil was to his administrative assistant, often leaving her in tears. "Nobody deserves that kind of treatment," Sharon said.

I told you before: When Sharon Tackett—the nicest, most honest, most discreet person in the world—thinks it's important to tell me something, I take it to heart. And I agreed with her completely—nobody deserves to be treated like a doormat. But if that had been the only charge against Phil, I probably would've simply given him a talking-to—at least the first time. That's not how we treat people in this company.

As it was, what Sharon told me fit a bullying pattern that I had uncovered about Phil. When I told some close staff people that I'd decided to let him go, they inevitably said things like, "Charles, I'm glad you finally saw the light. Phil was really screwing this place up." So why hadn't anybody come to me about it? The answers usually went like this: "Well, I actually work for Phil and didn't want you to tell him I said anything bad about him." The message I got was that Phil Carter was a vindictive man. Whether he fired you or not, he made it really clear: *Don't cross me or you're in deep shit.*

"So one Friday I get a call from Charles," recalls Jim Womble. "I'm in Corpus Christi on a little beach vacation with my second wife and our children. 'You got to come back,' Charles says. 'I want to fire Carter, and I want you to be with me in the office Monday morning when he walks in.' Then he told me what Sharon had said to him."

Jim got back on Friday night, and that weekend he and Rodger and I met on both Saturday and Sunday and worked out a script. You have to be careful with things like this; you can't just go in and wing it. So on Monday morning when Carter arrived at his office—it was about 7:30—the three of us were sitting there waiting for him. "Phil," I said, "I'm going to have to let you go for the following reasons…." His face went white. It was a *very* short meeting. Then I had security escort Phil from the building.

Unfortunately, that was the easy part. Now I had to deal with the mess I'd let happen while Phil was in the president's chair.

□ □ □ □ □

"THE INSURANCE PAYMENT on the house was one and a half million dollars," says Jane. "So it was a fairly good-size problem.

"But I had to be grateful that neither Bill nor Rob was hurt. And Curtis, due to the fact that he sometimes worked for us, and had for many years—he knew where everything that we loved was in that house. He got my father's shotgun out from under Rob's bed. And he got things off the walls that he knew I loved. And I mean he just saved things that most people wouldn't have.

"And the firemen, when they thought they were going to lose the house, they pitched in and pulled furniture to the doors. It was pouring down rain, but our friends were out there. And A.J. Hambuchen, from Hambuchen Furniture, had brought trucks, and our friends would carry our furniture to the trucks, and A.J. would have the furniture taken down to his warehouse.

"But of course we didn't save everything—there was a corner cupboard that had some antique china in it. And the firemen were so anxious to get that out that they tried to move the whole thing and it broke a bunch of the china. But they weren't even family pieces. So I was just grateful to have what I have."

□ □ □ □ □

TOO MANY LAYERS of management. Too many titles. Too much command and control—those were just some of our obvious problems. But Acxiom was like that T-boned Mercedes I'd once rebuilt in my garage: It was easy to see the now-misshapen frame. The deeper you got into the wreckage, though, the more you found to fix. Critical internal problems—problems of philosophy, of self-image, of well-thought-out *design*—were preventing us from running at full capacity.

But while my senior executives and I were trying to think out solutions, all the daily business of a going concern—whether going well or not—was piling up on my desk. I needed help, dedicated help. And the way I found that help was by asking a young woman in our accounting department to prepare some numbers for a meeting I was going to attend.

"What are you going to do with these numbers?" Cindy Childers said. "I mean, are you going to analyze them? Are you going to try to put some action together?"

"I haven't thought about that," I said.

She volunteered to think it out for me, and in a day or so she brought me the numbers with a flexible plan for how to use and present them. "Wow, this is great!" I said.

By the time Cindy got back to her office, her phone was ringing. "You want to come work for me?" I said.

"Doing what?"

"I don't know—we'll figure it out. Stuff like we just did over the past couple of days." Fortunately, she thought it over and said yes. And that's when the real rebuilding of the company began.

Even before Phil Carter left, we had scratched the idea of Quality Circles and started looking for other ideas. "Quality Circles was a management fad at the time," recalls Cindy, "and for us a massive failure. My favorite story about Quality Circles was that we had a group of people looking for ways to shorten the amount of time it took them to accomplish something. So they did a lot of study, conducted a bunch of interviews, and gave their presentation to a group of managers. And the finding of this Quality Circle team was that they could best save time by buying a large trashcan and placing it in a certain area. 'Oh dear God,' said the managers, 'we've missed the boat here. Just go buy the damn trashcan.' For us, that was the turning point with Quality Circles. The idea of it—to decentralize decision-making—was spot on, but the Quality Circles concept itself was just an over-engineered way of doing that."

The next step was to see what other ideas were out there. We did that by visiting what Cindy called "benchmark companies—companies we thought had pretty cool stuff going on." Cindy and a handful of colleagues called on about a half-dozen firms whose main ideas ran the gamut from "accountability" to "recognition," with various impressive stops along the way. I visited two of these companies myself, and I remember being especially impressed with Milliken Carpets, which was strong at employee empowerment. Even in matters of cost control, Milliken allowed their employees to figure out ways to contain costs instead of imposing decrees from on high.

As a result of those visits, we formed a team that put together a 12-action plan to begin changing Acxiom's culture. In 1990 and early 1991 we started trying to implement this new, more enlightened thinking through a top-down *re*-education plan that we called the "Race for Excellence." It didn't stress getting the checkered flag first at all costs, however; it stressed running the race right, keeping the bigger picture in mind. In fact, we eventually changed it from the Race for Excellence to the *Quest* for Excellence, because a quest has no finish line.

We began the program company-wide in a dramatic way, with me having a big management meeting—there were probably 50 to 75 managers there—and I stood up on a chair and said, "I just want y'all to know that *I am the problem.* And I'm going to start trying to fix me, and we're going to try to fix this whole organization starting from the top down. We're going to spend the next few days talking about how we do that."

In the end, I taught all the senior leaders the concepts of the Race for Excellence and how we were going to implement those concepts—what everybody's role and responsibility was. I taught a one- or two-day class that all those guys had to attend, and then they had to go and teach their people. So it was a waterfall educational approach.

But even as we were engaged in this re-education program, we began realizing that our existing company structure was totally wrong for the company we wanted to become. "We had thirteen layers of management," Cindy says, "which meant every manager managed two-and-a-half people. By the late eighties it was not an engaged workforce, okay? People came to work, checked their brain at the door, did what they were told, and left. HR at that time was doing payroll and hiring, but nobody was doing any organizational planning. So before we could *really* implement any new thinking, we had to tackle our obvious existing problems—the superfluous management layers and their accompanying emphasis on titles."

Our goal was to create an organization around the concept of groups and business units—a flat organization, a more empowered, more fun place to work. I wanted our people to worry more about fun, productivity, and results for the customer, and less about what's-my-title, how-many-people-report-to-me, and how-do-I-climb-higher-on-the-food-chain. My own title became, simply, "Company Leader."

"We went from thirteen levels to three," says Cindy. "And we eliminated all titles so that people didn't have that competition thing going on."

Ah, but humans will be humans—won't we? "In hindsight," says Cindy, "we should've done it a little differently. Because what we realized was that to some people when you lose your title, you lose your identity. So it rocked the organization. Thirty percent of the people were, 'I don't care.' But seventy percent were, 'Oh no!' So we did replace it eventually, but not with traditional titles. We came back with you're a team leader or you're a business unit leader. We put leader in the title and that was intentional, because we wanted people to start leading. And we kind of adopted a motto—you manage things and you lead people. And if you can't lead, then we'll let you go manage things. But you can't manage people. So that's kind of how it started. That was a pretty big turning point, organizationally."

These changes let us be fast, flat, and flexible, and by 1992 we had organized into business units. Each business unit had a business unit leader coordinating the work of some 25 to 75 associates. Under the business unit leader were team leaders, and above him was a group leader, who had multiple business units working for him or her. The group leaders reported to me. The very lowest-level associate formally reported to a business unit leader but worked under the direction of team leaders—they could work on more than one team at a time. That allowed us to move people around to whatever section had the highest demand at any given moment. The smallest business unit was probably 15 people; the largest—this would've been in some of the operational areas, such as computer operations—might have been 100 people.

We "franchised" these business units with major franchise-signing events. Every person in the unit participated and signed the "agreement." It was a cool concept and people really rallied around it. A unit had to prepare and commit to be franchised, so it was a big deal to have the franchise signing ceremony. It gave the business unit leader and the associates "ownership" in their business.

Now, all of a sudden, I could look to a unit leader who had Citibank or Chase or First USA, and I could say, "You've got no excuses." Because these business units had most of the resources necessary to get anything done—programmers, operational people, whatever they required. They were essentially small businesses that outsourced their data processing to a bigger business, which was Acxiom itself.

Finally, with the excellent help of Cindy Childers and other colleagues, I felt I had come to terms with my old nemesis—structure. It was really disruptive, but there was no way we could've grown this business without doing it. Once an organization gets 1,000 people in it, it can choke you. So what we did was lob a 100-pound stick of dynamite in the middle of the organization. Just blew it up like it was a piece of overgrown ground, blasting off all the gnarly trees and jagged rocks and thick, clingy vines in a single explosion.

Then we covered up the hole we'd made and it was like we'd returned to a pristine field—clean and calm and flat and green. Green fields are good places for starting over.

□ □ □ □ □

"OUR MARRIAGE," SAYS Jane—"I can just say our marriage *before* about nineteen ninety-one and *after* nineteen ninety-one were two entirely different marriages. Over the years Charles became more argumentative and more interested in power, I guess. And it didn't get to the point that I thought I was having trouble dealing with him until about ninety-one. His narcissism began to get out of hand. I think it may have been when he decided to take over Phil Carter's place. And it just went out of sync. Carrie had said we never fought. But Rob was there those last few years and he knows we fought. Before that, we didn't fight. But we did those last few years."

Every story has two sides—at *least* two sides. Going into the 1990s, I felt that my life was expanding very quickly. It's shocking to hear how little Jane understood the significance of that period for me, either personally or professionally. The truth is, in the late '80s I thought I knew how to build and run a business, but I didn't know squat. The decade of the '90s was transformative for both Acxiom *and* me. Between 1990 and 2000, Acxiom emerged from a nice little business into an industry leader. And I, realizing now how little I really did know, learned—day by day and year by year, against tough odds and under the most trying circumstances—how to do my job.

I've already told you about some of the disastrous acquisitions we made in the late '80s—the letter shop, the fulfillment center. Fortunately, Alex Dietz and I had that all-important conversation about our "core competency"—our core business being data—so we were now more on track in terms of acquisitions. With the Race for Excellence we started attacking organizational issues, and from that effort we began to put in place more advanced thinking about what kinds of companies we ought to be buying.

It's important to understand that we weren't just buying to buy. We were buying to *grow*—to do more business better. So we had to develop a kind of three-pronged strategy for acquisitions: a strategy to identify a company that could help us in our core business; a strategy for making that acquisition; and a strategy for blending that company into ours.

Had that been all we were facing, it would've been one thing. But it all comes at you at once. We were also wrestling with how to get big city-based executives of prospective client companies to travel to Conway, Arkansas, so we could spend a whole day selling them on all our latest technologies and what those capabilities could mean to them. In the '70s, we'd lured a lot of top executives by flying them down in Charles Ward's jet. In the mid-'80s, we'd bought a little King Air that could accommodate four or five people, but New York in that plane was a five-hour flight one way, which made for a long day. So in the late '80s, we'd bought a Citation II jet. It would seat seven people, but it wasn't even five feet high on the inside, and it was pretty slow. And by the '90s, most of the big guys in New York were used to big airplanes. So the game had changed, and we had to change with it.

We also had to stay ahead on technology, or else what would we sell those CEOs when we *did* get their attention? One day back in the early '90s, Jim Womble and I were sitting in his office talking about our bank business. By then, we were working with seven or eight good-sized banks, each of which was sending us credit bureau data feeds. So we were receiving a lot of the same data over and over again, and we were doing the same things to the same data—except these projects were getting longer and more complicated, and we were continually buying more computers to stay ahead of the business. For the most part we were just doing current credit data, but the banks kept wanting to send us monthly data for five years—they never took their eye off that grand goal of theirs. *No!* we'd say. *We can't buy the computers to handle that! And there aren't even enough computer operators!*

"Jim," I said, "we've got to find a better way to do this." Our problem was what we call "data fragments"—bits and pieces of questionable data. Let's say we're tracking data on a John and Mary Jane Doe, currently of Little Rock, Arkansas. Let's also say this particular Doe family has also lived in Pittsburgh and Kansas City. But maybe, along the way, the information on Mary Jane inexplicably drops off—we can't find in the various data we have access to that she actually lived with John in Kansas City. We do, however, have a Mary *J.* Doe on the same Kansas City street as John, but at a slightly different street number. Is this the same person who lived with John Doe in Pittsburgh, and who now lives with him in Little Rock?

If you don't have any other data, you have to either *assume* that Mary J. is Mary Jane—or that she's not. But the problem with assumptions is that they have a chance of being wrong, and wrong information makes for inaccurate data, and inaccurate data puts the banks' credit card business at risk. And if the banks' business is at risk, then so is ours.

That was one problem with fragments. Another big problem, from our standpoint, was that the more data we were given to process, the more fragments we had to deal with, meaning that these ever-larger jobs were taking us longer and longer to do and requiring more and bigger computers. I could foresee a day when we would reach the breaking point—when we couldn't handle the work. That would be the end of us. So in the midst of everything else, I began conceiving of a plan to take Acxiom technology to the next level. Nearly a decade later, the result of this incipient planning would become a revolutionary product called AbiliTec. It would give us the extra data to help put Mary J. Doe and other fragments in their rightful place.

The ever-larger volume of available data also presented us with a more pressing problem—privacy. Data itself isn't possessed of morality, good or bad. How it's used is everything. I'm not talking just about intention. I'm talking also about care, and about respect for others. In the early '90s, partly through my new position as board chairman of the Direct Marketing Association, I was becoming convinced that with Big Data came Big Responsibility.

But the direct-marketing industry—starting with some of my DMA board colleagues—wanted to sweep the whole subject of privacy under the rug. I was appalled at their short sightedness. Every day, it seemed, we heard another crazy story of kamikaze risk. Citibank, for example, had hired some new whiz-bang marketing executive, and we learned that he and his people wanted to use their own data for things that weren't even legal. I thought: *Do I really want to find myself on the front page of The New York Times because of something like this?* I never once doubted that our big-name clients, if they got caught doing something wrong, would say, "Hey, it wasn't us. It was those guys in Arkansas. They're really bad guys." They would throw us under the bus in a New York second.

My sensitivity to the subject of privacy was no doubt heightened by an internal change that we'd made at Acxiom. As a service bureau, for years we had bought the same data over and over for various clients—for example, if Chase wanted a list of wealthy men and women in Manhattan, we bought it for them, from whoever owned the best list of that type; then if Citibank or another client wanted a similar list, we bought it again. One month in the late 1980s we bought the same list eight times, which prompted a revolutionary thought: *Why don't we negotiate a deal with the list provider to buy the list just once, and then sell it ourselves?*

So we did that, creating a database of composite lists we called InfoBase. This was in 1988. Soon an international advertising, marketing, and consulting company called Wunderman Worldwide expressed interest in a joint venture with us—we would build and maintain this InfoBase database and they would sell it to their many clients. Jennifer—by then she was Jennifer Barrett, married to my old friend and colleague Don Barrett—was our business development person in those days, so she took the point position with Wunderman and InfoBase.

The joint venture rocked along for three years, during which time I became increasingly unhappy with Wunderman; they really weren't doing much for us. Finally I fired them and we brought InfoBase into Acxiom as one of our products.

"I remember," says Jennifer, "Charles said to me at the time: 'You know, now we're a data company, not just a service bureau anymore. And that probably means we need to do something differently. Would you figure out what that is?'

The result was that, in 1991, I named Jennifer to the newly created post of Chief Privacy Officer. As a dedicated monitor ensuring the responsible use of all data in our possession, Jennifer Barrett broke new ground—she was the first such privacy officer of any company on the planet.

There was nothing at all altruistic about this appointment. I just knew that if marketers kept saying screw the public, one day we would have a big blow-up, and somebody would write a big privacy bill that would virtually shut down the industry. I decided to be proactive in confronting that possibility. I could already see that without a strong code of conduct, there were increasing opportunities for us to make the wrong decision and get into trouble. Jennifer's new job was to keep us away from that.

□ □ □ □ □

THESE WERE JUST some of the balls I was juggling when, beginning around 1991, Jane began to feel that our marriage was in trouble. I might add that some of this work pressure was occurring against a backdrop of the first Gulf War and a huge postal increase that turned our business on its head—in a single year we dropped from $117 million to about $90 million in revenue.

To add to my stress, the drop in revenue also dropped Acxiom's stock price, creating a personal financial crisis for Jim, Rodger, and me. A year or two earlier, Rodger had come to us with a "can't miss" investment deal—a beer distributorship with two locations in Little Rock and one in Shreveport, Louisiana. It wasn't cheap, and I was doubtful—for one thing, I didn't know anything about the beer business. But a pal of Rodger's vouched for the deal and Rodger urged us to invest. Against my better judgment, I said okay—as long as Rodger did all the due diligence and stood behind both the deal and the friend who had brought it to him. Rodger praised the soundness of the business plan and said his friend was a prince among men. So with that, we each put in about $5 million, give or take, which we borrowed from the bank and secured with our Acxiom stock. Rodger's friend, who was putting up no money, was also getting ownership in the company. What a deal—he gets us to invest so he can make a killing.

As it turned out, this guy was a crook. He stole from us—embezzled money that we didn't prosecute him for. But the real problem came in 1991, when

Acxiom's stock was taking a beating. Suddenly the bank put out collateral calls, which neither Rodger nor Jim could meet. They were beside themselves—if they couldn't cover the note with some other collateral, the bank would sell their Acxiom stock. But they had nothing else to put up. Take my word for it—they were *frantic*.

I couldn't stand by and watch my good friends go broke, so I took on their obligations—betting a whole bunch more of my stock to save them. In exchange, I took some of their equity in the beer distributorship. But then we also had to plow $5 million equity back *into* the beer business—it was broke. And now that I was the majority owner, I had to put up the majority of the equity that we used to recapitalize the business.

But guess what happened next. When things got better, I sold the majority of Jim's and Rodger's equity back to them for a token amount of money. And when the beer business was finally sold, they each made several million dollars on the deal. To this day, Jim has never forgotten the fact that I saved him from financial ruin. Rodger has never been quite as appreciative.

So, stress and worry? You bet, I had more than my fair share in that period around 1991, when Jane started finding me "difficult." And I don't doubt for a second that I brought some of my worry home with me.

But there was more on my mind than business. I've always protected myself in the future—it's just in my DNA to look ahead, to *plan* ahead. By 1991 I was 48 years old and had been married to Jane since I was 23. A quarter of a century. How many years did I have left to work? Fifteen? Twenty? And then what? Spend my retirement sitting around the house with Jane?

The first time I seriously thought of getting a divorce was in about 1985. Back then I figured it was about a 10-percent probability—someday, when the kids were grown, I *might* leave and find another life. But over the next five to seven years, the probability rose dramatically. By 1994, it was 100 percent. Bob Ingenito's theory of time was like a roar inside my head.

Rob had gone off to college in 1992. He'd also announced that he wanted to start racing cars—that, however, is a separate subject, at least for now. But Rob's leaving hadn't decided anything. It had simply removed an important hurdle, though there were still other hurdles I had to find a way to clear. I was worried about Jane. I knew she wouldn't take my leaving well, but what I feared was that it might be damaging to her mental health. By 1994, I thought about leaving all the time. But it was something I could always put off for another week...another week...another week.

Looking back, I think it's easy to see how my growing desire to make a break had developed. As an incidental byproduct of building a company, I had also begun creating an ever-larger life for myself. Call me narcissistic, but I discovered that I liked it. I liked having built that company, and I liked setting goals for it and continuing to meet or exceed those goals. I liked traveling to New York and London and getting to know other people with interesting and expansive lives. Of course, I *loved* my racing. And whether because of business success or racing success, I began to see myself and my company written up in prominent publications— *Success Magazine, The Washington Post, Forbes,* and the like. That was also part of the larger life I enjoyed.

In 1994, the Sales and Marketing Executives Association named me Manager of the Year. I liked that too—especially when I received a handwritten note of congratulations from my Uncle Ralph:

August 28, 1994

Dear Charles:

Your recent honor made news here in Fort Smith and I hasten to add my congratulations to you—It is really a signal achievement when you are selected as the <u>best</u> of anything in the U.S.A.!

I'm sure that Betty & Don are again patting themselves on the back for having such a famous & successful son. I assure you that I am a proud uncle & I may add grateful that my faith in your ability has been well repaid by the appreciation of my investment in Acxiom stock!

Keep up the good work—

Love,
Uncle Ralph

In my answer, I thanked him for his confidence in me and for taking time to write. "I always like to hear from happy stockholders!" I said.

My reason for mentioning these facets of the larger exterior life I enjoyed by then is emphatically *not* to blow my own horn. Rather, it's to help characterize how far apart I felt that Jane and I had grown. The more public my life became, the less comfortable Jane seemed to feel with it. I would want her to go with me to board meetings in New York or Washington, say, or events of the Direct Marketing Association, and she wouldn't want to go. Everyone else took their spouses to evening functions—that was part of the fun of it. "These are nice people," I would tell Jane. And she *would* go, because she knew it was her duty, but she went reluctantly. And often she did have fun once she got there. But she really dreaded going.

Even our own company events now put her off. When the company was small, she didn't mind having everybody over for beer and hot dogs. And when we first moved to the big new house in the country—the one that burned and was rebuilt—she threw great picnics. People would park their cars all over the property, and Rob and his friends would be out there with buckets of water in case someone's hot manifold caught the grass on fire. For winter parties, Rob and his friends would be our valet parking team, taking each guest's car at the front door. I think Jane still had fun then. Later, as we grew so fast and took on so many new people, it got much harder—I'm the first to acknowledge that. By the early '90s, when we had a Christmas party at that house, we invited some 1,800 people. They came in shifts, in 30-minute increments.

Mostly, Jane got so she just preferred to sit and read her books. Even at races now, she would place a lawn chair under the awning of the motor home and sit there reading while the cars screamed around the track.

No matter what I urged her to do or to be a part of, it seemed to make her angry. More than once she told me she felt like she was just that person following behind me—that every once in a while I would stop to notice her, but that I didn't really respect her. To punish me, she clearly wasn't going to do anything I wanted her to do, such as stop smoking or exercise. Instead, she would just sit and read.

We did argue quite a bit when Rob was in high school. Once, we had a tremendous fight because Rob had left some things on the back stairs and Jane had been telling him for a week to get that stuff off the stairs and take it to his room. Being a teenager, he ignored her—and the louder she ordered him, the more obviously he ignored her. She would be hollering at him as he walked through the kitchen, and he would be so pissed he would just look straight ahead and keep walking.

Finally, when he'd gone to his room, Jane turned her fury on me. She was in my face screaming that I hadn't taken her side by making Rob pick up his things. It's true, I hadn't. He was a *kid*, and I felt that her own behavior was so over the top on this issue that I didn't want to reinforce it. Jane turned the whole thing into "Rob doesn't respect me" and "You don't respect me either." Many of our fights were about Jane not getting the respect she felt she was due.

While some of those fights were bad, there are worse things in a relationship than fighting. "I don't really remember any fighting in high school," says Rob, and I'm glad to hear that—memory has its protective coverings. "But when I would come back from college for a weekend, I noticed they were both real short with each other. We'd be sitting down to dinner, and the communication level was just completely broken down."

□ □ □ □ □

HISTORICALLY, WHAT DID Jane and I do to bury our problems? Right. We built a house.

So in the fall of 1994 we decided to build a weekend home at Greers Ferry Lake. "This is hard for me to talk about," says Jane. "This falls under my Acxiom service. We were building that house really for Acxiom, as a retreat. I was supposed to find the house, four bedrooms, and I found some plans in *Southern Living*—though it was all backwards from what I thought it should be. But I figured out how to flip the rooms around, and we ordered the house plans and Charles put it on his computer—he had a program that would actually draw the plans. So we got it like we wanted. We did this together, which is something we'd never done before on a house.

"Then we went up and found the property and hired a builder. And we were going up there at least every weekend, every Saturday, to see how it was coming. It was a neat, neat house."

The lake house wasn't supposed to be what it became. We—I—began it in good faith. On some ideal level, I thought it would be a good place to bring our sprawling family together, in whatever iteration of "family" the passage of time presented to us. As for Jane and me, I still hoped we could become the kinds of friendly exes you sometimes see in the movies; then there were my elderly parents; my brother and his wife; Jane's sister and Ewell and their children; Carrie and Rob and their eventual spouses; our someday grandkids. I saw this place as a big old happy house for the comings and goings of generations. At the same time, it *would* be a convenient site for my occasional two- or three-day management retreats, and even for entertaining potential clients.

Then one day it hit me: *This is how I get out of here.* When the lake house was finished, I could quietly move into it. No hullaballoo, no lawyers, no headline-grabbing new house to buy. Just a silent and dignified separation, moving from one of our houses into another. Under the radar. And once ensconced there, I could take my time working with Jane toward an amicable divorce.

Now, for me, those weekend building-site inspections were fraught with internal drama. The workmen were really *moving* on the lake house, and my heart pounded with every finished wall and door frame. Now that the long-awaited day was so near, I felt courage failing me. In early June 1995, when they poured the driveway, my own feet seemed encased in concrete.

My reluctance baffled me, because by then I had a new and pressing reason for wanting to leave my cold, unhappy marriage—I had met a young woman, an IBM rep named Cathy Cook. Cathy was as warm and as loving as my marriage was not. We'd been together only twice, once in New York and once in San Francisco, and I was like a schoolboy—it was all I could do to keep from telling *everybody* about my wonderful secret. But of course I couldn't tell *anybody*— except Sharon.

"I usually went out and picked up Charles' lunch and brought it back to the office for him," says Sharon, "so it was odd when he suddenly told me he was taking me to lunch. He wanted to drive sixteen miles down to Morgan, where there was a good hamburger place.

"Charles has always been really good about being sure I was in the know about things. Sometimes he would tell me more than I *wanted* to know—in this case, I felt bad for Jane—but his attitude was, 'You're in a position where you need to know what's going on.'

"So when we got to the restaurant, he said, 'There's something I think you need to know—I'm having an affair with Cathy Cook.'

"'I know,' I said. 'I figured that out last week.' The week before, Charles had been on a business trip to New York. And Cathy Cook had called our office and needed some information or something. And when I called her back, I found out *she* was in New York—and she was booked on the same plane as Charles. *Hmmm*, I thought, which was the first time the light bulb had ever gone off like that. And a few days later, he took me to lunch."

The reason I told Sharon about Cathy was that I knew I was planning to move to the lake house, and I figured things might soon get a little crazy. But as it turned out, I never made my lake house escape. Other events superseded it.

□ □ □ □ □

BY THE MID-'90S, we had devised a business strategy centered on Acxiom's own data marketing product, InfoBase. To give you an idea of what InfoBase is, today it contains information on 126 million U.S. households and nearly 200 million U.S. individuals. All these separate nuggets of information—about 1,500 per person—have now been sliced and diced and shaken and strained, so that various combinations of these data elements create individual data *products*. These individual slivers of intelligence are then organized into umbrella categories, the main one of which is called InfoBase Consumer Enhancement.

So if you're a marketer who wants to reach customers with "Casino Gaming Propensity," you would purchase element 2777. If you want to target people who're likely to become wealthy when a family member dies, you'll opt for element 1801—"Potential Inheritors." If you're interested in "Heavy YouTube Users," that's element 2722.

With InfoBase, you can access vehicle purchase and ownership data from dealers selling every brand of car on the road, from Acura to Volvo. You can segment your audience by College Graduates (element 7471), Empty Nesters (7472), Entering Adulthood (7473), Recent Mortgage Borrower (7468), or Probable New Teen Driver (7480). You can target Book Enthusiasts (2805), Corrective Lens Wearers (9505), Christian Families (7842), and Vegetarians (7742). You can track your desired audience's buying habits with highly predictive data gleaned from consumer online shopping, retail store purchases, and catalog activity—consolidated by month and by type, from Apparel to Weaponry. If you want to know how they paid, you can order elements 6604, 6605, and 6610—cash, credit card, and retail card, respectively.

InfoBase wasn't as sophisticated in the mid-'90s as it is now, but the idea was generally the same. And the business strategy we designed around it, called "Lead with Data," aimed to streamline the selling process by converting new prospects to customers quickly, using InfoBase products. After all, prospects come to Acxiom for one reason—they want to improve marketing results.

One of the keys to this new business strategy was a concept called "briefing centers." If we had an opportunity to brief a big potential client—Allstate Insurance, say, which we landed in 1993—why would we want to beat the heck out of six or eight of our top people, our top assets, by flying them around the country for an off-site meeting that we can't control? They would have to go up the day before in order to be *sure* they make their flight connections. Then they'd spend all day the next day with the prospect and wouldn't get home until late that night. It wipes out a day and a half for each person, and it's just horribly inefficient.

But if we could bring the prospective customers to us, it's a completely different story. That's how the concept of briefing centers came about. These were rooms where our salespeople could conduct in-depth sales presentations to prospective customers—prospects who couldn't suddenly end the meeting because they had something else to do. They also paid closer attention when they were away from their own offices. If we could get the CEOs down there, we could wow them with our various capabilities and they would go home and tell their team, "You senior managers, I want you *all* to go hear what they can do for us!" This concept proved very successful—at the Acxiom campus in Conway, we built a 15-room briefing center, and many times I saw every one of those rooms full.

Now, though, how do you fill those rooms? The answer was a bigger, better airplane. In that way, the jet, the briefing centers, and Acxiom's success became inextricably linked.

In 1995 we took the plunge and bought a Falcon 20, a larger, sleeker plane that could seat nine people and had a cabin nearly six feet high. But we were still a fairly small company with a lot of debt on the books, so before we bought it we evaluated different ways of acquiring the plane. One was to lease it, which turned out to be insanely expensive—it was going to cost us something like $200,000 a month. That didn't even include pilots and maintenance.

"Well, hell," we said, "if we're going to use it for a long time, the best thing is just to buy it." Even so, there was a lot of resistance to loading on more debt. We were buying a lot of computers at the time, and our debt load was growing to an uncomfortable level. So there was considerable hand wringing: *What are we going to do, what are we going to do?*

Finally I said, "Look, I'll buy the damn airplane." And the way it worked out was that the board and I made an agreement for me to buy and refurbish a used Falcon 20 and lease it to the company at below-market value. If I used it for a personal trip, I would pay for the flight. If it was a business trip, Acxiom would pay. As I write this, that was nearly two decades ago. And I want it on the record that this *remains* the worst decision I've ever made in my life. Not because the plane didn't turn out to do everything we thought it would be for the business—it did. But it also came back to bite me in a million different ways.

The foregoing is a long preamble to the pivotal story I'm going to tell you now—the story of how my lake house escape plan became superseded by other events.

In late June 1995, I was due to have a meeting at the Little Rock airport about our new corporate jet. As with the other Acxiom aircraft before it, this plane wasn't just for executive travel; various business units would use it whenever they had to go somewhere to close a deal, have an important meeting, whatever they required. We continued to have naysayers in regard to the planes, but not only had our jets helped our business, they'd also *brought* us business. "It's very hard to get to Conway from other parts of the U.S.," says Jim Womble. "There was this one account in Richmond, Virginia, and the guy refused to come to see us. Changing planes, all of that. So we sent our jet for him, brought him to Conway, hot-boxed him, and sold the account. That account was worth ten to fifteen million dollars a year, running a twenty-percent profit. So we made two million a year from one round-trip flight."

At the Central Flying Service facility at Little Rock airport, I was to meet with a couple of aircraft designers from Springfield, Illinois, who were flying in to discuss the finishing-out of the plane. They'd already given me specs for the built-in furniture, and I'd been working on that on my computer. It was a very interesting puzzle, this plane redesign, because we couldn't change the actual configuration of the airplane without going through a laborious—and expensive—process involving the FAA. But within the parameters that these designers had given me, I could change the shape or the width of individual drawers in a cabinet as long as the overall cabinet remained where it was. So I wanted to discuss that with these designers; they were also bringing boards to show me their thoughts on an overall interior color scheme.

I knew Jane was good at this sort of thing—how many homes had she decorated by now? I also thought it would be good for her to get out of the house a while. So I asked her to drive down to Little Rock with me. We could look over these designs together.

The designers were nice guys, but they were also strangers; I could feel Jane pulling into herself around them. For a long time she listened to the rest of us talk. Then: "I think those cabinets should be moved to the back," she said.

"We really can't do that," I explained. "All the cabinets are fixed in place."

She remained quiet for a while, then made another suggestion—I can't recall what it was. But the response from the designers was that it couldn't be done on this particular airplane. It was a perfectly polite answer to a matter-of-fact business problem.

When they showed us their color boards, the designers specifically asked Jane what she thought. "Oh, you know," she said, and went on to say something that reflected her now-intense disinterest, or disdain. I could tell she was really irritated with us all.

When the meeting was over and we got in the car, she started in. "Why do you bring me to things like this to embarrass me and ignore me?"

"I brought you here," I said, "because I thought you could actually help. You know I'm not very good at colors, so I thought you could pick the side panels and stuff. You were just asking us to do some things that weren't really practical."

"You just want to ignore me."

"No, it's because of the plane's certification...."

"You're full of shit."

"Jane, I'm telling you—what you asked today really was impossible."

After that it escalated, with her telling me *I* designed the cabinets, so *I* would've been able to add this or that. Soon she was screaming at me: "You do this all the time! You embarrass me in front of people and ignore me in front of people!"

"I wasn't ignoring you or trying to embarrass you," I said. I was determined to remain calm.

"You just put me down! You tell me I can't do things!"

"Jane...."

Screaming at me, at the side of my head. Finally I broke. "I don't know what you don't fucking understand about what I'm telling you—*what you wanted to do is impossible! How do I say it so you think it's okay?*"

"Oh, that's what you always do—you never respect me and you *belittle* me! *It's just your way of making me feel bad about myself!*"

It's about 30 miles from Little Rock to Conway. I've driven it thousands of times, coming and going, and even after all those miles I still find the drive pleasant and soothing. Coming from Little Rock, you first descend through a curvy slash of black stone forming cliffs that introduce the wide Arkansas River. Once across the bridge, you soon bear a gentle left onto I-40, through woods and farmland, eventually passing exits to Morgan and Mayflower and coming upon pretty Lake Conway on the right, with its stubs of trees jutting above the water, clues to good fishing below. Finally, the sprawl of Conway itself edges south to meet you. On your left, the handsome Acxiom building, with its blue awnings, is easy to see from the interstate. Then comes exit 129, which was my exit. At the stop sign I turned left and crossed over I-40, and from there I either headed home or back to the office.

That's the way the trip is supposed to go—easy and peaceful; *pastoral* even. But on that late June day in 1995, Jane and I were in a full screaming match by the time we reached Mayflower. The words made no sense, and no further clarity comes from my recounting any more of that argument here. It was simply a sputtering, spittle-ridden version of the argument we'd had over and over and over for *years*, in one form or another.

As I bore right and entered the exit ramp, I said to Jane—so quietly that I think it scared her: "Jane. I'm done. I have tried, but I'm through now."

Her head jerked back slightly toward the passenger window. "What do you mean?" she said.

"I'm not having these arguments anymore," I said. "I am done. This will be the last one."

"I don't know what you're saying."

"I'm saying I've decided I don't want to have any more fights with you."

"Well, what are you going to do?"

"I don't know, exactly," I said. "I'm upset now and I need to think about it. But I'm telling you, this is the last time."

As CCX becomes Acxiom, we stress fun and fitness as a path to productivity. At right, Jeff Pascoe and CFO Bob Bloom celebrate winning the ninth annual company golf championship. Below, left to right, board member Rob Walton, me, and Steve Sheperd on what might be called the Tour de Acxiom—an executive exercycle race.

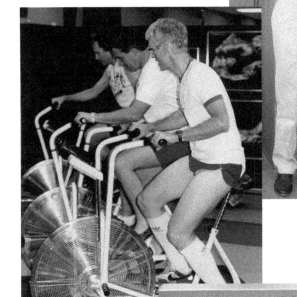

In our company fitness center, Acxiom execs Don Barrett (famous for his adage "It's the data, stupid"), Rodger Kline, Kent Manion, and Jim Womble plot their assault on the next company championship.

Racing, circa 1993, on my way to what would become 19 International Motor Sports Association career victories. What I didn't know was that I had only four more years to race.

Photo: Al Steinberg

Above: Jane and me at the racetrack in 1993, amid increasing turbulence in our marriage. That's Acxiom colleague and family friend Scott Hambuchen standing behind Jane, and Carrie is seated at right.

Left: The house we were building at Eden Isle, circa 1995. I began to see that house as my escape hatch.

The mid-'90s brought both personal loss and personal gain. From left to right: Mother, Speer, and me after Father's 1996 funeral. At a race with Susie Peeples, whom I met months after Jane and I split.

Right: Rob and me after the 24 Hours of Daytona in 1996—we drove the Oldsmobile team second car to victory, beating out the factory drivers!

Left: Rob and Canadian superstar Ron Fellows being interviewed after they won at Canada's Mosport in 1997. I was the crew chief, and people thought I was crazy to let Rob drive as much as he did. He did a great job.

Acxiom, late '90s: We were among the first companies to provide an in-house fitness facility—here a step aerobics class—and on-site day care.

Below: I held regular "campus days," making myself available to all Acxiom associates. They could ask me anything—and did!

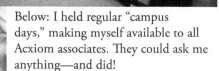

Left: We were widely recognized as being one of America's best companies to work for. Here, Jerry Adams presides over yet another Grand Opening, another ribbon cutting for our expanding campus.

Right: Alex Dietz and I participate in a session of the companywide re-education program we launched in 1990— "The Race for Excellence."

Right: With Susie at Lime Rock, May 1997, in my last major professional appearance. I thought my career had ended after my crash at Sebring, but was called in to substitute for Rob's co-driver, who couldn't make it.

Below: I had fallen hard for Susie. When she was about to make a decision out of fear, I wrote her this check—now she had the security to make the right decision.

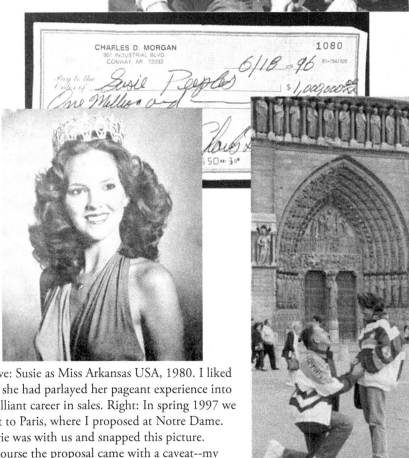

Above: Susie as Miss Arkansas USA, 1980. I liked how she had parlayed her pageant experience into a brilliant career in sales. Right: In spring 1997 we went to Paris, where I proposed at Notre Dame. Carrie was with us and snapped this picture. Of course the proposal came with a caveat--my divorce from Jane wasn't yet final.

Left: Susie and I married on May 1, 1998, in the stunning E. Fay Jones-designed Thorncrown Chapel in Eureka Springs, Arkansas. Jones, an Arkansas boy, had apprenticed with Frank Lloyd Wright.

Photo: Marty Sikes

Above and Below: We took our honeymoon in Cabo San Lucas, the beginning of a whole new chapter in our lives. Susie and I had no plans to buy property in Mexico, much less to build. A year and a half later, we'd built this!

Hobnobbing: Above, with Rob and Carrie at the engagement party for Rob and his now-wife, Vici. Left: Presidential candidate Al Gore, Inventor of the Internet, meets the Big Dude of Big Data. Next to Susie is Acxiom board member Mack McLarty. Below: Susie and me with board member Bill Dillard, of department store fame, and President Bill Clinton at the McLarty home.

Above: Rodger Kline, Sharon Tackett, and I enjoy a Thanksgiving potluck.

Right: With Cindy Childers, architect of much of Acxiom's 1990s self-reinvention.

Left: Following Acxiom's work in the wake of 9/ll, former President Bill Clinton flew to Little Rock to view our findings.

Below: Jeff Stalnaker, president of our financial services division, makes an apparently sobering presentation to Cindy, me, and corporate counsel Jerry Jones.

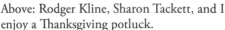

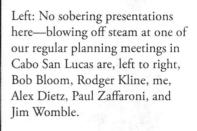

Left: No sobering presentations here—blowing off steam at one of our regular planning meetings in Cabo San Lucas are, left to right, Bob Bloom, Rodger Kline, me, Alex Dietz, Paul Zaffaroni, and Jim Womble.

For Rodger, Jim, and me, our last days at Acxiom were anything but sweet (Alex worked there until July 2014!). But three years later, new CEO Scott Howe summoned us to a packed Acxiom auditorium and unveiled the above painting of the four of us. It now hangs in the Acxiom lobby. Then he called me up and read the plaque at right. The word proud doesn't begin to cover my feelings at that moment.

MORGAN AUDITORIUM

THIS AUDITORIUM IS NAMED IN HONOR OF
CHARLES D. MORGAN, JR.

CHARLES, A TECHNOLOGY VISIONARY, LED THE SMALL, PRIVATELY-OWNED LIST MANAGEMENT PROVIDER, STARTED IN CONWAY, ARKANSAS, TO A PUBLIC, BILLION DOLLAR INTERNATIONAL MARKETING SERVICES COMPANY. UNDER HIS 36-YEAR LEADERSHIP, ACXIOM ACHIEVED MANY MILESTONES, INCLUDING MULTIPLE RECOGNITIONS IN THE INDUSTRY AND NAMED ONE OF AMERICA'S BEST PLACES TO WORK.

BECAUSE OF HIS PASSION FOR THE BUSINESS, HIS LOVE FOR THE PEOPLE AND HIS UNWAVERING COMMITMENT TO THE COMPANY'S SUCCESS, WE HONOR HIS LEGACY AT ACXIOM.

We've sustained a lot of bumps, but at the end of the day, we're lucky people. Above: Carrie with her husband Rod Ford and children Jules, left, and Yale; Right top: Rob and Vici with daughters Lainey and MaKenna and son Chase; Right bottom: Susie's son Aaron and wife Ashley with son Carson and daughter Morgan; Below: Susie and me with all the grandchildren at Hilton Head.

Recently our big family got bigger. In addition to our Chihuahua, Demi, Susie brought home another girl, a Papillon we named Calli. Life is good.

Photo: Malise Perrilliat

11

MARRIAGE
ON MY MIND

1001010010110010100010010110010101110011

FOR THE NEXT 10 days I lived inside myself, pondering the next step. Meanwhile, I saw a side of Jane that I hadn't seen in years—quite possibly not since those solicitous, seductive months leading to our marriage. She was upbeat, cheerful, accommodating: "Can I make you a drink?"

It was a Sunday morning when I told her. I woke up early and waited for her to get out of bed. By the time she did, I'd been up about three hours. "I'm going to get my stuff and move out," I said. She was shocked and started crying. "Look, Jane," I said, "I've tried and tried and *tried*. You know we're both miserable. Life's too short to squander being unhappy. I want *both* of us to get out of this stress-filled house and find happy lives."

And here's the part of the narrative where I told Jane about Cathy Cook, just like that time years before when I confessed to being with that girl in Chicago. Stupid, perhaps, but I certainly didn't want Jane to hear about Cathy from someone else.

I didn't say a lot about Cathy, just that there was someone I thought I could care about. "He went into pretty much detail," recalls Jane. "That she worked for IBM and had a little child and where she lived and how old she was. I was reeling—I didn't really need to know all those things."

"I'm going to get an apartment," I continued. "And what I'd like us to do is work toward getting a quiet, amicable divorce. I'll make you a very fair settlement and we can do this without raising the roof, which would be better for the kids. Maybe we don't get the divorce in Conway, where it would be big news. Maybe Little Rock or somewhere else is better.

"And I'm not even talking about doing anything right away. We can think about this a while."

Jane left to take a shower, and while she was gone I went upstairs where Rob, home from college, was still sleeping. He'd had a late night. I sat on the side of the bed and shook him, and when he seemed awake enough, I told him I was moving out. In the middle of this, Jane came in and was furious that I hadn't waited for her. I took that as my final cue. Today Rob says he thinks I mishandled that situation by not waiting for Jane. No doubt he's right.

After I packed a few things and left, I drove straight to my parents' place to phone Carrie. Of course I had to tell Mother and Father first. That was hard to do. They and Jane had been close for decades, especially Father and Jane. Now Father was in very poor health—he'd just had a stroke—and he'd been showing signs of dementia for quite some time. Not long before his stroke, he'd gotten into his car one day and just started driving. He ended up in Missouri with no idea where he was or how he'd gotten there. We had to go up and get him.

Carrie was married now, living in Atlanta. "I had been sober seven years," she recalls—it had been a long battle she'd waged, from age 14 to age 21. But now she was finally clean, and Jane and I were very proud of her for that. "My husband and I had a condo in Atlanta, and I had a great job," says Carrie. "And I got the call from my dad that he had left my mom."

The first thing she said to me was, "Dad, I can't believe it took you so long." Her words hit me like a brick. I thought that was very perceptive of her—she was aware that it had been very difficult for a long time.

Then, of course, she was immediately concerned about her mother. These things are complicated beyond belief.

There was one final required call to make that day. "We were celebrating my youngest son's first birthday at my house on a Sunday afternoon," recalls Sharon, "when the phone rang and it was Charles. 'I just told Jane,' he said, 'and I left.' The date was July the eighth, nineteen ninety-five."

On that beautiful summer Sunday in Arkansas, the drive from Conway to Little Rock was a journey I'll never forget. Even from the interstate, the terrain was calm and peaceful—fishing boats on a lake, forest leaves lightly rustling, crops full in farmers' fields. And then, as I rounded that gentle curve, I came upon the wide, impressive river with its magnificent bluffs dotted with homes, some barely visible in the lushness of summer. I drove on across the bridge and up between the handsome black cliffs, and soon I exited, headed west to my new life.

My first night away from that big, sad house in the Conway countryside was spent in a small, furnished apartment that I had rented in west Little Rock. It was really nothing special, just a temporary solution. But it was an extraordinarily welcome one.

The next morning, Monday, I was so excited that I got up before dawn and drove back to Conway, to Acxiom. "Charles called me very early," recalls Alex Dietz, "and he never did that. 'I need to see you in the office this morning before work,' he said. So I got dressed and showed up in his office. 'What is it, Charles?' I said.

"'Well,' he said, 'I love Cathy Cook.'

"'I do, too, Charles,' I said. 'I think she's great. You know, she's just one of the coolest reps I know.'

"'No, Alex. I really *love* Cathy Cook. And I'm going to divorce Jane.'

"I was floored. I had no idea. My wife, Lee Ann, and I were married in Charles' and Jane's house that very year, and I was oblivious to any kind of issues that they were having. I had no idea until that day that he had even started a liaison with Cathy and that he was on the verge of divorcing Jane. Of course, then it progressed quite rapidly. Because he told everybody."

I did. And apparently I told others in the same way I did Alex, because several people now reading this will think that was *their* story: same scene, same basic dialogue, same innocent wonderment that after so many years I could find myself the lucky recipient of such tenderness—even mechanical engineers need that! So of course I told everyone my good news.

But before that first week was out, I received word that Jane had hired the meanest, most tenacious Jack Russell terrier of an attorney in our part of the country, and she had filed for divorce. So much for slow and amicable.

Two-and-a-half years—that's how long the hell would go on. It would disrupt not just my personal life, but also the corporate life of Acxiom itself. Nearly everybody I knew would undergo grueling, insulting depositions, and several people in the company would have to drop their regular duties and focus on my divorce—because Jane's accusations and claims regarding "her part" in the building of Acxiom would actually become threatening to the future of the company itself.

□ □ □ □ □

BY THE FALL of 1995, I had bought and furnished a 2,500-foot condo in west Little Rock, and I had started enjoying my life. I loved my new home—*I could live here forever*, I thought. Even with the impending divorce, I couldn't stop smiling. It was early yet.

My infatuation with Cathy Cook hardly survived the summer, and soon I was seeing several women. "The big joke around the office," says Cindy Childers, "was that because Charles wasn't good with names, we should get name tags for his dates to wear so he didn't get confused. He was going out with somebody new or having drinks with somebody different every night."

But I was working hard, too. I always need a project, so on weekend days and on weeknights when I wasn't going out, I threw myself into the tech project I'd been mulling over since Jim Womble and I had first discussed it in the early '90s—the project I eventually called AbiliTec. "We just can't keep doing this the same old way," I'd said to Jim, speaking of the challenge of processing ever-greater amounts of data, with ever-greater numbers of confounding data fragments. "But what if we could give everybody in the United States—or every address—a number?" If we could come up with a series of constant numbers, we could eliminate much of the time, computer power, and uncertainty then inherent in data processing.

Jim and I thought the idea had potential, so I had actually put three people on the project to test my constant-number theory. They'd worked on it for a year or so, but finally reported that the data then available just wasn't good enough to let us create reliable individual numbers. I filed the idea away, but I never gave up on it.

By the mid-'90s, better data was available. And instead of assigning the project to someone else to work on, I decided to do it myself.

I had started working on it even before I left Jane. The basic premise of AbiliTec was simple: *As long as you're alive, you're you.* You can get divorced and remarried, change jobs, decide you're gay, move across country, take early retirement, reinvent yourself as a painter or a shaman—it doesn't matter, you're still you. The challenge for me was how to track you—accurately, and without question—along all the highways of your life. Such a feat had never been within our power before.

But two important data breakthroughs had made me believe that AbiliTec's time had come. First, in the interest of greater efficiency the U.S. Postal Service had refined its addressing system, adopting the more specific Zip-plus-four codes. It was like they had zoomed in on all neighborhoods coast to coast, and the result was a list of all valid addresses in the United States. While Zip-plus-four hadn't caught on with the general public, it was very useful to me. But it was the second development in tandem with the first that made the big difference. Acxiom now had a deal with TransUnion, one of the big-three credit bureaus, whereby they would share with us all the credit data they kept in their vast archives. TransUnion maintained a decade's worth—maybe more—of data on millions of people, and this included Social Security numbers.

That was my "aha!" moment.

My first small step in the long, arduous journey of trying to create a permanent AbiliTec number for every address in the United States, and an AbiliTec number for every possible individual, was to take on the small city of Conway, Arkansas. Once I coded the data and demonstrated to myself that I could build address-and-people links there, my next obstacle was figuring out how to update those links; they would have to be refreshed almost daily.

I was still working on the Conway portion of the project when I moved to Little Rock. It was going well, so far so good, and I was trying to figure out how I should proceed after I'd proved that I could build AbiliTec links for Conway. I decided Little Rock would be a logical and serviceable next step.

There would be times over the next couple of years when this project saved my sanity. During the extreme difficulty of the divorce, the challenge of AbiliTec was a friendly constant, a comfortably complex conundrum in whose all-consuming company I could lose myself—or escape from what my real world had become, however you choose to interpret it.

During that charged summer of 1995, I was also—of course—still wrestling with the ongoing challenges of being a CEO. Earlier in the year, Jim Womble and Cindy Childers and I had attended a spectacular leadership conference in Orlando, Florida, where we were able to hear talks by some of the smartest people in the world—among them Margaret Thatcher, Alvin Toffler, Lee Iacocca, Tom Peters, Lester Thurow, and, via video, the estimable 85-year-old Peter Drucker. This was part of the searching I was going through in the '90s— how to be a leader; how to empower my people; how to guide a company as it grows.

Drucker was the main reason I'd gone to the conference. I still have my notebook from those sessions, and even today I get excited reading jottings on the pages devoted to Drucker's talk:

- We [the U.S.] are so far ahead in info that no country will catch up. Also ahead in finance.
- Moving to a society of networks—companies that are networks.
- Learn to watch your non-customers. Changes just occur among non-cust.
- Manage what we have. Improve. Innovate.
- Set up Innovation outside of business units that have cost responsibility.
- Abandon yesterday—don't sacrifice future for current products.
- To get good at something new takes 15 years.
- Companies must become more information literate.
- "What info do I owe to whom?" Restructure around flow of info.
- Advise people to "Find out what you are good at and become excellent at it."
- Tired of talk of leadership—want to hear more of competence, dedication, and hard work and RESPONSIBILITY!!!
- Test people in autonomous commands.
- Good CEOs start with purpose and mission.

I felt that we, Acxiom and I, were on target in many areas Drucker touched on—certainly innovation (AbiliTec came to mind); also our "Lead with Data" strategy echoed Drucker's philosophy of "restructuring around the flow of information." We also were edging toward the idea of "business networks," especially as run-ups to acquisitions.

In the early '90s, we finally figured out that the best acquisitions were companies in our industry, in our technology; and that the best way to buy them was to contact those guys directly and not to go through investment bankers. We'd had very poor luck with investment bankers. It was far more useful to contact the companies ourselves to see if they had any interest in doing something jointly. "Hey," we'd say, "is there any way we can work together? I know we're competitors, but we've got some data technology that you don't have, and you may have something that we don't have. Maybe, without colluding, we can do some sharing of technology."

It was a way to get to know each other. If we liked what we saw, most of the time this partnership turned into an effort for us to acquire. We made two new acquisitions in the summer of 1995. In July, we announced the purchase of the outstanding stock of Generator Datamarketing Ltd, of Hertfordshire, England, near London. Generator provided data and database marketing software and processing services to its customers, and we saw this marriage as a way of expanding Acxiom's footprint overseas.

In August, we announced plans to acquire DataQuick Information Systems of San Diego, California. Our largest acquisition to that point, DataQuick supplied property information for marketing, appraisal, real estate, banking, mortgage, and insurance applications. We estimated that the merger would add $20 million to Acxiom's annual revenue. "We are a supplier of data," I told *Arkansas Business* magazine. "It's not cost-efficient for companies to do this themselves. They choose Acxiom over their in-house system. We have more software and we do a better job of marrying software and data than anybody."

□ □ □ □ □

MARRIAGE, THEN, WAS the subject uppermost on my mind in 1995. Professionally, I was strategizing the union of corporations; personally, I was wondering how to achieve a peaceful dissolution of my own marriage to Jane.

In those days, I kept my thoughts in a Stuart Hall Executive notebook—things to do, priorities to achieve, opportunities to pursue. The notebook covering this time frame begins in August 1994 with notes about "InfoBase Data Strategy"; it ends in October 1995 with "Concepts" for getting this divorce done:

- Split everything 50/50 incl. Furn, all Businesses & stock, Jane signs up for all liabilities—
- Jane gets X shares Stock, transfer 2/3 of Beer Bus to Kids. I keep all liabilities Sell house & split proceeds
- Jane gets stock & X million cash

By the fall of 1995, I had already made several overtures to Jane—attempts at what I considered generous starting points for settlement. She and her attorney, Steve Engstrom, wouldn't even discuss them. At one point I sent her a check for $10 million, as a "good faith advance" on a mutually beneficial settlement. My attorney, Phil Dixon, handed the check to Engstrom, per Steve's strict warning that we were *never* to try to contact Jane directly. The next thing I know, the kids are telling me Jane is saying I'm "trying to buy her off" for $10 million. Where would she get that idea? I surmised then that she was out to humiliate and punish me, with the eager participation of her attorney. That, I soon learned, wasn't just paranoia on my part—Carrie and Rob told me it was true.

My feeling, right or wrong, is that Steve was very good at milking his client for every dime he could get from her. Anyone could see that Jane had a chance at a lot of money, but she was also sad and crying. Soon, though, sad and crying turned to anger, to *I'm going to get that son of a bitch*. I can imagine Steve saying, *I'll help you get him. We're going to embarrass him; we're going to humiliate him.* And Jane saying, *Let's get him, let's hurt him, let's humiliate him.* As I understand it, for two-and-a-half years Steve billed Jane something like $250,000 a year. So where was *his* incentive to settle?

For the longest time, we didn't even know the basis of their case, what they were trying to achieve. They just asked for this document and that document, providing no clarity whatsoever, and no conversation. Finally we decided that Jane sought to depict herself as the savior of Acxiom. Being the former bookkeeper she was, Jane had kept every scrap of paper—every canceled check, every check register, every bank note, every IOU, every tax return, every ledger book—from the '60s on. So she and Steve had a veritable field day sifting through all those documents and building a case claiming that Jane was the power behind Acxiom's success—that without her, it wouldn't have happened. It was absurd. Between 1991 and the end of that decade, our annual revenue would grow from $100 million to $1 billion—and that was thanks to Jane?

"The Oprah show called to invite Dad on," says Carrie, "because the question in the legal culture in that period was, does staying home and raising children and taking care of a household entitle you to fifty percent of what in Dad's case was then about $100 million? That's what Steve saw at the time—let's go back and show what Jane's contribution through the years was…besides the well-adjusted children!"

We were in no way contesting the Arkansas law that said she gets half of all community property. The question was, how do you define half? Half of what?

But what really made my attorneys nervous was that it looked like she was trying to build a case that she should get *more* than half—because, as we interpreted what we knew of her argument, she came into this marriage with money, which she put in, but she never received stock, so I really ripped her off. That was the reason for all the depositions. I think it was a negotiating ploy mainly designed to inflict pain on me, because we certainly couldn't ignore her claims that she should be getting more than half. Of course this ploy also created big legal bills.

We did borrow money from Bob Dills a couple of times early on. And Jane and her dad did buy us a piece of equipment once—an IBM S/360 channel controller—for which they were reimbursed. It wasn't an enormous amount of money, but it was certainly something we needed, and we appreciated it.

In general, though, Jane's "financial support" of Acxiom was in the form of co-signing, or guaranteeing, loans. For example, she once co-signed on a bank loan for a computer we were buying, and she never lost any of her money because of Acxiom. But in the divorce she presented herself as vital to the company's success. I think she misunderstood her role in these co-signings of loans, these guarantees. When someone is a senior executive and controlling shareholder of a private company—as I was after Charles Ward's exit—anything the corporation does in terms of leases or bank loans *has* to be signed by that shareholder and his spouse. It used to be an old trick for shady shareholder-execs to take assets from their companies and put them in their spouse's name in a private company, but the banks figured that one out. That's why they required Jane to sign, too. Once we went public, that requirement went away.

In any case, after 30 months of nastiness—during which time Acxiom stock dropped, to Jane's detriment—she would actually settle for less than what I'd offered her initially. But, then, she'd had the satisfaction of punishing me. As the credit card ad says, *Priceless.*

"It was a very, very acrimonious divorce," says Alex Dietz. "Jane was devastated by it. But once Charles has made up his mind, you might as well just get out of the way. When he decides what he's going to do, he's going to do it. Her reaction to it was just great indignation. If you heard Jane tell it at the time, she was personally responsible for the fact that Charles owned as much of Acxiom as he did. But the success of the Acxiom Corporation had nothing to do with Jane. As far as the business is concerned, she had no involvement at all. It was Charles' genius that made the company what it is."

"Jane felt that she was integral to the early growth of Acxiom," says Jerry Adams, "and I don't believe that. Bob Dills' money helped us bridge payroll. And Jane was Charles' support, so she probably knew a lot about what Acxiom was doing. But she was never integral in sales, never integral in product development."

The atmosphere became so poisonous that Carrie and even Rob didn't talk to their mother for a while—so furious were they at the way she was acting. They weren't allowed to say my name in her presence.

"The kids tended to be more toward Charles," recalls Jane. "I told myself that it was because they saw this as an opportunity to actually be with him."

In fact, the kids and I had always spent special time together. For years, Rob and I had had racing in common, whether motocross or cars. Even in high school, he'd been pressing me to let him drive—it reminded me of me with my dad. I told Rob he had to go to college, which he did. And when he reached college age, I started allowing him to drive. I would rent cars for him to drive on weekends when I was racing.

By the time of the divorce, Rob and I had our own racing team together. I loved spending this time with him, sharing our common interest. I believed he had real talent, and I enjoyed helping and watching him develop as a driver. Especially during the divorce, racing with Rob was for me a great escape.

As for Carrie, she still talks about certain moments that she and I shared—some happy, some not so, but all of which brought us closer. "Besides taking me to boarding school," she says, "Dad also saw me off to France when I spent a semester abroad. He took me to New York and we stayed at the Waldorf the night before I left. We had a wonderful dinner and the next morning he took me to JFK and sent me off. Months later, he picked me up in Paris.

"I also remember a night in a hotel room in Portland, Oregon, when I was about sixty days sober. I was so fragile and so vulnerable and I wanted to blame *him;* I wanted to be a victim and have it be *his* fault that I'd gotten so messed up. I remember Mom left the hotel room, and Dad and I cried and had it out. I said, *You sucked,* and he said, *You've been drunk for six years—you were the one who disappeared, you've been stoned and drunk and high on drugs, I've been building my business. I didn't know what to do. I love you.* So I just want to take my share of the responsibility—I'm not a victim of him. I was a messed-up kid, and I was wasted most of the time."

□ □ □ □ □

IN OCTOBER 1995, WHILE attending a civic event, I ran into an old acquaintance named Jack Fleischauer, CEO of a local bank. I had always liked Jack, but we hardly ever saw each other; both of us were always too busy. He was divorced, however, so now we would have that in common. That night we compared notes on starting over in mid-life—I was 52, Jack 47—and agreed to get together for dinner.

After a few back-and-forth weeks of working through our assistants to find a mutually agreeable night, we finally settled on an upcoming Saturday in mid-November. On the morning of the appointed day, I phoned Jack to finalize our plans. "You bringing a date?" he said.

"I wasn't planning on it," I said.

"Well, I've started dating somebody, and I've asked her to join us," he said.

"Okay," I said. "Sure."

"Tell you what—I'll ask her to find you a date."

It wasn't really what I expected or wanted from the evening. I'd thought it would just be Jack and me, catching up.

In a while he called back: I now had a blind date. We would all go out to eat—but first I was to show up early at Jack's place for drinks and a briefing on my date, an interior decorator named Becky. She'd gone to Purdue and was smart enough to plan on meeting us at the restaurant in her own car, in case she didn't like me.

Welcoming me in, Jack led me back to his den, where the most beautiful woman I'd ever seen was sitting on a bar stool. She was wearing a black dress with a very deep slit up the side, revealing a considerable amount of shapely leg. This was Jack's date, Susie Peeples. She was vice-president of a big temporary placement firm. I guessed her age as mid- to late-30s.

"So I'm sitting there," recalls Susie, "the doorbell rings, and I don't know what Charles looks like. I know that's crazy, because he's the CEO of Acxiom, but that's in Conway and I'm in Little Rock and even though I'm calling on his company, you don't go to the CEO, you go to the human resources people. So, I hadn't seen pictures of Charles. He could've been short and bald.

"Then the door opened and Charles came in. The minute I met him, I knew there was chemistry. At that time, his hair was longer, it was darker, he was really tall and really, really lean. I was like, *Wow, okay*. I mean, I'm in the placement business, I've set him up with somebody and he's going to be okay—*she's* going to be okay. So he sits down and we start talking, but he wouldn't make eye contact with me. He wasn't comfortable yet. He later told me it was because of my skirt."

Over the next few hours I learned that Susie had been divorced about five years, had a son, lived in west Little Rock, and was the main person at the largest staffing company in Arkansas, ProStaff. She had basically built the organization by opening 25 sales offices across the state. She had opened all those offices herself. ProStaff was billing more hours than any staffing company in Arkansas, so she was not only good looking, she was a kick-ass business developer.

At the restaurant, I was sitting across from her. *I really like this girl,* I thought. My date from Purdue spent too much time trying to impress me with how smart she was. After dinner, I didn't want the evening to end. "Hey," I said, "why don't we all go to my place for a nightcap? My condo is all finished and I'm proud of it. Come on."

I took them all—Jack, Susie, and Becky—on a tour of the condo, with special attention to my racing photos and memorabilia. "Jack had told me Charles raced cars," says Susie, "and I'd thought, *Oh, God, not that stock-car track out on I-30.* Before I met him, I'd thought Charles might turn out to be a redneck."

But Susie was impressed. I remember she and I were standing in front of a particular racing photograph and I was telling her all about it; suddenly we glanced at each other and locked eyes for a moment. Then she quickly went to look at something else, and soon we all went back downstairs.

We all drank a little too much that night. But I had to get up early the next day and leave for Dallas, where I would be in flight school for the next two weeks. My new Falcon 20 was going to be delivered the first of 1996, and I had to get certified to fly it—my latest obsession in the joined realms of speed and technology. During the evening, I had mentioned that to Becky and she'd said she was going to be in Dallas at market and we should get together. Fine, I said.

"The next day Becky called me," says Susie. "'Oh, I think he likes me, I'm going to see him in Dallas.' And I'm thinking, *Wow, he's moving fast.* 'He *must* really like me,' she said, 'because he gave me Sharon Tackett's number.' Well, I didn't know anything about Charles Morgan then, but now I know that if Sharon Tackett doesn't have your number, you're not getting *anywhere* with Charles. He can't find you because he doesn't keep up with it. But anyway, Becky went on to Dallas to do a shopping trip, and he was down there doing flight training. They had a couple of dates."

I got back from flight school on December 2 and saw Becky one or two times more. One night I said to her, "Why don't we ask Susie and Jack to go out with us?"

"Well," she said, "I'm not sure that's going to work. I think Susie has broken up with Jack."

"Oh, that's *awful,*" I said. "I am *so sorry* to hear that."

◻ ◻ ◻ ◻ ◻

THE NEXT MORNING at work, I asked Sharon to find Susie. I couldn't remember the name of her company—I just knew she worked in staffing. "Call around," I told Sharon. "Somebody's going to know her. Call around and find out."

"I'll never forget that day," says Susie. "It was an afternoon at ProStaff, and I've got all the sales team in because now I'm vice-president of sales, I'm helping everybody. And suddenly, over the intercom, I hear, "Susie, Charles Morgan's on the phone, he wants to talk to you." Well, I just grinned. Everybody else was like, *Oh my God, we've done something wrong, he's fixing to fire us from Acxiom.* I just grinned all the way back to the phone."

When she answered, I said, "It's taken me all day to remember the name of your staffing company. I've had everybody looking for it and we finally found you. I just wanted to thank you for setting me up with Becky." Then, after some hemming and hawing, I got to the point. "I don't know what your status is, but I'm really interested in Jack's date."

"I'm completely available," she said. No games—I really liked that.

From then on, it was all about trying to figure out when we could see each other. We were each busy that night, and the next and the next. By then the obligatory office Christmas parties were starting, and I even had to go out of town for a couple of days—it looked like we couldn't get together for nearly a *week*. It was nuts. Finally, on a day before we each had Christmas functions, we set a date for dinner the following night, after our events were over. We agreed to meet at 8 p.m. at a west Little Rock restaurant called 1620.

The next night—December 7, 1995—I couldn't wait for my party to wind down. As soon as it was acceptable for me to leave, I broke away and *raced* out to 1620—I didn't want Susie to get there and me not be waiting. Well, I walked into the place a few minutes early and she was already sitting on a bar stool sipping a drink. *Man,* I thought, *that's confidence.*

They showed us to a booth in the back, and that night we told each other the stories of our lives. I learned that Susie had had a hard upbringing—a middle child and only daughter of an Air Force man and a nurse who never worked the same shift, so the family was seldom all together. For a while they lived in a two-and-a-half bedroom trailer. Her father was depressed and jealous, and he drank; the parents fought constantly, and whenever trouble started, Susie's brothers ran and hid—she was the one who stepped between her mom and dad. Twice, her father threatened to kill himself in front of the children. There was love there, Susie said, but no know-how—they didn't have a clue how to be parents. They couldn't be counted on.

Her father was killed in a motorcycle accident when Susie was 12, so she didn't really have a lot of memories with him. "Except I knew he loved all of us kids," she said. "He just didn't know how to focus it. He was kind of like a shotgun, all over the place—one time it would be, wow, this is the best thing in the world, and the next time he would be depressed."

As a result of her home life, she began to live two lives. On the outside, she projected a happy, confident persona—she didn't want people to know what her life was really like. But on the inside, she yearned for what she imagined as normalcy. She always wondered what was going on in somebody else's house. What did they do when the doors closed at night and they had to get ready for school? Were they having their baths and getting their bedtime story read? Or were they like her, eating dinner at eight o'clock at night, maybe in the middle of a family fight, maybe needing help with homework but there wasn't anyone to ask? "I didn't have the structure," she said. "I didn't get to develop those routines and those disciplines that most people get. So I had to find that somewhere else. I had to look at other people, and experience it, and be exposed to it, and think, *That feels right, that feels good, that seems right.*"

It was a sad story in many ways—but I was impressed with how Susie had managed to turn it into something positive. "Sometimes I think all of that was for a reason," she told me. "Because of it, I learned how to be a good sales person. I learned early that when I walked into my house, my mother and dad were either going to be fighting, or he was going to be either happy or sad—*something* would be going on, and I would have to adjust to it. So I was always the sensitive one, the one who had to be sensitive to the house. Now I think maybe that was a gift. At an early age, whenever I walked into a room I could tell you who was happy and who wasn't. I always had to juggle adult people in my environment."

The second she said that, I heard an echo from my own days at the motel. I realized then that despite the vast difference in our family situations, we had some elemental things in common. "We experienced some of the same loneliness, the same *We're-going-to-have-to-do-this-on-our-own* type of attitude," says Susie today. "I mean, I really felt like, *I'm going to have to do this. If I'm going to get anywhere, it's going to be up to me. No one is going to help me get there.*"

The way she did that was through beauty pageants. "I started the pageants at thirteen," she said, "because after my father was killed, my mother wanted to do something that she thought would keep me focused. She put me in pageants because she wanted me to set goals and stay out of trouble." Susie won pageants all through Jacksonville (Arkansas) High School and in college at the U of A in Fayetteville. But the pageant life began to wear on her—she began to question what she was doing, and why. "My mother, my school, my sorority—I realized I wasn't doing these things because I really wanted it; it was because somebody *else* wanted it."

Her chaotic home life hadn't equipped her with the study habits she needed to succeed at the university, and during Christmas break of her sophomore year she decided not to return to school. But what would she do? That spring, 1980, she fell back on her pageant experience—"selling people on *me*," as she characterized it. She tried out for Miss Arkansas USA and won the thing. Next thing she knew, she was in the Miss USA Pageant.

"You would think this was my lifelong dream," she said. "In all my yearbooks, from junior high on, it was, *You're going to be Miss Arkansas, you're going to be Miss America.* That's how people defined me. Not, *You're going to be a doctor, you're going to be a scientist.* Because where I excelled was in front of everybody, so that was what I was supposed to be. Now I found myself at the Miss USA Pageant, where I got a helpful dose of reality. In the naïveté of my 21-year-old self, I had always thought girls who reached that level must come from perfect places, perfect homes, unlike me. And, you know, I got there and they were just regular people, with as many problems as I had."

Her year-long tour as Miss Arkansas USA opened many doors for her, and she became adept at interacting with government and business leaders all over the state. After that year was over, she applied to a trade school called South Central Career College and started teaching personal development and modeling. "It was a sales job," Susie said. "The college also offered word processing and interior design, but everybody took personal development—how to do make-up, how to walk, how to do wardrobes. So I was one of their instructors. I worked there, and I sold. I learned from the guys at the college how to sell people what they want, not what they need. In the psychology of selling, people *always* buy what they want, but they don't always buy what they need." It was the process of trying to place the college's graduates that led her to the staffing business.

At about that point in her story, Susie and I were startled by what sounded like a distant roar. We looked up to see a man vacuuming the restaurant. It was 11:30, and not a single other customer was left in the place. I apologized to our waitress. "Yeah," she said, "the last people besides you left an hour ago."

"We had no idea," I said. We'd been too engrossed in each other to notice anyone else.

12

TURNING
POINTS

1001010010110010100010010110010101100 11

THE YEAR 1996 marked several important milestones, for both Acxiom and me. For Acxiom, early that year we changed the company dress code from "professional" to "business casual." I was immensely proud of that, and our people responded just as I'd hoped they would—by feeling lighter, freer, more energized in their work. As we pioneered in data, so did we pioneer in corporate culture. We already had a day-care center for our employees' use. In 1996, *Working Woman* magazine listed Acxiom among its "Top 100 Companies," and in a couple of years we would also see ourselves included in *Fortune's* prestigious list of "100 Best Companies to Work For."

These were important distinctions, valuable recognitions, especially starting in the mid-'90s when more and more tech companies were appearing on the scene. I may have come late to the table in understanding the importance of structure and core competencies, but I had *always* preached the necessity of hiring the best people we could get. I, personally, would go to a campus day at the University of Central Arkansas in Conway or the University of Arkansas at Fayetteville, and I would tell the staffs, "I want to talk to your smartest prospects." I'd do a day at each place. Then I would come back and tell my senior people, "I just interviewed four of the sharpest young kids, and I want all of you to get *your* asses out there and start doing campus interviews, just like I do." So I was pushing them by example. And one year at the University of Arkansas, we hired 15 of the top 15 computer science kids in IT and computer science—a clean sweep.

In May 1996, we made an acquisition that felt very special to me: We acquired Direct Media, our oldest customer and earliest partner, the company that had given us our first big break nearly 20 years before. Dave Florence was still there, and the company was the U.S. market leader in the mailing list industry; it also had operations in Canada and the United Kingdom. We paid $25 million to acquire Direct Media, estimating that it would generate approximately $40 million in net revenues for us.

In hindsight, our purchase of Direct Media calls to mind a particularly challenging facet of the whole business of acquisitions: Once you get these companies, what are you going to do with them? How are you going to integrate the sales, the technology, the accounting? How are you going to get the leverage out of them? And just as important—maybe even more so—how are you going to blend the various corporate cultures?

These were issues we were already wrestling with in regard to some other acquisitions we'd made. But on that happy day in 1996 when we announced the agreement with Direct Media, if you had told me we would have similar problems with these old pals of ours, I would've said you were crazy.

□ □ □ □ □

DURING ALL THE early divorce wrangling, I was determined to go on with my life. I felt that I had no jeopardy—I was getting a divorce, so why stay home and wait for it to be final when it was obvious to me that it was going to be a long road? So if I wanted to go out, I went out. Life felt almost normal at the beginning, during the discovery period, when I wasn't getting hit in the face with something every day. Occasionally I would feel a twinge of alarm, like a man who knows his floor is being gnawed by termites. But it hadn't caved in yet.

In the week after our long get-acquainted dinner at 1620, Susie and I started seeing each other whenever we could. We got along really well, but it was frustrating for me because we were both so busy with work that we often couldn't get together even at night. Finally I said, "Are you ever in Conway? Could you come have lunch with me at my office?" As it happened, she planned to be traveling through Conway to one of ProStaff's offices in a few days, so we made a date for her to stop by Acxiom on the way. Since I forgot to ask what she wanted to eat, I had Sharon order in a variety of things.

"We had soup, we had salad, we had everything," recalls Susie. "It was like, *I don't know what to get her, so I just got everything*. I thought it was very funny."

Before lunch we had what I actually called a business meeting. I realized I didn't know Susie well, but I'd been around her long enough to figure out there wasn't anything about her I didn't like. "So," I said, "I'd like to offer you a business proposition."

"Go on," she said.

"'I can't make any long-term commitments now, you know, until I get this divorce. But I know enough about this town to know there's nobody here that I would like to date more than you—at least long enough to get to know you well. And what I don't like to do is play games. I've had enough of that in my marriage. So I'd like you to be honest and straightforward with me: If you want to date somebody else, don't do it and not tell me. Just tell me what you're going to do and be honest with me. But my plan would be not to date anybody else until we figure out if we want to be more steady. In the meantime, we just take it day to day."

"I thought, *That's a simple proposition*," Susie recalls. "I mean, I wasn't pressed, I was financially secure on my own, I was happy with my life. I enjoyed him, but I wasn't desperate. So, fine."

"Okay," she said, and then we ate lunch.

With that agreement out of the way, we started having fun. We spent Christmas together and began making plans for the coming year. I had a bucket list of things I wanted to do now, and one was to see the famous Monaco Grand Prix in person. That was coming up in May 1996. I asked Susie to go with me.

"I thought, *That's five months from now,*" says Susie. "*How do we know we're even going to be together?* But, sure, we're taking it one day at a time. 'You're lucky,' I told him. 'I don't have anything on my calendar for May.'"

Also, Rob and I were scheduled to race in the 24 Hours of Daytona in February, which meant we needed to go to Daytona for testing in January. I asked if she would go with us to that, and she did. When we got to Daytona, I told her I was buying her what's called a "hard card"—a season pass. "I don't want to put any pressure on you about long-term commitments," I said, "but it's just easier if we get the hard card." So she got her picture taken and was issued her hard card. She was now officially a team member.

We hit a bump sometime around late January, when I got word that Jane and I would have our separate maintenance hearing in March. "You mean you haven't even gotten to court yet?" Susie said. I think that was the first time she realized this was truly going to be an endurance race.

"I'm sure people were starting to wonder about us," says Susie. "He'd been saying, 'I'm getting a divorce,' but if you're getting a divorce, the process is *underway.* My divorce was over in thirty days. So I thought, *Oh my God, this has not even started yet. He and Cathy Cook were undercover, so I'm the first one anyone sees. Everybody thinks I'm the reason he's leaving his wife.* So I'm feeling a little weird. I have a son; it's that whole reputation thing."

Fortunately, we got past that rough patch. But just as we thought we could see our way clear to the fun of Daytona and Monaco, Susie was confronted with a crisis of her own. Actually, she didn't know it was a crisis until I told her.

Her company, ProStaff, was taking steps to go public. The plan was for ProStaff to join up with several other staffing firms—one in Fayetteville, another in Oklahoma City, and probably a couple more—to form a big regional staffing operation, for which they would issue an IPO. All the individual owners expected to get filthy rich in the stock market.

Susie had been with ProStaff for more than a decade. She was the number-three person in the firm, behind the two owners, Ed and Steve Schulte. She had spearheaded the company's growth to 25 offices statewide. "How much ownership do you have?" I asked.

"Well, I don't have any right now," she said. "But Ed's always told me that if we ever monetize or sell the business, I'll get fifteen percent of the price."

"Do you have any documentation of that conversation?"

"No, but we've discussed it several times, and he assures me. Ed has almost been like a father to me. I trust Ed completely."

"Well," I said, "I'm going to tell you something you don't want to hear. When money starts getting to be big numbers, either up or down, the nicest guys lose their nice guy. They look after themselves and their families. And suddenly being a good guy is secondary to the money."

She was certain that Ed would never betray her, but I urged her to go talk with him. She did, and he backpedaled. He said he'd told his partners she needed to get a big percentage, but now he wasn't sure he could do 15 percent. He was thinking more like "at least ten percent."

"Susie," I said, "aside from his just giving you ten percent, he's not telling you the truth. He may not know it, but he certainly hasn't gone to lawyers and checked it out. Because you cannot redistribute stock in a six-month period prior to the IPO; it'll bust the stock pooling and make it a taxable transaction. But they're not going to wait six months anyway. They're about to do this thing. I beg you, get a lawyer to help you. Otherwise, I think you're going to get screwed."

By this time, Susie was really getting nervous, but she did hire an attorney. Meanwhile, the IPO was getting closer and closer. And the nearer it came, the more Ed said, "Just trust me. Just trust me."

"He's going to screw you," I said. "Trust *me*—it's going to happen. You need to tell them you'll sue them if they don't do what's right for you." The thought of a lawsuit made her come unglued. "Susie," I said, "it's the only right thing to do. You built this fucking business, but these guys are going to walk away with twenty million dollars."

□ □ □ □ □

THESE CONVERSATIONS TOOK place over a period of months, wherever we happened to be. In February, Susie went to Daytona with Rob and me, and I was proud she was there to see us win the International Motor Sports Association (IMSA) GTS-1 category in the 24 Hours. It was one of my four biggest career wins at that point. The funny thing was, the previous year, in August 1995, Rob and I had won a big race together at Mosport Park in Canada, driving our Oldsmobile Cutlass Supreme to Oldsmobile's 100th racing victory in IMSA competition. We won that race by beating out the two-car Olds *factory* team. As a reward for that momentous win, we were asked to drive the factory team's second car at the 24 Hours of Daytona in 1996. And we beat the factory drivers again!

In May, Susie and I spent two weeks in Europe. I did some business in London and Paris, and then we went to the Formula I race in Monaco. After that, we explored the Riviera—Nice, Beaulieu-sur-Mer, Antibes, Cannes. As it turned out, we were there during the film festival, which was fun. "I'd never been in a place like the South of France," says Susie. "I'd never seen so many people with so much money. I'd never heard so much hype about racing. I mean, the beautiful boats out there and being able to experience the countryside. It was a once-in-a-lifetime experience."

We were abroad for 17 days. The interesting thing to me was that we didn't have a single fight the whole time. *This is working out pretty well*, I thought. *She's agreeable. She'll try anything one time. She's the experimental sort.*"

Returning to the U.S., we flew directly to New York, rented a car, and drove to Lime Rock, Connecticut, where Rob and I were racing over Memorial Day. Rob was already there with our car and crew. The 1996 season would mark a turning point in my racing with Rob. For four years, starting in 1992, we'd often driven in the same races, though not always in the same class. We did a couple of races in 1992 and maybe three in 1993. Then in 1994 Rob moved up to my division, IMSA GTO class. It was a very competitive, very expensive division to run in. These were production-based race cars that were anything *but* production. They looked like cars you might see on the street—Mazdas, Mercury Cougars, Nissan ZXs, Camaros, Fords, Oldsmobiles—but under the hood they were monsters with enough horsepower to take you to the moon. I had won the IMSA championship in that class in 1993.

In 1996 I partnered with Rob Walton, of the Walmart Waltons, to buy IMSA, but at the last minute it was sold out from under us to a man named Andy Evans. Andy was a former Wall Street financier who loved cars and racing and was able to enjoy that costly pursuit partly by managing hundreds of millions of dollars of Bill Gates' money. I knew Andy. In fact, in my early days of racing he had paid me to drive for his team for a year.

Long story short, I think Andy felt bad for snatching IMSA away from me, and he knew and respected my son Rob as a driver. Andy's California-based race team, Team Scandia, ran a series of high-powered Indy cars with some of the world's top drivers. They dominated the 1996 Indy 500. But Team Scandia also raced Ferrari prototypes in the World Sportscar Championship Series, and Andy offered Rob a job driving Ferraris for him.

Actually, the deal sounded even more fun than that. Andy had a consulting arrangement with some video game makers who were developing a racing game. "I've already taken a bunch of money from these game guys," Andy told Rob. "If you'll go be their official consulting person and help them make sure the game is built right, I'll make you a driver of my second Ferrari."

Rob, who had just graduated from the University of Arkansas with a degree in marketing, could hardly move to California fast enough. So now as I look back on those 1996 races we ran together—Daytona, Sebring, Road Atlanta, Lime Rock, Mosport—they feel a little bittersweet. Starting in 1997, he would be driving Ferraris for Andy Evans.

□ □ □ □ □

AFTER LIME ROCK, Susie and I had to return to Little Rock to face all the real life that was waiting for us there. On the divorce front, progress was frustratingly slow. The wife of Phil Dixon, my attorney, had been diagnosed with cancer, so that was throwing Phil behind. Of course I understood—but I also really needed to get this divorce done.

As for the ProStaff IPO, guess what happened: Before the big day, Ed came back to Susie and said that "the law" only allowed them to do a certain amount for her—$200,000 and a three-year contract paying her about half of what she'd been earning before. "We have to be fair to everybody," Ed said. And then he made the horrendous mistake of saying, "Susie, this is a lot of money for a girl like you."

"You've *got* to sue them," I said. We were sitting in my condo.

"*I can't*," she said. "I've got a house payment. I've got a young son. I'm driving a company car. And I'm going to tell these people to get screwed? What then? This is a job where I've been financially secure. And you're telling me to tell them to forget it? Charles, you're *married*. What am *I* going to do?"

I just looked at her. I even teared up. "You know," I said, "I never thought about it like that. Men, when they get mad, they just say screw it, and they go on and they make another life and living. But women—you're going to need the security. You're not making the right decision right now because you're afraid. And I want you to make the right decision. So I'm going to write you a check. Now, you need to call Sharon before you cash it, if we don't work out. But I want you to have this check to show you that you're going to be okay no matter what. Don't do anything out of fear. Whether we make it or not, or if you sue them or not, you're okay."

"He wrote me a check for a million dollars," Susie says. "I still have it—June eighteenth, nineteen ninety-six, check number ten-eighty. It's in my jewelry box, all folded into little pieces, the way he folded it when he gave it to me. Even at the time, it wasn't like I suddenly felt, *I've got money*. What struck me most was that Charles wanted me to hold these people accountable. Instead of making the wrong decision out of fear, he wanted me to make the right decision, based on the facts and because it was the right thing to do. They owed me. And if security was what I needed in order to do the right thing, then here it was—a check for a million dollars. And he folded it, folded it, folded it, until it was just a little square."

In the end, Susie didn't have to sue Ed Schulte. Walter Smiley, who was on Acxiom's board—and who I think was secretly in love with Susie—knew about Ed's promise of 15 percent to Susie. When we told Walter what was going on, he went to Ed and delivered the message: *If you don't do right by Susie, she's going to sue you. And I'll testify for her in court.*

Susie wound up with about $1 million in stock. After the IPO, the stock shot to about 30 dollars and then plummeted to around three, but Susie managed to sell in time to net probably $500,000. It wasn't what she was worth, but it also wasn't nothing. And she left the company with her honor intact.

□ □ □ □ □

ONE OF THE hazards of being a CEO is sleep deprivation—you sometimes lie awake obsessing about problems, counting them like sheep. And if you do sleep, you likely toss and turn dreaming fitfully of Achilles' heels.

Acxiom had several vulnerabilities that worried me. One was that we couldn't develop anything that was a totally repeatable product. We couldn't just build something and go sell it in general. The closest we came to that was our InfoBase data products. Our problem was partly technical and partly political. Technically, what worked for Citibank wouldn't work for other financial institutions, much less another kind of business like Allstate Insurance. We couldn't just shrink wrap our Citibank work and say, "Here—one size fits all." And even if we could, Citibank wouldn't stand for it.

The politics of client relationships was a fine art, one that I now spent much of my time practicing. You don't delegate the important things, and nothing was more important to Acxiom than our customers. Moreover, in a hiring market our top banking customers increasingly expected to have regular contact with the Acxiom boss. So by the mid-'90s, Rodger Kline was acting in the general capacity of a Chief Operating Officer, while I concentrated on broader issues. In addition to pursuing acquisitions and driving our core business strategy of "Lead with Data," I paid special attention to building and maintaining strong relationships with the senior executives of our top 25 accounts. I made regular trips to New York, mostly for the banks, stroking the egos of such customers as the head of global credit card operations at Citibank or Chase. I also worked at becoming a larger presence in the everyday lives of our associates. One way I did that was by developing a weekly newsletter called "Morgan's Minutes," through which I kept associates abreast of everything we were doing. I also engaged in a lot of management by walking around.

With acquired branches of the company now scattered from California to London, the "walking around" sometimes also required an airplane.

Another Achilles' heel that I worried about was our incessant need to buy more and more computers. If you're a public company you've got to grow, and we were certainly doing that. But servicing that growth was sucking up boatloads of money in computer purchases. It was this circular issue that first got us interested in the concept of "grid computing."

The idea of linking many computers to create one powerful server was pioneered in academia. Desktop computers had changed the world, but many desktop systems are used only a few hours a day. The rest of the time, they're just sitting there. It was probably some bright Ph.D who came up with the notion of linking all those computers into a network. Then when the university's data center had a big computing problem to solve, they could harness the computing power of many machines to accomplish their task. All they had to do was break down the overall job into pieces and assign each piece to a different computer. Afterwards, they would put the completed pieces back together again.

This technique gave new meaning to the phrase "divide and conquer," and by the second half of the '90s I had assigned our own Ph.D, Terry Talley, and his tech team to work on developing such a system for Acxiom.

Despite my focus on broad issues, however, I still stayed personally involved in Research & Development. I even had a desk in that department, and a couple of days a week I would abandon the CEO's office and work out of R & D to make sure I knew everything that was going on. The engineers and I talked a lot about my ongoing, obsessive work on AbiliTec.

"He worked on it all the time," Susie recalls. It's true. If I wasn't at the office or racing, I was either working on AbiliTec or *thinking* about working on it. Jane and I had agreed that I would finish up the lake house, which I had done. So on summer weekends Susie and her son and I would sometimes go up there for a couple of days. "He would get up at six in the morning, or earlier if it hit him, work on it all day long until it's time to go to bed. He wouldn't even talk sometimes. He was so focused on how to make this thing work, how to connect it, how to make it do what his vision was."

Working on AbiliTec kept me from being driven crazy by this divorce, though I'm sure I would've been working on it anyway. Today, I know that Susie was thinking, *Once the divorce is over, he'll be normal again.* She just didn't realize that this *was* normal. Whether I'm going through a divorce or not, I'm going to have a project.

I finished the first successful test of AbiliTec, the Conway prototype, in the summer of 1996. After that, I started working on Little Rock. So instead of only having to program Conway's single Zip Code, now I had to deal with the postal service's SCF (Sectional Center Facility) 722, which encompassed maybe two dozen Zip Codes.

A good way to start is with the addresses, because the key to this whole idea was for the post office to have a consistent street address numbering system. Let's say I'm processing a Charles D. Morgan who runs a business called PrivacyStar at 111 Main Street, which I think must be a good address. But it turns out somebody has mis-keyed and it's really 1111 Main Street. So now I'm going to have data about

Charles D. Morgan and PrivacyStar at two different addresses. Too many times I'll find similar names at similar addresses, and I can't automatically assume they're the same. I have to have a positive way to link them.

So the challenge is to consolidate all those fragments. If I know, through post office data, that 111 Main Street is an invalid address, I can say, "Aha, it must be 1111 Main Street." So now I've got an address error, and a name, and one other valuable piece of data—both addresses have the name PrivacyStar, and it's very unlikely that PrivacyStar is in both locations. Now I have a preponderance of evidence that says these two addresses should be consolidated. I should fix the 111 to make it 1111. Any time I see that error, I consolidate the data to the one Charles D. Morgan.

Of course you can't do this manually, for every person. That's what a prototype is—figuring out all these things in a general way so you can program it. The system has to be 100 percent automated.

I would work on the Little Rock prototype from 1996 to 1998, trying to assign a number to all the postal service's valid addresses. Believe it or not, though, the postal service makes errors, and I have to be able to deal with those, too. I can't physically go out and *look* at every address to make sure it's there. But I also can't just assume that what the postal service says is gospel, or I'm going to end up with a lot of unusable data.

The bottom line here is that no data is flawless. When I build a prototype, it won't deal with every single one of those questionable situations. But the goal isn't perfection; it's to build a prototype that does a good enough job that we can reasonably believe *this* process will get better results than our old process.

□ □ □ □ □

THE FALL OF 1996 marked a couple of major turning points. The first came in October, when my father died. He'd been ill for a long time, bedridden and hooked up to a feeding tube. As most people say in such situations, it was a blessing when he finally passed. But the death of such a central family figure inevitably shines a light on the cracks in a family's façade. Not that we had much of a façade left.

Before we took Father to the hospital for the last time, Jane asked to come to the house to say her own goodbyes. She loved my dad. She requested that I not be there when she came, and I respected that. "Carrie called me," says Jane, "and I went over there with her. Don was unconscious, but you never know what somebody can hear. Don and I were always very close, and I said my goodbyes. After he died, Charles told me I couldn't come to the funeral unless I sat on the back row with the children."

That's absolutely false. Not just false, it's ridiculous. I knew Jane cared for my father, and I wanted her at his funeral. As a matter of fact, in trying to calm the insanity surrounding the divorce, I'm almost certain I told Carrie to be sure Jane knew she was welcome. This silly story about my banning her from the funeral, or banishing her to the back row, is just Jane manipulating the kids into feeling sorry for her.

In Father's last moments, Mother, Carrie, Susie, and I were in the hospital room with him. I'd sent my plane to Missouri to pick up Speer and his wife, and they did arrive in time. Only Rob, who now lived in California, wasn't able to get there before he died.

It was the strangest thing—"a very spiritual moment," as Susie described it, and it really was. Once Speer arrived, we were all gathered around Father's bed and we took turns saying goodbye—"Dad, it's okay, you can go. It's okay." When the rest of us had said what we wanted to say, Mother held his hand and spoke to him softly: "Honey, it's okay, you can go."

Susie and I were standing at the foot of the bed. Father looked straight at me and a single tear came down his face, and he smiled that great smile of his. At that moment, the biggest windstorm you've ever heard blew up outside the hospital window. It was crazy. And at the instant Dad closed his eyes, that storm was gone. "His spirit just left this room," Susie said.

There was a service in Conway and burial at the cemetery in Fort Smith. After the graveside service, Speer and I took a drive around our old neighborhood. We didn't recognize much. Our motel house was now a car wash—in fact, our whole stretch of Highway 22 had been razed and rebuilt and reconfigured and fast-fooded and urban sprawled. Where the strip pit had been was now a mall. Our old reality now existed only in our memories.

We traded stories about Dad and all his great schemes, and we laughed a lot. But there were also sobering stories told that day: Speer reminded me that I had shoved him—several times—through the glass of our small shower, breaking it to pieces. "You were a real asshole to me when we were little," he said. I had forgotten about all that and hated hearing it.

"I'm sorry," I said.

"He expressed genuine embarrassment," Speer says today—laughingly, I might add. "I don't want to say shame, but something *like* shame about what a bully he was toward me as a kid. The truth is, I didn't particularly remember it that way. I remember us having fights and him throwing me through the shower door, but for me it never felt like I was oppressed by a bully. I just felt like it was part of reality.

"We ultimately had to come together against the rest of the neighborhood. And then I remember—I think it was my thirteenth birthday—Charles did what became more typical of him as a growing young man. I wanted a bicycle, but Father couldn't afford one, so Charles built a bicycle for me for Christmas. I mean it was a studly, well-made bike that he made out of parts. And he made it in secret. It was the best Christmas gift I ever received in my life."

That night we all—16 or 20 of us—had dinner at the Hardscrabble Country Club, where Uncle Ralph was a member. I couldn't escape the irony—here we were celebrating my dad's life in the very place that Uncle Ralph had prevented Dad from joining. I urged everyone to get whatever they wanted, and I ordered several nice bottles of wine and we toasted Dad over and over. "It was getting expensive," recalls Speer, "and I guess everybody thought Charles was going to pay. But he wasn't a member of the club, so he couldn't actually pay the bill. Anyway, at the end of the dinner Uncle Ralph made the usual noises about theoretically getting the check, and Charles said, 'Fine! Thank you, Uncle Ralph!' and got up to leave. Uncle Ralph looked a little green around the gills. I guess it was Charles' sublimated version of vengeance."

The second big turning point of that fall was that Susie and I moved in together. It was in December 1996, just before Christmas. There must've been jaws dropping all over town.

I'd first broached the subject with her in the summer. "Look," I said, "the way this divorce is going, it could drag on for years. So we've got some decisions to make. I'm pretty sure we'll get married. If we don't—if you end up throwing me out—at least you've got your million-dollar check. But in the meantime I've got my condo, you've got your house, they're both way the hell out west, far from Acxiom"—we were already in the process of moving the company headquarters from Conway to Little Rock, on the river near downtown—"so what I propose is that I buy a house in the Heights and you and your son move in with me."

She was very reluctant. "I had a lot of problems with this," says Susie, "more than I ever let on to Charles. My son, Aaron, was in the ninth grade. So this was a really hard thing for me to do. At my house, Charles absolutely could not stay the night at the beginning. I didn't let any of that go on. I wasn't going to have a situation where Aaron saw relationships come and go, and Charles respected that. Finally I talked to Aaron about Charles staying over, and he went crazy—*That's not right. You're not supposed to do this.* I just kind of backed off, and we waited until Aaron told Charles he could spend the night. That happened one night when Charles was over, and the three of us were laughing and having fun. 'If you want to stay the night sometime,' said Aaron, 'you can.'"

Now I was putting her on the spot, asking that she and Aaron *move in* with me. I understood the pressure Susie was feeling: Aaron's father wasn't at all happy about this plan, and even Susie's friends kind of thought, *Wow.* But nothing was happening in the divorce—Jane just wouldn't let go, and her lawyer wasn't about to push the thing through. "This is crazy," I said to Susie. "We can't stop our lives. *Let's do this.*" Finally I convinced her to at least discuss it with Aaron.

"I had decided it would be okay as long as, in my mind, Aaron was okay with it," says Susie. "So I had a conversation with him—I told him that sometimes people love each other and situations keep them apart, that that was the only thing keeping Charles and me from being together. 'I know it's bad and it's not right in God's eyes,' I said. 'But I'll be the one to deal with that.'"

13

THEATER
OF WAR

100101001011001010001001011001010110011

THE DEPOSITION PROCESS is a form of theater. Opposing attorneys preen and parry, while the poor subjects sometimes feel as expendable as extras in an Off-Broadway show. The supposed reason for depositions is to uncover the truth, but whose truth? In the choice of an attorney's questions, in the emphasis he places on facets of the whole, in his body language and his tone of voice, the truth can be twisted to look however *he wants* it to look.

Our divorce depositions began in earnest in 1997. There'd been a few earlier, but they were glancing blows compared to the full-on assault that now commenced. And not just against me—most of my friends and colleagues were compelled to endure unspeakable insult. "My *wife* was deposed," recalls Jim Womble. "And they were going along about Acxiom or something, and suddenly Steve Engstrom switched gears: 'Mrs. Womble,' he said, 'do you do your own laundry?'"

Jane's team even tried to subpoena Susie, in spite of the fact that she wasn't on the deposition list that both sides had agreed upon. "It was before Charles and I ever moved in together," Susie says. "I was leaving for a planning meeting when all of a sudden they met me out in front of my house at five p.m. I said, 'What do you want me for? I'm not the reason these two are getting a divorce. I'm the result, but not the reason.' Ultimately, we got it cancelled because I wasn't on the list."

I'm sure they were just trying to embarrass Susie by meeting her outside her house in front of her neighbors, who were coming home from work; it was an exercise in punishing me by punishing her.

On the first day I was deposed, Jane came to hear my testimony. Steve put on a stellar performance for her, gleefully leading me through hours of insistently prurient questioning about my liaisons with Jennifer and Cathy. I brought that part on myself, of course—I couldn't very well object to my wife's divorce attorney questioning me about those relationships. But what I *did* object to—strenuously—was the way in which it was done. Sensitive subjects weren't just covered, they were *re*-covered, *re*-approached, *re*-stressed, *re*-emphasized.

When we broke for lunch, I went over to where Steve was sitting, shuffling his papers. He's a little guy, and I'm 6-foot-3. Towering over him, I said, "Steve, you define scumbag lawyer. You're the worst excuse for a human I think I have ever come in contact with."

"You can't say that!" he said, jumping to his feet. "You've got to show me respect! Court reporter! Court reporter!" He just lost it. I calmly walked away, leaving him there waving his arms and screaming for the court reporter.

If there was any change in his manner after lunch, I'd say it was for the better, not the worse. I felt like he toned it down a bit. Maybe I frightened him some. You just don't do what I did.

Speaking of the theatrical nature of depositions, maybe some of the acting is in the eye of the beset beholder. Just as I felt that Steve was working me over for Jane's benefit, Jane felt that *I* was overdoing it to injure her. "By now my contact with Charles was just through lawyers and through a couple of depositions," Jane recalls. "In one of them, he proceeded to tell about taking the woman that he left me for to New York and taking her to Victoria's Secret and what all he bought her—with me sitting there. He had to go into great detail about everything he bought her at

Victoria's Secret. Steve wasn't asking him all those questions. I thought Charles was embellishing to rub it in."

I don't remember *ever* taking *anyone* to Victoria's Secret, so when I heard Jane had accused me of this I found it hard to believe I'd committed perjury for the purpose of incriminating myself. Sure enough, I didn't. I have confirmation that the words *Victoria's Secret* appear nowhere in my deposition. Instead, I think this tells us a great deal about Jane's mindset at the time: "Victoria's Secret" is a veritable cliché of the unfaithful husband. It also may tell us a thing or two about the flame-fanning counsel she was receiving from her attorney.

"It was getting very nasty," says Susie. "Steve Engstrom was clicking the clock away, and there were times when the kids, especially Carrie, and Jane got mad at each other. Then there were times when Jane would tell Carrie what Charles was saying in a deposition and Carrie would call Charles out on it—*'Why are you doing that to Mom?'* There was a lot going on that I tried to stay out of. But it was becoming constant, and Charles' original lawyer had a wife who was dying and things just kept getting put off."

Meanwhile, Susie and I were trying to blend a family without being married. I'd had the bright idea of our joining the Country Club of Little Rock. In hindsight, I see that this could've been like throwing ourselves into the lion's den—all those "proper" society types just waiting to chew up sinners like us, people who step out of line. But it went well. If they chewed us up, they did it the traditional way—behind our backs.

The Country Club membership was full, but they said there might be "an accommodation" for me. I was going to be the member, but I wanted Susie and Aaron to have full privileges like they were family. In that case, both Susie and I had to be approved as though we were man and wife. The vetting process was hilarious. We had to go to dinner with 12 members, who grilled us politely. In order for us to be approved, all 12 members had to vote yes.

"Well, Charles," one member said, "why do you want to join the country club?"

"I want a nice quiet place to go have dinner with Susie where people won't bug me."

"What about golf?"

"I don't play golf."

"Okay, so you just want to have a nice place to go to dinner."

"Well," I said, "Susie's son Aaron probably does play golf a little bit, and he might also want to use the swimming pool sometimes."

They asked Susie all these questions about herself—her background, her college years, her pageant history. At one point it began to sound like some kind of cheesy celebrity interview: "Susie, what are your likes and dislikes?"

It was a totally bizarre evening, but I'm proud to say we passed with the proverbial flying colors. They seemed genuinely happy to have us there.

Personally, except for the looming presence of the divorce from hell, I thought our life together was going well. The house was beautiful, and I even got on the computer and designed a new addition, a garage cantilevered out over the ravine leading down to the river, which we then commissioned to be built. It was another project I could lose myself in for a while.

Susie's view of our life together was more conflicted. "When we moved in with Charles, I told Aaron, 'Don't let this be something that you worry about.' I wanted to make sure he didn't carry that burden. But Aaron's father let it be known that *he* didn't like it and that he wouldn't condone it to Aaron. Anyway, what happened is that after ninth grade, Aaron went to live with his father in Cabot, a few miles northeast of Little Rock. It almost killed me. I thought, *Oh, it's because I've moved in with Charles. I'm a marked woman. He's not happy here. He didn't want this.*

"But in his young way, Aaron said, 'Mom, I've spent all this time with you and not Dad. Now you have someone, and I need to go be with Dad so he's not alone. I want to be at Cabot High School. I want to play football there—I know we can win the championship my senior year.'"

And he did—in fact, Aaron quarterbacked his team to the 5A state championship in both his junior *and* senior years. Susie and I went to his games, often sitting with Susie's ex.

"Looking back," says Susie, "I think it all turned out for the best. But at the time, there were moments when I was really depressed. I still watched over Aaron from afar. I made sure he was taken care of. I even followed him to Australia to watch him play in the Down Under Bowl. I tried to be there for his events, but it was hard because Charles has a busy life. And I was traveling around being the girlfriend of a CEO."

MY BRILLIANT CAREER as a race car driver ended suddenly on March 15, 1997, at Sebring—15 minutes before I would've officially retired. Rob was now driving Ferraris for Andy Evans, and Andy was never the best manager in the world. With Andy, the all-important crew chief job tended to be handed around to different people; Andy could also be chaotic when it came to drivers. He would hire them, get mad at them, and fire them. He was very helter-skelter.

Perhaps because of that, a driving position for his Ferrari team became available for a portion of the 1997 race season, and Andy turned to me. Six weeks before Sebring, Rob and I had driven at the 24 Hours of Daytona with Andy and a fine Spanish driver named Fermin Velez. In fact, Rob and I almost won the thing, ending up with the second-place trophy. After 24 hours of racing, we missed winning by about a minute.

Now came the 12 Hours of Sebring, a race that starts at 10 a.m. and finishes at 10 p.m. In 1997, I was 54 years old. My eyes weren't what they'd once been, especially at night, and I had decided that this would be my last race. No point in pushing yourself beyond the law of averages.

The venerable Sebring International Raceway was, I felt, an appropriate place to hang it up. One of the oldest road-course auto racing tracks in the United States, it had seen all the greats. The 12 Hours at Sebring, my final race, was one of the legs in the "unofficial triple crown of endurance racing"—the 24 Hours of Le Mans and the 24 Hours of Daytona being the others. Andy was fielding two Ferraris at Sebring that day, and I was to be the second driver in the second car.

By about 6 p.m., I had driven several legs of the race, and I felt great about it. We were in good position. But I'd told the team I didn't want to drive at night, so I had five laps to go before we changed drivers—five laps and it would be a wrap.

I tried not to let my mind dwell on that—*five laps, five laps, five laps*—but the words were practically shouting inside my head. Suddenly, as I was entering Sebring's infamous 17th turn, I saw a guy in a Porsche driving erratically ahead of me. This is a 130-mile-an-hour right-hand turn, at a spot in the course where three cars can fit side by side. But this guy was on the far left of the track looking like something was wrong, like maybe something was happening to his car. Having no idea what he was going to do, I slowed down significantly—way more than you want to do on a racetrack where cars are coming up behind you at really high speeds. But I didn't want to be anywhere near this Porsche if there was trouble. So I braked. I wanted to give him plenty of room.

The next second he jerked the steering wheel hard right and drove across the track in front of me! I did the only thing I could do—I absolutely T-boned the son of a bitch in Andy's million-dollar Ferrari. I was still doing 80 when I hit him, so of course the Ferrari was torn to hell. And I broke my hand. It was the only time in my whole racing career that I broke a bone. Eighteen years of racing, five laps to go, and that's how I ended it.

But it had been a good run. While I would get behind the wheel a few more times after this, never again would it be at the level of my professional IMSA years. In IMSA GT class, I finished my official racing career ranked third in the all-time driver point standings. I had 19 IMSA career victories, including one class win in the 24 Hours of Daytona, and two class wins in the 12 Hours of Sebring. Yes, it was a *very* good run, if I say so myself.

□ □ □ □ □

IN MAY OF 1997 we went to Paris for Susie's birthday. Carrie went with us, which was major progress on the *other* side of the blended-family equation. "I always felt like Charles' kids wouldn't have a problem accepting me because I wasn't why he left their mother," says Susie, "so I never felt bad looking his kids in the eye. But Carrie was really an emotional rollercoaster during that first year Charles and I were together. She would be, I*'m not ready to see you with somebody else,* and then she'd be okay. For a while it would be kind of a good experience—then he'd be taking me somewhere and she would be upset that he was spending his money on me. I don't know what Jane was telling her.

"Rob probably had some of the same feelings but didn't show it—because I saw him more, going to the races. He was friendly but reserved. *I've got to find a way to talk to you,* I thought, so I worked at it. And he would be friendly and even laugh some. But I sensed that he felt guilty because of his mother. Racing had been something *she* did with them—it was *their* family thing.

"Finally, though, I just disconnected myself from the situation. I realized I could've been *anybody*. With Carrie, it wasn't personal, it wasn't *me*. She just didn't feel like she had a good relationship with her dad, and another person was in there so she felt insecure."

"I didn't trust her," says Carrie, speaking of her relationship with Susie back then. "But, you know, I'm now about her like I think my stepdaughter is about me. When my husband and I separated for a while two years ago, Rod's daughter came to my house and hung out with me. 'Isn't he an asshole?' she said. '*Please* don't go away—I love you.' I think that's probably what would happen now with me about Susie. She's a kindred spirit, and he needs her."

I don't know exactly when Carrie made that leap—maturity can be a wonderful thing. But even by May of 1997, when she was just months shy of turning 30, she'd mellowed enough to want to accompany Susie and me on this trip to Europe. Carrie's life was full of turbulence at the moment—she was divorcing her first husband and was in love with a married man. Maybe all of that made Europe look especially appealing. And maybe she felt that Susie and I would be less judgmental than others might be.

"I went to Europe much to my mother's horror," says Carrie. "At that point, she and I were in about a six-month period when we didn't speak to each other. She was horrified that I had 'followed in my dad's footsteps,' meaning my divorce. She loved my ex-husband. And she didn't know Susie. To Susie's credit, she tried very hard because she was real anxious about being with a man who had adult children. I think his inviting me on that trip was probably at her suggestion. Also, I speak French."

We were staying at the George V hotel, just off the Champs-Elysees. And on the morning of May 31st, Susie's birthday, Carrie had breakfast sent to Susie's and my room. It was an especially sweet gesture, given what was about to happen.

As we were eating breakfast, I pushed back from the table and said to Susie, 'I think we need to talk about this relationship.' She suddenly looked like a deer in the headlights—she had no idea where this was going. "I thought, *Oh my God*," she recalls, "*he brought me over here to dump me.*"

"I want us to get married," I said. Of course I had to qualify my proposal because of the never-ending divorce. But I wanted to marry Susie the moment I was free—even if I was a doddering old man by then. And I wanted her to know it.

"Dad had tipped me off a day or two before that he was going to do that," recalls Carrie. "I remember thinking, *Oh gosh, wouldn't you have wanted to do that when you weren't with your damn kid? What an absolutely romantic proposal in the most romantic city in the world—I kind of wish I wasn't bugging you guys.* They were so—and I still see flashes of this now—they were *so* in love. They were just absolutely giddy and silly and spontaneous, and I had never seen my father like that."

We spent much of the day wandering around Paris looking at engagement rings. "I was not about to let him buy me a ring at Cartier," says Susie. "I mean it was *ridiculous.*" So we agreed to look for the right diamond once we got home. But just to make the proposal indelible, I got down on one knee in front of Notre Dame and asked her again. Carrie photographed the moment for posterity.

□ □ □ □ □

DOMESTIC ISSUES ASIDE—like that was possible during this period—I still had a business to run. This divorce coincided with the most dramatic growth in Acxiom's history. Between 1990 and the year 2000, our customer base and revenue increased approximately tenfold, while the amount of data we were managing probably rose by a factor of a thousand. At the office, we were all stretched to the breaking point.

I continued to strive to grow the company, and one way to do was to make the right acquisitions. One company I was especially high on was Chicago-based May & Speh, a large, family owned business that did the same thing we did; we felt there was a lot of synergy between the two companies. Not only did May & Speh have technology and people, they had an excellent customer set—some big banks, plus Sears and Montgomery Ward and General Motors. We thought this would be a great fit for us, so we started laying the groundwork. Though the deal was only in the conceptual stage, we knew it would probably turn out to be our largest acquisition to date.

In 1997 we were also busy forging various "partnerships." One interesting one was with Oracle, the giant technology company founded by Larry Ellison. Oracle was building what it called "Data Mart Suites," designed to help its customers zero in on the most profitable segments of the consumer population. In a press release announcing overwhelming support for the product, Acxiom's role was described this way: "For companies that want to build a customer-focused, decision-support data mart suite, Acxiom Corporation will be a strategic partner to provide external consumer support data such as age, income level, occupation, marital status, etc., to enhance the Oracle database."

Sometime during our dealings with Oracle, my corporate counsel and I flew out to California to meet with Larry Ellison. Redwood City, where Oracle is based, is 27 miles south of San Francisco on the San Francisco Peninsula. This is considered Silicon Valley north now, and Ellison's property encompasses a vast swath of what must be some of the most expensive real estate in America. However many acres he has, his compound is surrounded by a very high wooden fence. You can't see in at all. You just pull up to this high board gate and there's a callbox that you talk into; we had instructions, so we knew what to do.

Once we announced ourselves, a male voice soon confirmed that we were expected and told us to enter through the gate, which was at that moment starting to open. We were then to drive to a parking lot, where someone would pick us up. Winding through lush woods, we eventually arrived at a lot that would accommodate probably 50 cars. Ours was the only one there.

Soon a golf cart came tootling up with one guy in it. He introduced himself as the head of security. "Mr. Ellison is still in his quarters," he said, "but he'll be ready in a minute. I'll drive you there." We climbed in and went through more woods and down a hill and emerged in what looked like a scene from a Japanese woodblock print—beautiful garden, graceful trees, a big pond. Larry's house was small, low, and sleek, and it was connected by a covered walkway to another structure, the meeting and entertainment facility. This was where we would be meeting. As we entered, the head of security instructed us to remove our shoes and put on slippers.

This room looked to be about 30 by 30, with a cute kitchen and other amenities, and on three sides it was glass. Beyond the window was the pond with a big waterfall, maybe two. It was really a beautiful little private world. In about five minutes we saw Larry approaching under the covered walkway in his black turtleneck sweater. I had met him before, and he greeted us graciously. "It's such a beautiful day," he said, "why don't we go out and talk in the yard under the tree."

It sounded like a lovely idea, but first we had to take off our inside slippers and put on outside slippers. That's when my corporate counsel got bitten by a brown recluse spider hiding in the outside slipper. But other than that, it was a total Zen experience. At one point I caught myself thinking that Larry Ellison's life sure seemed a lot more serene than mine.

"Charles was distracted," says Cindy Childers, remembering me in that period. Cindy should know. As the scorching summer of 1997 crawled to a close, it appeared inevitable that this divorce case was headed to trial in the fall. My attorneys had long since realized that this wasn't just a domestic dispute; it was about money, which meant stock—which meant if I were to lose this thing, Acxiom itself could be significantly impacted. So we had furloughed a couple of Acxiom people to work fulltime with our attorneys to counteract Jane's financial claims against the company. Cindy Childers was one of those Acxiom people.

"We worked in the Little Rock office of Charles' family lawyer, Phil Dixon, putting together 'the Acxiom story,' says Cindy. "Then, every day at six p.m. I would go to Charles' house and brief him on our progress. There was an upstairs room at his house that we used as a kind of situation room."

It wasn't going well. Phil Dixon's wife was really ill now, and he had turned much of the work over to a young attorney in his firm. This poor guy just seemed lost at Kmart. Things weren't happening as fast, or as well, as they should've been, and I didn't like my chances with this lawyer going up against Steve Engstrom. In early fall, when Phil finally told me straight out that he wouldn't be able to take this case to trial himself, I said, "What the hell do I do now?"

"Call Jerry Jones," he said. Jerry was a litigator at Little Rock's Rose Law Firm. A few years earlier, Phil and Jerry had faced off in one of the most high-profile divorces in the state—that of Jack Stephens, principal at the financial powerhouse Stephens, Inc., against his wife Mary Anne, who had left Jack for football coach Don Shula. Jerry represented Jack, Phil represented Mary Anne. "Jerry's an excellent lawyer," Phil said. "He doesn't take many divorce cases, but he really knows what he's doing."

I picked up the phone and called Jerry. His secretary said he was in Virginia taking a deposition and couldn't be interrupted. That wasn't going to work for me. I explained my situation with what I'm sure was a strained mix of charm and agitation. "My secretary insisted that I take the call," says Jerry. "She knew not to *ever* interrupt me in a deposition, but she was so insistent that I agreed to talk with Charles. I said look, I'd love to help you but I don't know that I can because this three-and-a-half-month antitrust case I'm working on is set to go to trial in a month and a half. And if it stays on track, I just cannot get involved in your matter. But the defendants want a continuance, which I'm going to contest. If the judge gives it to them, *then* I'll get involved.

"Well, a couple of days later the judge granted a continuance. So I went over to Charles' house, I think on a Saturday, and spent most of the day with him and took his case. I just jumped into it. The guys who'd been working with Phil were able to help get me up to speed very rapidly, and Cindy Childers was also very, very helpful."

I felt better with Jerry onboard. For one thing, he brought fresh eyes to this two-year-old problem. "It had gotten bitter," Jerry recalls. "The parties were entrenched. There was a wide gap between them and how they wanted it to turn out. I was able to look at the case very objectively and to start figuring out a path and some alternatives on how we could try the case. Because I really thought at that point that this case was going to get tried.

"Before I got involved in the case, Charles' team—and I'm not being critical—had been really focused on yes, no, or maybe regarding the financial support that Jane's family had given—the core of her case. *Okay*, I thought, *we've got to have something to counter that.* So our opposing contention was that all the money in the world can't create a successful company—that it was the unique genius and capabilities of Charles and the team that he'd put together that led to the success of the company. What a chancery judge does in these matters is try to find an equitable decision. So they're strongly guided by legal principles, but they get to apply equitable principles as well. So even if Jane prevailed on the money side of this, I wanted there to be a countervailing argument. That's what I really got focused on—how do we create all this other stuff? That's what I asked Cindy Childers to take a lot of responsibility in. She was working as my paralegal to take responsibility of putting together the story."

From then on, in the evening briefings it was Jerry, Cindy, Susie, and me. "Charles spent a lot of time crunching data," recalls Cindy. "Showing who contributed to the wealth generation—and also whose hand Acxiom was going to benefit most from in the future, because who made everything happen? So we put together the hours that Charles worked, the relationships he had, everything you can imagine in terms of his contribution to the company. It was quite amazing."

It was also frustrating, exhausting, exasperating, and debilitating. Finally, this divorce had taken over my life. But with Jerry there, at least I knew he understood. Beyond his brilliance as a legal strategist, he also had a feel for the intense human issues beneath the case's give and take. "These two people *needed* to be divorced," Jerry says. "They had grown apart. And so in essence they were asking for their future, both of them. They wanted their future. They had gotten married at a fairly early age and they had been married for quite some time, but they had grown apart. And when I say they wanted their future, that's what I know Charles wanted. Charles was my client, and he wanted to move to the next chapter of his life as rapidly as he could."

□ □ □ □ □

THAT AUGUST, I stole away for a few days, leaving both divorce and business behind. Rob had phoned to tell me that Andy Evans' Scandia Race Team had cut a deal with Ron Fellows, a legendary driver and a national hero in his native Canada, to drive with Rob at Mosport in August. This was not just the Canadian track where Rob and I had beat out the Oldsmobile factory team to notch Oldsmobile's 100th IMSA victory; this was also Ron Fellows' home track. The Ferraris weren't the fastest cars in this race, but with Ron sharing the driving, Rob felt they had a great chance to win. I told him I would definitely be there to cheer him on.

About five days before the race, I got a call from Andy Evans. He was cussing and carrying on about "this asshole crew chief" of his that he'd just fired. "I want you to be the crew chief for the race at Mosport," he said. I told him sure, I was going to be there anyway, and I certainly felt competent to act as crew chief. "Count me in," I said.

Crew chief for a racing team is a big responsibility. While it's a collaborative effort, the crew chief is the strategist and the organizer. He decides who drives first and who drives second, and who qualifies. He oversees the engineers and approves any major changes to the car. He makes sure he has the right people going "over the wall," which means servicing the car during a pit stop. The crew chief is the general manager of the race team with absolute control over everything.

This wasn't a big step for me—I had done all of these jobs with my own team in the early days. The only thing that made this kind of a step was that it was a big race event and a lot of the top international drivers would be there. That meant the media would be out in force. But I didn't overthink it.

On the day of qualifying, Ron Fellows did a brilliant job and put the Ferrari in the pole position—the first time all year that Ferrari had started at the head of the pack. Of course Ron's a very talented driver, and this was his racetrack. Rob was much slower than Ron at first, and I caught myself with a nagging worry as I watched him scream through the turns. Rob didn't know the track as well as Ron, but by the last session he was running nearly as fast. *Thank you, God*, I thought. We had a really strong team here.

I figured the race would last two-and-a-half, three hours. I needed to run both drivers, of course, and we could go for 40 or 50 minutes between fuel stops. So this became the framework for our strategic decisions. We would have maybe three fuel stops, which is a good time to change drivers since the car's already in the pits. But I didn't want to change drivers every 40 minutes. So what we decided was, any time after an hour and 15 minutes, if we had a yellow flag we would change drivers. Or we could change at the second fuel stop, which could be a little past an hour and a half.

The crowds were there to see their hero Ron Fellows, so we agreed that Ron would start. That meant Rob might end up driving a little less than Ron overall. On the other hand, we knew there was a good chance for a yellow flag, so maybe Rob would get in sooner. In any case, all agreed that this was a good strategy.

Ron Fellows had put us in the pole position. Now he went out and attacked the track again, holding the lead through the first fuel stop. Then he came in for a quick refueling before peeling back out, still ahead.

At about the halfway point in the race, we had a yellow flag. It was a long one, maybe 15 minutes. Ron was still leading, but according to our plan it was time to change drivers. When the media saw Rob head back onto the track, they got all over me. "What the hell are you doing?" "You've got the best driver in Canada and you put your son in?" "Are you trying to lose this race?"

"Everything's under control," I said. "We've got a strategy. We've got a strategy that I think's going to win."

They didn't want to hear it. "You're just putting your son in because he's your son!" one reporter said. I was beginning to wish I'd worn a bulletproof vest.

In fact, now I was sweating bullets. By the time Rob roared out of the pits, we had lost the lead. Rob is an excellent driver, but this was a whole new dynamic for the two of us. *Please, God,* I thought, *don't let him get out there and screw up*.

Rob probably did the best driving job of his career that day. With three laps to go, we were in second place. But the first-place car, another of Andy Evans' Ferraris—this one driven by the Spanish ace Fermin Velez—ran out of fuel! At that point, James Weaver, driving a Dyson team Ford, made a strong effort to beat Rob to the finish line. But Rob wouldn't yield, sprinting to the checkered flag. Here's a write-up from IMSA describing the race:

FELLOWS WINS MOSPORT FEATURE

31 August, 1997

BOWMANVILLE, Ontario, Canada—Ron Fellows of Oakville, Ontario and Rob Morgan of Conway, Ark. did something Sunday no other drivers had been able to do since September, 1964—drive a Ferrari to victory at Mosport.

Fellows who had put the Acxiom Ferrari 333SP on the pole Friday, built a strong lead early in the two-hour Exxon World SportsCar championship race before turning the car over to team-mate Rob Morgan. It appeared that Fellows and Morgan would have to settle for second place but the... Ferrari of Fermin Velez ran out of fuel with just three laps remaining, giving the race to Fellows and Morgan.

In hindsight, I'm just glad I wasn't the crew chief who allowed Fermin Velez's car to run out of gas.

□ □ □ □ □

RETURNING TO LITTLE Rock felt like marching to my execution. The divorce was really starting to wear on me. I got furious every time I read depositions that didn't reflect the way it really was. *'This isn't what she said!'* I was constantly having to re-live Jane's and my life together, and it was killing me.

Even Susie seemed to be approaching the breaking point. "This was right at the time that Oprah was trying to get Charles to come be on her show," she says, "so this thing was getting bigger and bigger and I was a person in it—I was *with* the person this was happening to, but for me it was like an out-of-body experience. I had no control. My son wasn't living with me and I didn't have a job anymore, because I needed to be ready to go when Charles wanted to go. So in the middle of all this, I no longer knew who I was. And then right around Halloween of nineteen ninety-seven, the article appeared."

The Article—in my world, the very words have become fraught with meaning. It shouldn't even have been able to happen, but it did. And there are definitely two ways to look at it.

Our court documents were sealed. Various reporters had tried to get them opened through the Freedom of Information Act, but the judge had been steadfast in her resolve—the documents were not to be seen by the public. So how did those documents find their way into an inflammatory article in a local tabloid newspaper called *Arkansas Times*?

"It was awful," says Susie. "I mean, *hurtful.* It talked about Charles jetting off with different women. Some of that was me, some of it wasn't. It talked about his affairs with Jennifer and Cathy, and it reported some of Jane's medical history. *Oh yuck,* I thought. It was full-blown exposure, and all this stuff was supposed to have been sealed."

The article was titled "For Richer, For Poorer." When I saw it, I was livid—and, of course, embarrassed. That had to be the point. I can't prove it, but I suspect that Jane's attorney leaked those documents to the *Times* editor, who wrote the story. I stomped around for a while, and then I thought, *What the hell, all my dirty laundry is flapping in the wind for all to see. Might as well have a drink.* So I called a bunch of friends, including Jennifer and her husband, and invited them over to the house for cocktails. It was quite the festive party. It felt like the air had been let out of something.

What happened next is a story best told by Jerry Jones:

"I remember I was having lunch in the River Market when I saw the *Arkansas Times* article on a newsstand," says Jerry. "I read it and thought, Well, this is unfortunate, that some of these things are being said publicly.

"Then that night I was driving somewhere when I started putting together the path to settlement. After you've been trying lawsuits for a long time, you get a real good feel of how things could come together if you nudge them in a certain direction.

"In my gut, it took me thirty minutes or so to get there, but then I absolutely knew, Okay, we've got three or four days to get this thing resolved. Because from Charles' perspective, hey, it's all out there. From Jane's perspective, she's kind of gotten her pound of his flesh. I just thought okay, there's been a lot of emotion in this case. Let's use this as an opportunity.

"Steve Engstrom was the lawyer on the other side, and, frankly, I can't recall whether I called Steve or he called me. But I know that I said, 'Steve, we ought to try to get this case settled. I think there's a way to bridge the gap. I think if you and I work closely together, our clients can find a reasonable range to get this resolved. But if we're going to do it, we've got to do it in a hurry.'

"So we ended up getting the Brooks and the Baxter conference rooms at Little Rock's Capital Hotel. Of course, those rooms have historical significance because of the Brooks-Baxter political war, where they were actually firing cannons at each other here in Little Rock. It was after the Civil War. There was a dispute over who was going to be our governor and they actually had a little war out here. And I thought, That's perfect. One team was in one room, and the other team was in the other.

"We did it on Sunday. The hotel had their Sunday brunch downstairs. It was very good. And then we went upstairs and negotiated all afternoon and into the evening. As I recall, Jane was there. So was Charles. And we had the accountants and the numbers guys and all that.

"We didn't quite get it done. We were close, but we didn't get it done. And I remember driving back to Charles' house that night with him and we were both a bit disappointed. Jane wanted more and Charles wanted to give her less. We narrowed the gap, but we weren't quite there.

"So the next morning, Monday, Steve Engstrom called me and he was kind of sighing: Oh, it's a shame we couldn't get this done. Yeah, I said, it is. Because these folks both need a divorce. And it's down to money. 'How are we going to get this thing done?' Steve said. I said, 'Let me think about it and I'll call you back.'

"Which I did, a little bit later. 'Steve,' I said, 'you and I are going to have to take some risks. I'm going to give you a number that I don't have the authority to give you. And I'm going to ask you to go to Jane to get her to say yes to that number. If she will say yes to that number, I'll get Charles Morgan to say yes to it. But you do not want me to have to go to him first. You've got to do what I'm saying, okay?'

"Steve saw that. He got it. Steve's a very, very good lawyer, and a very, very bright guy. And I said, 'Also, for us to get this done, you're going to have to pull back the nasty pleadings that you filed.' Late on the previous Friday afternoon, he had filed something that, as I recall, was very inflammatory. I don't even remember what it said. I just know it was something that was fueling the fire. If that came out, if it hit the press, then all bets were off—we were going to trial. But the press hadn't picked up on it yet. 'Well,' Steve said, 'I don't know how I'll do that.' 'That's your problem,' I said.

"So Steve did what I requested of him, and Jane said yes to the number, whatever it was—I don't remember. 'I'm good with that number,' I said. 'But you've still got to get those pleadings out of the file.' 'How am I going to do that?' he said. Again, I said I had no idea, but that it had to be done—that was a condition to this settlement.

"So Steve calls me back about an hour later. He'd jumped in his car and set a land speed record from Little Rock to Conway. 'Okay,' he said, 'I got them.' I think he'd told the judge that the pleadings had mistakenly been filed before they should've been. 'Good,' I said. 'We're done.'

"Now I called Charles. 'Charles,' I said, 'you're getting divorced tomorrow.' He said, What? And I said here's the deal—we agreed to this. He said something like, 'Well, you didn't have the authority to do that.' 'I know,' I said, 'but you're getting divorced tomorrow.'

"At the end of that conversation, I wasn't sure if he'd ever speak to me again. But I knew that after he calmed down, he would be pleased. I knew that. I also knew that if I had gone to him and said, 'This is the number it's going to take to get this thing resolved,' it would have taken a superhuman effort for him to be able to say yes to it, psychologically. He needed Jane to come in his direction instead of the other way."

As is often the case with memory, my recollection of these events varies slightly from Jerry's. My memory, and Susie concurs, is that the whole business about "the number" was acted out during that Sunday's epic exercise in shuttle diplomacy at the Capital Hotel. I remember being annoyed with Jerry when he presented me the number. I also recall having great doubt that Steve Engstrom would follow through with the crucial condition of removing the offensive filing. *That* was why I didn't feel happy about our prospects on the drive home.

But early the next week, Jerry phoned to say it was a done deal. Even then I wasn't sure. "So I was kind of sitting around in my office," recalls Jerry, "and an hour later, maybe two hours later, Sharon Tackett called. 'Jerry,' she said, 'we're having a party at Charles' house. He wanted to know if you're free to come have a drink.'

"*Whew*, I thought. *Whew!*"

14

DAWN OF
THE LOST
DECADE

100101001011001010001001011001010110011

SUSIE AND I were married six months later—May 1, 1998. Our wedding took place in the beautiful E. Fay Jones-designed Thorncrown Chapel in Eureka Springs, in northwest Arkansas. Fay Jones was an Arkansas boy who had apprenticed with the legendary Frank Lloyd Wright, and Jones' chapel blends elements of Wright's Prairie School architecture with a very modernist point of view. Constructed of native wood and stone and some 6,000 square feet of glass, Thorncrown looks like a soaring open-air pavilion but is in fact fully enclosed. It was this open look—this utter transparency—that attracted Susie and me to Thorncrown to take our vows.

For our honeymoon, a friend recommended Cabo San Lucas at the southern tip of Mexico's Baja Peninsula. And so began a chapter of our lives that has become interwoven with all the other succeeding chapters, and that continues to this day. Susie and I both fell in love with Cabo. It's beautiful, dramatic, peaceful, and *close*.

But we didn't go down there planning to buy property; during our honeymoon, looking at real estate was just an enjoyable way of getting to know the area.

It all started when we met a realtor, Bernard, who was selling condos; he showed us various properties along the coast. At the end of our trip we told him we would probably be back in the fall, maybe at Thanksgiving, and would call him to find us a place to stay. We did, and he did, and during our Thanksgiving visit Bernard also showed us about 20 houses, both old and new, and several parcels of land. By now, Susie and I were generally committed to at least the idea of having a vacation home in Cabo. "But I don't want to spend more than a million, a million-and-a-half," I told Bernard. "I certainly don't want to *build* in Mexico."

What do you think happened? Of *course* we ended up building in Mexico. But that sentence hardly begins to describe our immersion in the place.

We looked at houses along the southern coast and even as far east as San Jose. We looked on the beach, away from the beach, at houses with a view, at houses without a view. Nothing felt right. I particularly worried about the security of beach property—*anyone* could pull their boat up in the dark of night and be right in our space in no time flat. More and more, I was leaning toward something in a protected community. That just made the most sense, especially since we wouldn't be there all the time.

"Well," said Bernard, "there is this one lot that just became available in Pedregal." Pedregal, we now knew, was the original luxury residential community in Cabo. Situated at the tip of the peninsula, it offered a 360-degree cliff view of the Pacific washing into the Sea of Cortez. The famous Land's End rock arch was just sitting out there beyond the bottom of your cocktail glass, almost as an afterthought. "This piece of property has been around for a while," said Bernard, "but they've just dropped the price. A lot of people are looking at it, but I think you can get it for six hundred ninety-nine thousand dollars. It's probably the last best cliff lot in the whole area."

"Well," I said, "I'm not going to build, but I don't mind looking at it." So we drove over there and parked the car and walked to the edge of this high, sheer cliff—it was 240 feet above the sea. The view was spectacular. Land's End was *right there*. The lot faced due south, so you wouldn't have glaring sun either morning or night to make you miserable. The lot was huge, and someone had cut into it already. You could almost build on it as it was.

I looked at Susie and she looked at me. We were both thinking the same thing: *Oh my God, now we're screwed.*

The next day I offered $675,000 for the lot, and within two days it was ours. Now what? I had no idea. How was I going to build a house on a drop-off like that? What were we thinking?

Then a friend in Little Rock put me in touch with a lawyer pal of his who'd had work done in Cabo by a pair of brothers, Antonio and Jorge Carrera. Antonio was an architect and Jorge was a civil engineer and a builder. "They're really good, and also really good guys," the lawyer said. "I'll be glad to help you negotiate a contract with them."

"I don't want a contract to build," I said. "I just want to contract with them to *design* the house, so I can see if I like it." And that's what we did. I was absolutely knocked out by their work—these guys in Mexico were using 3D AutoCAD, a computer program that allows you to see your design in three dimensions before you build it. *I* was using AutoCAD, but I hadn't even seen architects in Little Rock using it at that time. These brothers were in their 30s, though, so they were very well versed in all the modern tools. I was impressed watching them work out and work through the various permutations of these house plans. And since I knew AutoCAD, Susie and I were able to discuss the fine points with them without difficulty.

The house the Carrera brothers designed was amazing, and they very much wanted to build it. It would be the largest and probably the most complicated house they'd ever built, because by the time we finished the plans the house encompassed a total of 31,000 square feet, including decks and terraces, on five levels descending the side of a steep cliff. It looked like a hillside village. The main entrance was at street level, and three stories down was the second garage entrance. I wanted this as an extra garage for other vehicles, and for the help; that would be the level where the people who worked for us would enter. Right beside and above that second garage would be the caretaker's home.

I told Antonio and Jorge that I wanted them to get the caretaker's house finished first, so Susie and I could stay there during construction of the main house, which would take probably a year and a half longer to build. We were willing to live with the dust and the noise as long as the house was tightly sealed. And that way, we could watch over the construction process. So I worked out an incentive plan with them, with payments upon completion of various segments of the whole job.

Crazily enough, Antonio and Jorge were so good, and so motivated, that it was probably the easiest house I've ever built. We started construction in mid-1999, and Susie and I were able to spend Christmas of 2000 in our new house. We named it Villa la Roca. As I write this, it's been our special hideaway for 14 years. And as you'll soon see, in times to come we very much needed a hideaway.

□ □ □ □ □

ON THAT PORTENTOUS note, we leap forward to the start of the next decade, the 2000s. Cindy Childers calls the 2000s "The Lost Decade" at Acxiom, and while I hate to think of it in those terms, I suppose she has a point. After the amazing growth of the '90s, when our revenue shot from $100 million to $1 billion annually, the 2000s felt somehow jinxed. What went wrong? So many things, most beyond my control—but not all. As a company, we had never led a charmed life. We'd worked hard to create our breaks. But now it was as though some dark force had come home to roost. And I didn't even see it coming.

Why would I have? Leading into the Millennium decade, we had accomplished remarkable things. By May 1998, we were in our new headquarters building on the Arkansas River in Little Rock. We'd moved there partly because of our increasing need for workers; we knew that a lot of the kinds of people we wanted to hire lived in Little Rock and wouldn't want to make the round-trip to Conway every day. Also, I now lived in Little Rock, though that didn't have anything to do with it. Well, maybe a little bit.

Of course, moving our executive offices to Little Rock created some problems for people who lived in Conway—Sharon Tackett, for example. "I wouldn't say I was furious at him," says Sharon, "but I was really aggravated. But I couldn't very well complain about wear and tear on my car—Charles bought me a new one!"

By August of 1998, we had finalized our largest acquisition ever, Chicago's May & Speh, for $625 million in stock. "Acxiom and May & Speh are complementary data management businesses with similar vision, strategic focus, and business culture," said I in the press release announcing the merger.

Also, by 1999 we had finished building the AbiliTec program, and I was spearheading a topnotch development team to take this revolutionary concept to the next level—integrating it into our existing systems. Once that was accomplished, AbiliTec would finally allow us the *ability* to give the banks the five years of monthly credit data that they'd been dreaming of for more than a decade.

In 1999 we had also announced the commissioning of a new 12-story, $35 million office building in the River Market district of downtown Little Rock—a modernist symbol of our increasingly impressive success. Anyone looking at us from the outside would've thought we were poised for yet another brilliant decade.

In short order, though, the complexities of our achievements began to reveal themselves. Despite the ostensible "complementary" nature of May & Speh with Acxiom, we soon ran into difficulties. It wasn't just a conflict between Chicago and Arkansas. Family-owned May & Speh had a patriarchal culture, totally different from us from top to bottom. That resulted in considerable head butting. Acxiom in 1999 was a company of 5,000 people, including our newly acquired 800 May & Speh employees. We were learning—and not just from this acquisition—that buying a company is the easy part. Integrating it into Acxiom's culture and systems is a whole different problem.

We finally turned the integration over to an associate named Holly Marr, a good friend of Cindy Childers. I thought of Holly as a "utility player," and I mean that as a glowing compliment. She was gifted at taking on challenging jobs, getting them done, and moving on to the next one. She had developed Acxiom's quality assurance program and our competency-based review process. "Holly, go kill that," we would say, and she would take the task in hand and stay with it until she whipped it into submission. If anyone could bring May & Speh into the fold, it would be Holly Marr.

Unfortunately, none of us had been able to ameliorate the severe culture clash between Acxiom and our old partners Direct Media. They had bridled at our systems; moreover, they hadn't produced satisfactory revenue for us. In 1999, after three turbulent years together, we had decided to divest ourselves of them. By early 2000, Dave Florence and a group of Direct Media employees would consummate a deal to buy the company back from us—a sad end to a long association.

Even our completion of AbiliTec brought unexpected complications. You'd think that figuring out all the coding would be the hardest part of the process. But in hindsight, what I remember most about the creation of AbiliTec was difficulty with other people. With Susie, it brought us to a marital understanding. With my Acxiom team, it nearly brought divorce.

Susie's reaction made sense to me. Finally, my divorce from Jane was over and Susie and I were in real life together. But my version of real life was hard for her to deal with. "I had been waiting all this time for us to be together," she says. "I mean, when is it my time? It wasn't my time before, because he was running a company and trying to get divorced. But wasn't it my time now?

"Well, it's *still* not my time. But that's okay because now I understand. We had these conversations where I said I feel like we're disconnected, and Charles would say, 'Don't do that with me. I'm not responsible for filling your day. You've got to find that. I'm not going to find that for you.'

"I knew he was hypersensitive to that because he constantly had to help Jane. So he was not going to find projects for me. Now, every once in a while he slips up and tries to find a project for me. And I go, 'Oh, no, no, no. I don't need you to find me projects!'"

Some at Acxiom seemed to feel the same way. AbiliTec was certainly "a project," but to my mind it was one that we had no choice about—we had to implement it. In a world increasingly powered by Big Data, we either moved forward or we got left behind.

Earlier I talked about structured data, the kind of data we mined in the early days. But since the late '90s, the term "Big Data" has generally, and increasingly, been understood to refer to extremely large masses of *unstructured* data. Take email, for example—all the emails that have ever been sent in the world would be Very Big Data. You can't even collect it all in one place. Or look at streams of video; it *is* digital content, but it's content that's very hard to extract. Just imagine the amount of content in a single hour of a high-definition television show. Then you have all the messages that are sent, texts and otherwise; they too represent massive amounts of unstructured data.

Realistically, however, in a business context Big Data is typically a combination of structured and unstructured data. For example, a company might want to take a look at its call center data to find out what customers are saying on the telephone. And what complaints are people making on their website? Some of that information will be structured and some will be unstructured.

But it's really hard to create value from unstructured data. Not only is it expensive to capture, it's also difficult to analyze. You have to have an objective, and you have to find ways of meeting that objective. So in the modern context, I define Big Data as a combination of structured and unstructured data. And the biggest Big Data problem today is how to make use of that information in an actionable way.

□ □ □ □ □

ABILITEC WOULD HELP with that. But integrating AbiliTec into our system was going to be like building a new foundation on our house after the roof was on.

We could sell AbiliTec to new clients, because it was relatively easy to design a whole new process flow for them. The problem was with our existing clients. Every process we had involved a whole bunch of computer steps—applying Zip Codes, doing address hygiene, running data matching. Every single one of those processes had to be redesigned to use AbiliTec. With Citibank alone we had *thousands* of processes that had to be modified and tested and verified. Yes, when it was all done, we would get rid of a lot of steps and everything would run faster. But to get to that point was a staggering job.

The pushback I got was, "Man, you're talking about a huge thing. We're going to have to invest millions and millions in new computers." It was true, and we eventually figured out that the cost of computers was going to kill us. Fortunately, we already had Terry Talley and his team working on that grid computing system pioneered in academia. More and more, that was looking like our salvation. In fact, the story of AbiliTec and the story of what became known as "the grid" are fully intertwined.

Our tech team had recommended that we buy a bunch of Intel computers—no cabinets, no monitors, no keyboards, just the computing machines themselves—and set them up in racks, one computer stacked on top of another like bottles in a giant wine rack. Each computer was called a "grid node," and eventually we had thousands of nodes in racks. Each rack was connected to a Cisco router that had access to all the nodes in that particular rack.

Then we just had to convert our software so that it could break jobs down into parcels—primarily geographically, by Zip Codes. One computer could probably handle all the Zip Codes of a small place like Little Rock, but it might take 10 or so computers to deal with New York City. After which, we would consolidate all the results. If AbiliTec promised to give us the ability to process massive additional amounts of data, the grid promised to allow us to process that data at a low cost.

By 2000, we had an operational system of AbiliTec, but we hadn't yet built the infrastructure to run all of Acxiom's work on it. We had used AbiliTec to enhance InfoBase a little, and we had converted some, but not all, of Citibank's processes. So, basically, we were half pregnant. In that condition, the benefits were almost negative. Because now we had additional costs and additional processes that had to interface with all the old stuff, but we weren't getting enough benefit.

"Guys," I said to my leadership team, "we've got to get a broad implementation of this technology. It's demonstrating such a tremendous benefit where it *is* being used that it'll transform Acxiom when we get it done."

And everybody would say, "Yeah, yeah, we know, but we're really busy right now and it's going to impact this year's business plan, and we're going to have to hire more people." They had excuse after excuse after excuse: "I just put in for a vacation." "I'm going to have to work extra hours." "My wife's not going to be happy." I could go on for hours about the excuses I heard.

I'm not a guy who clings to an idea just because it's *my* idea. It all depends on my conviction level. Leadership is partly about empowering people, and you can't tell them what to do all the time—you've got to hire good people, point the way, and let them run. If my conviction level on a particular idea is low, I might hand it off to an associate with a suggestion about how he should approach it. If, later, he comes back to me advocating a different approach, I'll listen to his reasoning. If it seems sound, we'll do it his way.

But if my conviction level is high, it's a whole different ballgame. It's more like, *Don't bother me with opinions or facts—we're doing it my way.* It came down to something like that with AbiliTec.

I can remember this meeting like it was yesterday. I had all my leadership team in the conference room, maybe 20 people, and they were going on and on about how problematic it would be to integrate AbiliTec. Finally, I reached my limit. And I broke my one long-term rule—that you never, *ever* threaten to divorce somebody.

"Look," I said, "I've been busting my ass working with you guys to try to figure out how to get this thing done—how to get everybody on board. And I just feel like I'm pushing rope uphill. So this is what I'm telling you motherfuckers: *As long as I'm running this company, we're going to move forward with AbiliTec!* Because I believe so strongly that if we don't, this company's in deep trouble. It has no true future without it.

"If all of you disagree with me, then maybe I'd better go somewhere else. But I am sick of this. You either get onboard, or get out, or all come together and say you want me to leave. I don't give a shit which it is. But we're going to resolve this, and I mean *now*."

Well, that was quite a meeting. And it didn't take long before they came to me and said, *We know we have to do this, it's really important, yada yada yada*. Okay, I said. And so we started in.

It was worse than pulling teeth, and it took years to complete. But once AbiliTec was fully integrated, we were essentially a new company. We could now handle twice the data as before, with less sweat. Our competitors tried to copy us, but we had leapfrogged way too far in front of them. Nobody could even touch us.

□ □ □ □ □

THE DECADE OF the 2000s began brilliantly, with AbiliTec being touted as something akin to the data industry's Holy Grail. In 2000, the year the dot-com bubble burst and sent the NASDAQ into a 30-percent plummet, Acxiom stock was up 65 percent. Clients using AbiliTec included such giants as Microsoft, Citicorp Credit Services, Mercedes-Benz USA, Palm Inc., Rodale Press, Bank One Services Corp., and American Express. In the first quarter of our 2001 fiscal year (April 1, 2000 to March 31, 2001), earnings from AbiliTec amounted to an estimated $5 million; in the second quarter, the first time AbiliTec's contribution was separated out from other earnings, the figure was $40 million. AbiliTec, I told the business media, "is changing the heart of Acxiom."

And there was no limit to our ambition. "If you look at Acxiom today," our strategic-alliances head Andy Griebel told *Arkansas Business* magazine in late 2000, "we're at about one-point-two billion dollars in revenue. Charles' vision is for Acxiom to grow to a five billion dollar company in the next two to five years. And the sooner the better."

But by the end of that 2001 fiscal year, we had stumbled. In Q4 we posted an operating loss. There were many reasons—most prominent among them a one-time contract write-off of nearly $35 million, stemming from our former client Montgomery Ward's bankruptcy. But also the general economic downturn was catching up with us. Some potential clients that had planned to sign lucrative contracts for AbiliTec had postponed their commitment until their own financial prospects improved. In our British operation, the investment in building a European AbiliTec contributed to a loss of $500,000 for fiscal 2001—compared to profits of $5.1 million the year before.

Our stock had been trending downward for months. From the high-water mark of $43.87, set on November 14, 2000, we dropped to just below $30 on February 20, 2001. On April 2, 2001—the first trading day after we issued a revenue-and-earnings warning for Q4—the stock hit $11.50.

So instead of spending the first quarter of fiscal 2002 counting our triumphs, we devolved into crisis mode. We immediately announced five-percent pay cuts for most Acxiom employees. "If you made less than twenty-five thousand dollars, you were exempt from it," recalls Cindy Childers, who had the tough job of overseeing this and other employee measures we were forced to take. "But in exchange for that pay cut, we gave new stock options. And then you could volunteer to reduce even more of your pay. If you took more than a five-percent cut, we would double down for you on the money. I'll never forget sitting in the conference room with Charles during this time. We were talking about the double down, wondering how many people we could get to do it. We thought if we could get ten percent, that would be phenomenal. Well, we had thirty-eight percent sign up. So those guys got stock options somewhere between eleven and thirteen dollars."

In addition to the pay cuts, we started trimming expenses wherever we could—in advertising, travel and entertainment, consulting and outside services. We had to do everything possible to regain the confidence of analysts and stockholders.

To that end, on May 16—the day after our Q4 results were official—we held a conference call for stockholders, analysts, and media. I began my talk with an admission and a promise:

"Good morning…Q4 and fiscal year two thousand one were certainly not business as usual times at Acxiom, as all of you are well aware.

"The fiscal year was filled with ups and downs. We made great progress with AbiliTec in its first year of general availability. We signed up many blue-chip customers, and our strategic partners are making good use of our AbiliTec technology, also. We built infrastructure. We've done the branding work to assure AbiliTec's long-term success. And, of course, there are a number of other highlights I'll go over throughout my comments.

"Q4 and fiscal two thousand one represented the first earnings miss in our business in almost a decade. And I can assure you that we are making changes in our business, starting with the way that we report revenue so that our performance is going to be more predictable and our business more easily understood.

"In addition, we're continuing to take actions to deal with this current economic climate. These include the pay cuts that we already talked about and other expense cuts, as well as focusing on the sales side to improve our revenue picture. And I can tell you, you have our commitment that we're going to continue to work very hard on these issues in the future."

But by the end of Q1 of fiscal 2002, we weren't where we wanted, or needed, to be. At the end of June 2001, we announced a significant layoff—412 people, out of our worldwide employee population of 6,000. Issuing pink slips is always hard, but we had no choice. "We did it with as much integrity as anyone possibly could," recalls Cindy. "We tried to help people find jobs. We met with the local companies and got several people placed. So while we didn't exactly come through this period unscathed, we were still named one of *Fortune's* best companies to work for at the time—because of the way we handled things."

In response to the layoffs, our stock dipped to $10.25, the lowest in years. I did what I could to put the best possible public face on our situation. "We continue to be very excited," I told the media, "about the long-term prospects of our business and the impact AbiliTec will have in the customer data integration space, and we believe these expense actions make Acxiom much leaner so that when the economy recovers we will be positioned extremely well for significant long-term success."

□ □ □ □ □

IF LIFE AT Acxiom was going less than smoothly, outside the office I had ample reason to be thankful. In February 2000 my son was involved in a horrible wreck at Daytona. Since 1998, Rob had been driving in NASCAR events. "In nineteen ninety-seven," says Rob, "my mom had been to a NASCAR truck race at Texas with some friends. Afterwards, she called me and said, literally, 'Fuck the Ferrari. You need to drive in NASCAR.' So she ended up funding my first few NASCAR races."

The year 2000 was the first year of the NASCAR Truck Series, which featured trucks that were anything but street vehicles. Beneath the truck body was a flat-out race car engine and chassis, and these trucks went even faster than the cars. "They're bigger, they're taller, they're a little bit heavier than cars," says Rob, "and NASCAR thought that was going to be a restrictor and slow us down. Well, it didn't work that way—it actually made us faster because it punched such a big hole in the air. And then you get two or three trucks together, we were going two hundred six miles an hour. The cars didn't even hit two hundred that year."

After a restart with Rob in seventh position, on the 56th lap Rob got tapped by rookie Kurt Busch trying to pass under him on a banked turn. All hell ensued. Rob veered onto the apron, then swerved back and hit veteran Geoff Bodine's truck, driving Bodine into the retaining fence. Bodine's truck burst into a fireball and tumbled end-over-end nine times down the track, parts tearing off the truck with each flip. Meanwhile, in Bodine's wake a dozen other trucks began crashing into one another. Bodine finally landed upside down, only his roll cage intact; his engine came to rest more than 2,000 feet from the point of impact. There's a video of this spectacular accident, and once the melee is ignited, the usually energetic commentators become hushed and reverential, like witnesses to sudden death. One clip on YouTube shows Rob's truck right behind Bodine's fiery, ripping wreck.

Jane watched this race on TV at home, by herself, and she says she didn't know for a long time if her son was dead or alive. "I'm very, very bitter about that," says Jane today. "I was sitting in my living room watching it and there was a wreck of thirteen trucks, and Rob was the second truck hit. I followed him for a while and then I lost him. And the last truck they showed before they went to commercial was a truck that was nothing but a burned-out hulk with a driver that looked like he was dead, slumped over and burned, burned, burned. It was so bad that when they came back on the air they wouldn't replay it. I sat there for forty minutes, and his father was there at that race and never called me and told me he was all right."

All I can say in my defense is that I was caught up in the moment. Fortunately for us all, Rob was okay—for that matter, so was Geoff Bodine. After being hospitalized for a few days, he was back racing a month later. "More than a year after the crash," says Rob, "Geoff and I were invited to tell about it on Montel Williams' 'Brushes With Death' show. I was young and invincible then, and Geoffrey was older and had won a lot of NASCAR races. So we're doing the interview and he says, 'You know, Montel, I saved Rob's life.' And I just kind of laughed. 'No, really,' he says. "If I hadn't been there, he would've hit that wall head-on at about one-hundred-eighty miles an hour.' And I just went, *Holy shit.* I would've hit harder and faster and more straight on than Dale Earnhardt did when he died at Daytona a year after Geoff's crash."

After Bodine's spectacular wreck, restrictors became a requirement on all NASCAR trucks, slowing them down a good 20 miles per hour. Also, Rob began rethinking his involvement with NASCAR; he quit the series the same year. "There were a couple of reasons," he says. "One, it got very expensive. Two, I decided to get married, and my wife, Vici [pronounced Vicky], got pregnant very quickly. It was a time in the sport when a lot of guys were dying—Kenny Irwin, Tony Roper, Dale Earnhardt, Adam Petty. Vici had been to a lot of my races, and I had a real bad wreck at Texas, probably worse than the Daytona wreck. And then she was standing next to Tony Roper's wife at Texas when he died right in front of them. A couple of weeks later Adam died, and we were there. I just quite frankly thought, *getting married and having my life on the line.* I decided I really didn't have to do that."

My children's marriages brought about some surprising changes in my personal life. Carrie had married Rod Ford in 1999, and Rob and Vici Abajian followed a year later. Marriages beget babies, and babies have a way, at least in theory, of making grownups want to put the painful past to rest and focus on hope for the future. That theory applied even to Jane and me, though not instantaneously.

In 2000, Carrie gave birth to our first grandchild, a son named Yale. Susie and I were in Cabo at our new house when Yale was born, so we missed the family scene at the hospital. But when Vici and Rob had daughter MaKenna in 2001—in Little Rock—we were excited to be a part of it. "So we go busting into the hospital room," recalls Susie, "and I see Rob and tap him on the rear end. And then I see Jane, just sitting there. This is the first time we've ever been in close proximity to each other. She immediately gets up and walks out. She didn't say a word, just walked out. And never came back."

So much for putting the past behind us.

The next grandchild—Juliette, Carrie's second child—was born in April 2003. This was a turning point. Carrie was in labor, and Jane knew that Susie and I were coming to the hospital. She and I hadn't spoken to each other more than a handful of times in nearly eight years, and those occasions were generally fraught with tension. But now we were told that she was okay with our coming to the hospital.

Susie tells this story better than I do. She didn't miss a nuance. "So we get to UAMS," Susie says, meaning the University of Arkansas for Medical Sciences hospital, "and Jane's in the hallway. Carrie's in labor. Jane's in the hallway, and Charles is in the hallway. They even *talk* to each other a little bit. And I'm just being quiet. I'm feeling a little sick. *If they can just talk and be cool, that's what I want.*

"So it was really funny—Jane kind of forgot for a moment. We're sitting in the waiting room and Carrie's in-laws are there, and Charles and I are there, and Jane's there. And Rob calls from California, to Charles' phone. Rob wants to speak to Jane. So Charles hands her his phone and she's talking away to Rob, and then she says, 'Okay, I'm going to give you back to Daddy.' *It's like they're a family*, I thought. *And he's always going to be their Daddy.* I realize then that Jane has let her guard down. She's not mad.

"After that, Charles is walking around talking a lot and being the proud grandfather-to-be, and Jane looks over at me and catches my eye. I wink at her and she rolls her eyes, like it's our joke about Charles.

"But the best was when they rolled Carrie in with the baby. Jane gets on one side of her and I get on the other, and we're both bending down looking at Carrie and telling her how pretty Jules is. And I remember looking up at us all and thinking, *This is a moment. This is just really neat. This is forgiveness.*"

□ □ □ □ □

NO ACCOUNT OF the decade of the 2000s will ever again be complete without some discussion of the September 11, 2001, terrorist attacks on the United States. That day changed us all. And in hindsight, I'm inclined to say that those tragic events led Acxiom to perhaps its most unqualified success of this difficult decade.

In 2001, even the U.S. government didn't understand the power of data. The FBI guys who moved into our office were international counter-terrorist experts, and they knew nothing about computers. It was like I was speaking to them in Greek. And what a cyber-odyssey I had to tell them about.

By this time, I had persuaded my divorce lawyer, Jerry Jones, to join Acxiom as our corporate attorney. On Tuesday, September 11th, Jerry had been in Connecticut for a meeting, but in light of the terrorist attacks his meeting was cancelled. With no planes flying, he rented a car and drove back to Arkansas, arriving sometime on Thursday.

"On Friday morning," recalls Jerry, "Charles and I were sitting in his office talking, and a young man who worked with us, Jonathan Askins, popped in to say that the FBI had posted pictures of the 19 terrorists on their website. 'Should we,' asked Jonathan, 'run them through our database and see what we have?' Charles and I looked at each other. 'Oh, hell yes!' we said."

After Jonathan left, Jerry and I talked about what we would do if we did have information on these guys. We decided that Jerry should get some advice from people we knew who'd been in the U.S. government—Mack McLarty and Rodney Slater. Mack, who was on our board, had been President Clinton's chief of staff. Rodney, besides being a law school classmate and a good friend of Jerry's, had served as Clinton's Secretary of Transportation. Both knew how the levers of government worked.

"So," says Jerry, "I reached out to both of them and said we're doing this, what's your advice? Should we call up the government if we find something? And both of them said yes. This was a big decision for Acxiom because we'd never really done anything with the government. There were good and legitimate reasons for that. We didn't want to always be responding to subpoenas for records and things of that nature. But this was a matter of obvious national security implications.

Our country was under attack. We felt an obligation to do something and help if we could."

A short time later, it turned out that we did have data on many of the terrorists—data that we thought could be useful. And there would likely be lots more to come. Jerry placed a call to a former law firm colleague, Tom Mars, who had once served as director of the Arkansas State Police. Mars pointed him to several people who might be helpful, starting with the U.S. Attorney's office in Little Rock.

"I called them up and told them what we had," says Jerry. "I suggested to them that it might be appropriate for them to deliver to me a subpoena, asking for certain information. And if they would do that, we would comply with that subpoena posthaste."

In that way we managed to provide the United States government with information that certain interested parties found helpful. Very soon we had those six FBI counter-terrorism experts living in our building with us, for a couple of months. We worked very closely with them. As time went on, we also coordinated with a number of our customers to access their data under an appropriate legal structure.

Chief Privacy Officer Jennifer Barrett was working out of our London office when all this post-9/11 work began, and I phoned her and asked her to come home. "It was Friday afternoon," Jennifer recalls, "and I was flying to Manchester to spend the weekend with friends. After that I was going to hop over to Florence, Italy, where my son was spending his junior year abroad. Then Charles called. 'You need to come back,' he said. 'We're doing some work for the government and I'm sure there are some privacy implications.' So I flew back to the States on Saturday. I wasn't necessarily involved in all the technical analysis of the data, but I was there to say what we should and could do, who we could give it to, that sort of stuff."

For the first month after the terrorist attacks, I almost lost myself in sleuthing. Operating mostly from home, I all but gave up running the company to work on our so-called Bad Guys Database. Centering our search in Florida, we tracked our targets from there to New Jersey; another group was set in Chicago. Sometimes I stayed up all night, following this lead and that lead, breathlessly going where they took me. And thanks to AbiliTec, they took me to some very interesting places.

In the weeks after 9/11, there was a lot of talk about the Saudi connection to the attacks, and one of our most intriguing data threads involved a Saudi national. I can't say for sure what this particular person was up to, but he had two Saudi passports. Same man, same birth date, two passports—I double and triple confirmed it. The identification numbers were off by one digit, like somebody had done a quick scrub so the two passports wouldn't match.

This man owned a house in the suburbs of Washington, D.C., and had cars in Washington and Florida. He would enter the country on one of his two passports and the address where he was going to be staying was always a different hotel in the D.C. area—never his home address. I tracked *him* to Mohamed Atta's Florida apartment building, too. Here's the same man traveling in and out, always through Washington, and one of his cars is listed as having the same address as Atta's apartment building. Now what was that all about? Couriering money was my guess.

As our dedicated team of researchers pursued the suspects, we were able to learn a number of things about the way the government brought information together—mainly that there needed to be significant advancements in that area. "As we all now know," says Jerry, "there were disparate pieces of information that if the systems had existed to bring all that information together in a usable format in front of a person, the attacks could very well have been preventable. But it's very, very difficult to be able to bring all that information together—that somebody had taken flying lessons in Florida and somebody had gotten a speeding ticket somewhere else, and somebody used credit cards in these locations and these people had lived in close proximity to the same group in different places. With the benefit of hindsight, you can say, 'Ah, we should've figured this out.' But that's totally unfair. That's not the way the world works."

But our world—the world of Big Data—*can* work that way. So even as we hunted down the bad guys, we began thinking about techniques and strategies that, if implemented, could increase the probability of heading off terrorist attacks in the future. And we began formulating a plan to put our special capabilities on the table, in front of the people who needed to know such things. They could then decide whether or not they wanted to take advantage of them.

□ □ □ □ □

WE MADE SOME phone calls and took some meetings. Tim Griffin, then an assistant U.S. Attorney and later a U.S. congressman from Arkansas, was very helpful. So was retired general Wesley Clark. Former President Bill Clinton came to town with Mack McLarty and spent an afternoon with us going over our findings. Our two U.S. senators, Blanche Lincoln and Tim Hutchinson, were also very keen to know what we'd uncovered and, even more importantly, how we thought such a tragedy could be averted the next time. Being a Republican, Senator Hutchinson had more of an in with the Bush Administration, and it was through him that we secured a private meeting with Vice-president Dick Cheney.

That meeting took place in the summer of 2002, in the Vice-president's room at the United States Capitol. Our team included General Clark, Senator Hutchinson, Jerry Jones, and me. Cheney was accompanied by one of his senior aides. Cognizant of the Vice-president's time, General Clark opened the meeting and got right to the point—that government agencies had embraced information technology over the past 30 years, but that as the individual agencies' systems had grown, the ability to share this information within and between agencies had not grown with it.

Then General Clark introduced me. I made a short presentation explaining how the government could solve its massive data integration problem in a manner that would be respectful of individual privacy rights, which was critically important and technologically feasible, and at a cost that we thought would be acceptable, all things considered. The Vice-president seemed to find this plan quite intriguing, and in fact the scheduled 20-minute meeting stretched on to nearly 45 minutes.

At the end of the presentation, we left the Vice-president with a 13-page single-spaced memo called "Data Integration in Government Agencies"—subtitled "Facilitating Information Sharing while Protecting Privacy and Agency Autonomy." Here's a paragraph from page one:

The September 11 terrorists looked and acted like many others in America. They used our education systems, our financial markets, our transportation systems, and our societal freedom to attack us like we have never been attacked before. This is certainly frightening, but it is also encouraging.

Because our society, for the most part, is an electronic society. Every credit card transaction is captured; every airline ticket recorded; every financial transaction stored, and most every government activity recorded in some type of electronic media. If all these activities could be integrated, would it be possible to use information technology to discern aberrant behavior and then to track the activities of individuals and capture them *before* they inflict harm? Today, it is common to use computer-generated models to predict the likelihood of fraud in financial services. Could similar models be used to predict the likelihood of terrorist activities? The answer is absolutely yes, but many are frightened by the "big brother" implications of such tracking. There are many legislative and constitutional hurdles surrounding the sharing of information....

The rest of the memo explained the capabilities of AbiliTec and demonstrated, through examples, how various agencies within the United States government could share vital information legally, responsibly, and quickly. Certain keys would keep the databases separate until the proper authority was given to integrate them. Our recommendation was that such authority needed to rest with Congress.

As the meeting was breaking up, Vice-president Cheney expressed curiosity about Acxiom. "You guys aren't the typical government contractor," he said. "What's it like dealing with the federal government?"

Unknowingly, he had walked into a buzz saw. "Well, sir," said Jerry, "if you have a minute, I have a story to tell you."

One day a few months after 9/11, I had received a phone call from U.S. Attorney General John Ashcroft. He'd called to thank me, and the whole Acxiom team, for our work in putting together the Bad Guys Database. Jerry was in my office when I got the call, so he heard the whole conversation. Attorney General Ashcroft was very complimentary, and as he was hanging up, he said he was going to have FBI Director Robert Mueller phone us as well.

About 10 minutes later, Sharon announced that the Director of the FBI was on the line. So Jerry and I talked with him a while, and he thanked us profusely for the contribution our company had made. "You know," he said, "you guys ought to get paid for that."

"Oh, no sir," we said, "our nation was under attack. It's a national crisis. We're more than happy to be of assistance."

"Well," he said, "you should get paid for the work you do in the future."

"Sir," I said, "that'll probably just mess things up. Your contracting officer is probably not going to like us."

"No, no," Mueller said. "Just send a proposal to me."

"Well, sir," I said, "with all due respect, I doubt you'll ever see it."

"Just send it to me," he said. "Wait about sixty days and send it to me, and we'll see where it goes."

So that's what we did. And sure enough, some weeks later I got a phone call from the chief contracting officer of the FBI. "You're violating the law," he said.

I immediately called for Jerry. "I could hear Charles hollering at me from the other side of the building," Jerry says. "*Jerrrrrrrrryy!* Come *heerrre!*"

He quickly showed up in my office, and I told him what the man was saying. Switching the phone to speaker, I then introduced the chief contracting officer to our corporate attorney and asked him to now tell Jerry the problem. "You're violating federal law," he said again.

"With all due respect, sir," said Jerry, "there are a lot of federal laws. Where do you think we're in violation?"

"Well," the man said, "you're unlawfully supplementing the federal budget."

"I didn't realize that was a crime," said Jerry.

"Yes, it is," said the chief contracting officer. "It's a serious matter. You have to cease and desist immediately."

"Well, sir," said Jerry, "again with all due respect, I don't think we want to do that."

The chief contracting officer didn't like that answer. "I don't even know if there's a need for what you guys are doing," he said.

"Well, sir," said Jerry, "I think the Director of the FBI believes there's a need, and I think the Attorney General of the United States believes there's a need."

"You guys have just got to stop!" said the chief contracting officer. We could hear exasperation in his voice.

"Well, sir," said Jerry, "unless you tell me that you have the authority to immediately call downstairs and have the six agents of the FBI that are housed in our building, working directly with us, with our people, to immediately come up here and arrest Mr. Morgan and myself; again, sir, with all due respect, we're going to politely ignore you."

"You can't do that!" the chief contracting officer said.

"Well, sir," said Jerry, "again, with all *due* respect, that is what we're going to do."

"I have to write you a letter!"

"Okay, fine. Write us a letter."

"I'm going to," said the chief contracting officer of the FBI.

And that's the story Jerry told, verbatim, to Vice-president Cheney after our meeting. Cheney, who had spent his life in government, was visibly upset by it. "What do you guys want me to do about this?" he said.

"Mister Vice-president," said Jerry, "we're not in government. You are. You guys have to figure this out."

That was our meeting. By the way, the letter from the FBI's chief contracting officer arrived a few days after our phone conversation. "It got filed," Jerry says.

15

THE LONG
GOODBYE

100101001011001010001001011001010110011

WE MOVED INTO our shiny new office building in June 2003, just about the time my longstanding fear of a blowup over privacy finally became reality.

"When I created the privacy office," recalls Jennifer, "I probably spent three weeks a year on it. I was still doing all these other things, and privacy was just another project. I thought it would be something I would work on for six months or a year, get it done, and then look for something else interesting to do. Well, I never got past it; it stuck. It stuck because it just kept growing. So by nineteen ninety-five it was probably full time and by ninety-six or ninety-seven I started having to build a team. And in the late nineties we started doing more international work. About the time we would get everything in place, we would move into another part of the world, and we would have to figure out what *that* meant."

Throughout the '90s, we had seen more and more abuses of data. The telemarketers were the worst. They would get you on the phone and harass you and make you feel guilty. You couldn't get rid of them, and most people are too nice to say, 'I'm hanging up now.' So we began to see laws. The first do-not-call registry was in 1986 in Florida because telemarketers were calling and harassing older people. "Later came the automated dialers," says Jennifer. "If they didn't have an operator to take the call, then the person would pick up the phone and say hello and there would be dead space and they would think *ghost stalker.*" That was the start of what turned into much state legislation around telemarketing, ultimately culminating in the Federal Trade Commission's do-not-call registry.

Not only were the 1990s an aggressive time for marketers, but a lot of big databases were also being created, raising the stakes for privacy advocates. In 1998, the European Union passed its "data protection directive," establishing privacy rights for Europeans. The U.S. was far less regulated at the time, though in 1999 the Gramm-Leach-Bliley Act (also known as the Financial Services Modernization Act of 1999) began requiring financial institutions to establish protections for their customers' data.

That act passed the same year as "the first online ad privacy scandal," in the words of *Advertising Age* magazine. That was a reference to the brouhaha launched when DoubleClick, an online advertising company, bought Abacus, a co-operative database of catalogers, and privacy rights advocates went nuts. Worrying that personally identifiable information would become available in online selling, the protesters appealed to the FTC and finally got DataClick to promise that they wouldn't connect such personally identifiable information with online browsing data. "But," says Jennifer, "while you couldn't buy, say, Lands' End customers, you *could* buy people who bought blue button-down shirts with monograms on it—shirts that just happened to come from Lands' End. The cataloger's intent was to merge the online business with the catalog business, but they didn't think through the privacy implications. And it blew up on them."

Our privacy office was designed to avoid such explosions. "The team sets policy for the company," says Jennifer, "and that policy is based on either a law that we have to understand—so I have lawyers on the team—or on self-regulation such as the DMA code of conduct. So we set up the policy, we train our business people on that policy, and we help them establish the procedures we'll need to make sure we follow that policy. We then audit the business to see that it's doing what it's supposed to be doing. We also consult with clients, because as a service bureau we have a deeper body of knowledge about a lot of the laws than the client does.

"In addition, my department deals with the media—I would say we talk to the media a hundred times a year—and we field inquiries from consumers who contact us. I also testify about privacy issues before Congress in Washington."

Acxiom's greatest privacy crisis began one otherwise normal morning in the summer of 2003. Jerry Jones was sitting in his new office in our new building when one of his staff people popped in and said, "You're not going to believe what we think just happened."

The staffer had answered a phone call from a detective in the sheriff's office in Hamilton County, Ohio, which is Cincinnati. They had seized the computers of a young man, and Acxiom's name was on many of the files. "Who is Acxiom," the detective said, "and why would your name be on these files?" The detective was on hold, wanting to speak to our corporate counsel.

"I asked what was in the files, and he told me," recalls Jerry. "That's when we realized this was a serious issue."

The man whose computer contained our files was named Daniel Baas, and he had worked for a Cincinnati company with ties to us. "These files were on an FTP server," says Jerry, "which is basically an electronic mailbox for things coming in and going out. We had made a mistake. For some reason, passwords were encrypted but they were stored on that server, and Daniel Baas had figured out how to decrypt those passwords. As a result, he'd been able to take a lot of data off that server. He couldn't infiltrate any other Acxiom assets, but he'd been able to open what was on that server. Baas was claiming that all he'd done with those files was show them to his girlfriend."

Before long, Jerry was flying to Cincinnati in the company of Jamie Holt, an investigator we employed in those days. "I had always told Jamie that whatever we were dealing with, we had to find out what the truth was," says Jerry. "*Then* we could deal with it. Now Jamie and I were going to Cincinnati to find out the truth from Daniel Baas."

At the Hamilton County Sheriff's Department, they walked into a conference room filled with men packing guns. "We convinced them to let us go to the jail and interview Baas," says Jerry. "I asked him if he had sold the data, or if he had posted it on a website somewhere. His story was that he'd just shown it to his girlfriend. And we eventually became convinced that that was it. He never did anything with the data. But he went to jail for forty-five months and was ordered to pay restitution."

□ □ □ □ □

THAT WASN'T THE end of the problem, however. As a result of the Baas incident, we launched a comprehensive investigation to find out if this had happened at other times. And we discovered some IP addresses that had hit the FTP server that were anomalies. We didn't know what these addresses were, only that they probably shouldn't be there. So with the benefit of law enforcement, we tracked the IP addresses to a company called Snipermail, in Boca Raton, Florida. Snipermail was in the spamming business.

Understand, even then Acxiom was starting to be known as "the Big Data guys." We were getting talked about as this relatively low-profile company in Arkansas that had data on *everybody*—especially bank data. Among our clients were 14 of the 15 biggest credit card companies; seven of the top 10 auto manufacturers; and five of the top six retail banks. We analyzed consumer databases for such multinational companies as Microsoft, IBM, AT&T, and General Electric. So as the Internet increasingly became a vast, interlaced world of infinite promise, it naturally attracted opportunists the way gold mines once attracted prospectors and con men. Data became the new currency. And if you were the kind of person who preferred to steal data rather than mine it yourself, where did you go? To the mother lode.

Jerry had a preliminary conversation with somebody at Snipermail, and then we contacted the U.S. Attorney's office, the FBI, and the Secret Service. They jumped on it, put together a task force, and worked very closely with their counterparts in the southern district of Florida. We first met with them here in Arkansas on a Wednesday or a Thursday, and by Sunday evening they had obtained search warrants to go into Snipermail's offices and conduct a search, including taking their computer equipment.

It soon became clear that these guys had done something very similar to what Daniel Baas had done. The difference was that they weren't stealing this data just to show their girlfriends. In 137 hacking attacks between January and July 2003, they had stolen 1.6 billion customer records, including names, physical addresses, and email addresses. The purpose, apparently, was to beef up the Snipermail contact lists so as to make the company more attractive for acquisition. They had also sold some of the information to a broker for use in someone else's spamming operation.

Very thorough in their investigation, the FBI and the Department of Justice decided to bring a criminal complaint against Snipermail. Various people in the company agreed to cooperate with the government, but not the CEO, Scott Levine. So the government took him to trial, charging him and Snipermail with the largest theft of personal data recorded to that time. Levine was convicted and sentenced to eight years in prison.

This was a sickening event for Acxiom. Fortunately, Snipermail hadn't done enough with the stolen information to create many real-life problems for the consumers involved, but that's beside the point. Those people should never have been compromised *at all*, and the reason they were was that we had gotten a little lax. We had inadvertently left a hole in our security, and the hackers had found it.

At one point, Snipermail had had at least a quasi-legitimate relationship with Citibank, and that's how they were able to penetrate our FTP server. By the mid- to late-'90s, much of the mail between us and our clients that once would've shipped by FedEx or UPS—physical data tapes, for example—was now coming and going electronically. Let's say Citibank had 10 letter shops doing direct mail for them, all by email. Now they were dumping stuff out on the FTP server, and we gave them a password to access the necessary data. They didn't even have to have a second password. And instead of assigning a new access code every time somebody shipped data, we had lapsed into codes that people would use for extended periods of time.

This was especially dangerous with the big banks, because they were dealing with so many people who needed to access the data. Access wasn't a snap—you entered a code to get into the FTP server, then clicked on your file name, then entered, say, the Citibank mailing number, and then you entered the access code. But we were processing *so much data*—these banks were shipping out hundreds of files a week—and we just got sloppy by not regularly assigning new individual security codes.

So along comes this data company in Florida that has done legitimate work for Citibank, and they see an opportunity. In time they figured out what things were called and how we were assigning security codes, and soon they were downloading data to their PCs in Florida. They started with Citibank data, but eventually they figured out how to get into some of the other banks' files as well.

When the news of this breach broke to the media, Jennifer Barrett and our privacy team acted as the "public" face of Acxiom. "We didn't have a Chief Security Officer at the time," says Jennifer, "and I had dealt with the media on privacy issues, so I became our spokesman." I was glad we at least had a Chief Privacy Officer and that we could point to all the things we'd done in support of privacy. But the truth is, even though we had systems in place that were capable of protecting all the data, we didn't have enough audits in place. Our procedures failed our systems.

Our privacy team also coordinated the fallout internally. "We put a crash team together to coordinate all the activities with clients," says Jennifer. "We also created a security team to do the forensics and help law enforcement and others figure out exactly what had happened, and to whom. We dropped everything to do all this, and it was pretty much fulltime for at least six weeks."

For me, the hardest part of this whole disaster was calling Citibank and telling them we had a colossal problem. Trust was a vital issue in our relationships with the banks, and it had taken *years* for them to let us have their inside data. Now, if Citibank had had an alternative, they'd have been out of here, but they had no alternative. It changed our relationship, though. They sent their own people out to investigate, and they stayed for weeks, mostly choosing not to believe anything we told them.

We learned from our mistakes. We realized that there was no single point in the company where all of our systems came together. If we'd wanted to fire someone for this, who would it have been? Me, probably, since there was no Chief Security Officer. But the more positive way of looking at this is that we realized we needed to centralize our information security in someone who had helped build our systems, someone who knew how all the information flowed. That person turned out to be Frank Caserta. He serves as Acxiom's Chief Information Security Officer to this day, and to my knowledge the company has never suffered another breach.

Ironically, even though this episode was traumatic for a lot of people, our hacking incident soon looked almost small time. I think the headlines we made must've woken up the hacker community, because within a year several big banks and even the government itself had been hacked to greater damage than Acxiom sustained. Today hacking is even more prevalent—as I write this, the retailer Target is still reeling from the damage done by its massive breach.

In hindsight, we plugged our holes after getting off relatively easy. Taking the long view, you could say we have Daniel Baas to thank for that. I hope his girlfriend was impressed.

□ □ □ □ □

BETWEEN JUNE AND December 2003, my attention was mainly trained on hitting our quarterly numbers. The economy seemed to be cooperating for a change, and our stock was slowly climbing. By the end of Q2, we had paid off $240 million of debt, which really helped our financial picture. Now we had $400 million of free cash flow.

Another priority was convincing our clients to make use of our new grid computing system. By the time I had that knock-down, drag-out, near-divorce scene with my leadership team, we had gotten our grid development to the point where we could apply hundreds of millions of AbiliTec links per day at a relatively modest cost. For the grid to fulfill the promise we saw in it, however, it needed to be able to do much more, such as postal coding, another very tedious job on our big computers. But the grid was a one-trick pony at the moment—all it could do was apply AbiliTec links.

Alex Dietz, Terry Talley, and I had a much bigger vision for the grid. It needed to be able to do many different kinds of computer jobs, such as store data and manage the work that it was doing, along with accomplishing all the other tasks a computer operating system like Windows does. Our grid, we realized, needed an operating system like Linux to manage the entire grid complex—a daunting challenge to set up, but one that I felt we had to meet. So under the able leadership of Terry Talley and 30 other engineers, including Chuck Howland, Acxiom made the commitment to push the grid to the next level. I met regularly with the team to help solve knotty problems wherever I could, but my big job was to push the entire organization to use the grid.

Today, the grid system we created would be called "cloud computing," except ours was a private cloud, just for Acxiom's use. We were the first to develop such a system, though there was this small company out west called Google that had a similar idea. Today when you Google something, you're using that very secretive company's acres and acres of linked computers.

Fast forward here a few years. In time, we realized that what we'd created had a potential far greater than just solving Big-Data tasks at Acxiom; we had something that could help the world—or so we thought. But we weren't in the business of building computers, and we didn't want to start offering grid services to others. To make the grid a truly general-purpose system would require a lot more investment, which meant that we needed a partner—someone like Sun Microsystems, Hewlett Packard, or EMC, which had the money to finish development and which could then sell and service the final product.

I met with the then-CEO of HP, Mark Hurd, and the co-founder and CEO of Sun, Scott McNealy. Both were initially interested, but at HP, anyway, our grid was a lot for the engineers to comprehend, and they eventually decided not to pursue it. Sun passed as well.

EMC was a different story. I was able to get a meeting with the legendary former CEO, Michael Ruettgers, who was still active in the company and on the board. Under Ruettgers' leadership, EMC had grown, in 10 years, from a $120 million company to a nearly $9 billion company, and they had shifted their focus from memory boards to storage systems. Ruettgers had been named one of the "World's Top 25 Executives" by *Business Week* magazine.

We met in a restaurant in Washington, D.C., and over quite a bit of wine I warmed him up to the story of our grid. He immediately saw the potential for EMC, but of course he had to get the company's leadership and engineering team to agree. Thus began a long process that eventually led, in 2006, to EMC's purchasing our grid technology for $30 million, with further upsides for us as it became successful for them. They wanted Chuck Howland and our entire engineering team to work for them, while staying in Arkansas. That transition would turn out to be difficult for Chuck, because suddenly his primary boss was no longer Terry Talley, but, rather, some guy in Boston whom Chuck wasn't sure about. In any case, we closed the deal with high hopes that EMC would create some very cool commercial cloud products. But it was not to be.

Just recently, I attended a meeting in Silicon Valley of the Software Enterprise Roundtable group, and there I met a man named Mark Lewis, who had worked at EMC at the time they acquired our grid. As Mark and I discussed why the grid died at EMC, I learned that it was way too disruptive for them because it could store data and do things that EMC's enterprise products already did, only cheaper. Instead of selling a storage solution for $1 million, now it might go for $100,000. And even if they sold twice as many of the grid products, it still didn't amount to $1 million. So the danger, as seen by the individual product executives, was that the grid could make obsolete much of the EMC product line, while also killing their revenues and probably their profits.

Mark Lewis told me that he and Michael Ruettgers and others were big believers in the grid, but that CEO Joe Tucci wouldn't fight his product executives; the grid died at EMC after they'd spent tens of millions of dollars on it. Mark Lewis is now the CEO of a cloud services startup.

□ □ □ □ □

IN DECEMBER 2003, WE made a couple of major announcements. Thanks to our lighter debt load, we were purchasing the global information and media company Claritas Europe for $40 million. Finally, we felt, this was the right company to help us expand our services in Europe. We estimated that this acquisition would bring us an additional $100 million in annual revenue.

We also announced a partnership with Accenture Ltd., a $12 billion management and technology consulting company based in New York. With Accenture's considerable U.S. telecom business and extraordinary global reach, we saw this alliance as a means of growing our already strong client base.

By this time, we had taken two important steps to help facilitate our work with acquisitions. In 2002, I had hired Jorge Carrera, the civil engineer/builder who, with his brother, had designed and built our house in Cabo, to centralize Acxiom's purchasing. At the time he arrived, every one of our acquisitions still had separate purchasing departments and separate accounts payable—a sure recipe for disaster. Jorge, a very resourceful guy, joined Acxiom and started consolidating those processes.

We had also bought a bigger airplane. Since the late '80s we'd had an office in England, and in the '90s we bought two more European companies: Generator Datamarketing (UK) and Normaddress (France). When I traveled to these companies, I either went commercial or flew the Falcon 20; if the latter, we had to hop from Little Rock to Goose Bay, in Newfoundland, to refuel; then from Goose Bay to Iceland for more fuel; and from Iceland I could complete the Atlantic crossing and land near London. It was a long haul, and a grueling one. About the only benefit was that Iceland had very cheap jet fuel.

Now, in 2003, we'd decided to step up our presence in Europe, which led to the Claritas purchase; by the spring of 2004 we would also acquire Consodata in Italy. With Claritas and Consodata alone, we would now have offices in England, France, Italy, Germany, The Netherlands, Spain, Portugal, and Poland; in England, Germany, Spain, and The Netherlands, there would be multiple offices to visit. (We would also expand into South America and China in 2004, but that's a whole different story.)

Suddenly the old Falcon 20 was looking a bit like a covered wagon. With so much management by flying around to do once we *reached* the Continent, we needed something to get us there faster, with less hassle and more comfort. The plane we chose was a Falcon 900EX, which seated 11 and was roomy enough inside for six-footers to stand up. We could also say goodbye to Goose Bay—the 900EX could take us from Little Rock to London nonstop in eight hours.

As 2003 drew to a close, then, I felt that we were well positioned to begin the new year on a very strong note. After our problems of fiscal 2001, our stock price was now back up to nearly $20 and our annual revenue was again projected to surpass the $1 billion mark, a level we hadn't attained in the previous couple of years.

So that December, when I learned that one of our largest shareholders wanted to meet with me, I felt totally confident. His name was Jeffrey Ubben, and he was the managing partner of ValueAct Capital, a hedge fund with offices in San Francisco and Boston.

Jeff Ubben was no stranger to us. Since June 2003, when he and ValueAct had begun buying significant amounts of our stock, we'd been keeping our eye on him. He had a reputation for activism in some of the companies he'd been involved with.

His M.O. was to buy up stock in a company and use his shareholder clout to get himself on the board. Then he would play politics to establish a majority block among the directors, and finally he would orchestrate some event to increase the value of the stock—even selling the company—so he could make a killing. His approach to business boiled down to financial engineering, while I was dedicated to creating value. "Could be trouble," we said, as we watched him buy up more and more Acxiom stock.

Our stockholder communications people had been talking with him. He was considering increasing his stake in Acxiom, they told me, but first he wanted to fly to Little Rock to see our operation, and he especially wanted to meet with me. "Come on," I said.

Wary as I was, Ubben nevertheless struck me as a nice young man, about 40 I guessed, smart and well educated. He told me he and his partners at ValueAct liked our company and were thinking of making further investments in us. He urged me to make "a public commitment to continued improvement in Acxiom's return-on-invested-capital and cash generation," which I agreed to do. He also said he hoped we could have the kind of relationship whereby he could phone me from time to time and offer his opinion on one thing or another—he was sure he would have ideas for ways to increase our stock value.

"We've got a lot of experience," I said.

"Well," he said, "I'd just like to be able to call you occasionally."

"Fine," I said. "I look forward to it."

And so it began. Over the next year ValueAct did acquire more and more Acxiom stock, enough to make them the largest outside stockholder. And Jeff did phone me quite often, suggesting this and that. It wasn't onerous—yet.

In the meantime, it was business as usual at Acxiom. And with our new European holdings, I was a very busy man. "Charles had this unique notion that if you really want to know how things are going in your business, you go and sit down with the rank-and-file people doing the work and you talk to them," says Kelley Bass, who for most of the 2000s worked alongside me as a kind of "channeler" of my thoughts to the people, both internally and externally, who needed to know my opinions. Reporting to Cindy Childers, Kelley wrote the weekly "Morgan's Minutes" to all associates; he wrote press releases; and he prepared my remarks to the analysts. Since his job depended on his knowing what was going on, I took him with me most everywhere I went.

"We would do these things we called 'campus days' all over Europe," recalls Kelley, referring to our internal term for meeting with regular folks; the term came from meetings I often had with associates on Acxiom's own campus. "We'd do town hall meetings and then sit down with different account teams and talk about what was going on. I remember going to Lisbon, to an office that had only twelve people. They could not believe this guy from Arkansas, from the United States, had flown his airplane to see them. No one from Claritas had ever come *close* to that office. Charles gave them half a day of his time."

In general, I tried to go to Europe once a month, and each trip took about a week. We would leave Little Rock early on a Saturday morning, arriving London at approximately 8 p.m. local time. Whoever could help the cause would get a seat on the plane, whether it was a programmer needed at a European office or an internal payment systems specialist going to streamline a particular branch's processes. Acxiom kept some rented flats in London, so London would be our home base for the week. Sunday was a day to rest and get over the jet lag. Monday morning we would hit the ground running, and all week we would fly around to various offices. Then we would return to Little Rock on Saturday. "I did fifteen of those trips," says Kelley. "When we would get back, people would say to me, 'Did you go to Buckingham Palace?' I'm like, 'Are you kidding? I went to the office to *work*.'"

One day in late 2004, when I happened to be in Little Rock, I got the phone call I'd been dreading. "We're making a big commitment to your company," Jeff Ubben said, "and I want to go on your board." He launched into a pitch about how he could help us make money, how he understood financial structuring to increase shareholder value, how his analysts could help us do this and that. "Your stock should be worth a lot more," he said.

I attempted to put him off. "I'll discuss it with our nominating committee," I said. And I did. I told them I didn't want this jerk on our board. I figured he had an agenda, maybe to sell us to Equifax or somebody like that. At the very least, I worried that he would be a disruptive presence, given his history.

When I reported to Jeff that we felt it was a conflict of interest to have a representative of any institutional stockholder on our board, he let me know that he was *very* unhappy.

□ □ □ □ □

THEN SOMETHING HAPPENED that put the whole Jeff Ubben nuisance in perspective: I got a call from my brother Speer saying that he'd been diagnosed with terminal brain cancer.

Speer had suffered from epilepsy for much of his life. "I had my first seizure while teaching my first English class as a doctoral student at Stanford," says Speer. "While trying to explain the meaninglessness of the White Whale, my brain suddenly went into meaninglessness. In the ambulance on the way to the hospital, I looked out at the tops of trees, contemplating my new life—a life maybe not defined by epilepsy, but certainly hampered by it; by the constant threat of another seizure."

Epilepsy had indeed been a broad shadow in his life for decades. He's done well at the University of Missouri, teaching and writing award-winning novels and editing the prestigious *Missouri Review*. Along the way, he's become an internationally known man of letters. I'm not saying he ever wanted to leave, but if he had, he knew it was impossible. He couldn't chance stepping off base and losing his insurance.

In January 2005, a doctor told him he had brain cancer. "The doctor stood there pointing to an X-ray," says Speer, "telling me the seizures were caused by cancer, and that I was dying. My wife was crying and I was trying to figure out how I was going to wrap up my affairs in a month. All of this violated Charles' sense of logic."

My feeling was, if the doctor was saying that the brain cancer was causing the seizures, why hadn't Speer had brain cancer before? It just didn't make sense. So I sent my plane to Columbia, Missouri, to fetch Speer and his wife, Kris, and I flew him to the best neurosurgeon in the world, Dr. Gazi Yasirgil, who just happened to work at the University of Arkansas for Medical Sciences in Little Rock.

Born in Turkey, Dr. Yasirgil received his medical training in Germany and worked for many years in Switzerland before becoming, in 1994, Professor of Neurosurgery at UAMS. In 1999, the medical journal *Neurosurgery* named him "Neurosurgery's Man of the Century 1950-1999" and devoted an entire issue to covering the doctor's contributions to the field.

There was no cancer, just damaged brain tissue. And in a nine-hour surgery, Dr. Yasirgil, a man then in his 80s, cured Speer of epilepsy. "Nine weeks ago I had a brain operation," Speer wrote in his diary on March 13, 2005. "Something was taken out deep in the left temporal lobe. It was tissue damaged in birth trauma. This is the most frequent cause of epilepsy. The brain swells during surgery, and I had one post-op seizure. That was it. Now no more seizures and no more meds. Charles saved me from the doctors in Columbia."

□ □ □ □ □

THAT SUCCESS STORY remains *the* high point of the decade for me. Unfortunately, the low points were very many, and *very* low.

Sometime in the second half of 2005, ValueAct made two premium offers to buy all remaining shares of Acxiom stock at some percentage over the then-current price. The first offer was at $23 a share; our Board ultimately decided to reject it. The second offer was for $25 a share, and that was rejected as well.

Now Jeff started playing rough.

As I write this, I've been reading an article from the Summer 2007 *Journal of Corporation Law* called "Corporate Governance and the New Hedge Fund Activism: An Empirical Analysis," by Thomas W. Briggs, a corporate lawyer who represents hedge funds. It's terrifying reading. "'Hungry' hedge funds with outsized war chests and egos to match are said to be the 'new raiders,' or even the 'new sheriffs of the boardroom,'" writes Briggs. "Hedge fund activists are not 'normal' institutional investors. They threaten and even actually launch proxy fights for corporate control. They attack in wolf packs." Briggs, who clearly knows the character of his clients, dates the emergence of such activism to the year 2005, so at least we can say we got in on the ground floor.

The proxy battle was Jeff's next move. In April 2006, he made it clear to me that ValueAct Capital would put up its own slate of directors for election to the Acxiom board at our 2006 annual shareholders meeting. The ValueAct candidates were Ubben himself; Louis J. Andreozzi, a consultant to the hedge fund; and J. Michael Lawrie, a ValueAct partner.

Mud was slung—that's the nicest thing I can say about what happened next. Ubben and his band of raiders first mounted a phone campaign to contact other shareholders, seeding their ranks with rumors about Acxiom, its board, and most especially me. Then they put up a website called "Change @ Acxiom." This was full of the most ridiculous stuff you can imagine. They had tracked my airplane's comings and goings, for example, and said something to the effect of, *The plane arrives in Paris just in time for Fashion Week...of course Morgan's beautiful young wife has to be there....*

I didn't know *what* Fashion Week was, much less *when* it was. Unless I was on vacation, my trips to Paris were to visit our two businesses there. And Susie wasn't even with me on the trip in question.

I was clearly the main target of the ValueAct website. Here's how it opened:

Bring "True Independence" to the Board at ACXIOM

"True independence—meaning the willingness to challenge a forceful CEO when something is wrong or foolish—is an enormously valuable trait in a director. It is also rare. The place to look for it is among high-grade people whose interests are in line with those of rank-and-file shareholders—*and are in line in a very big way.*"

Warren Buffett

Berkshire Hathaway

2003 Chairman's Letter

"It is the policy of the board that no representatives of institutional investors that have significant holdings of Acxiom stock...will be submitted for nomination by the board due to the possibility of conflicts of interest."

Acxiom Corporation

Notice of Annual Meeting of Shareholders

June 2005

Which view of board representation do you think is the right one—Warren Buffett's or Acxiom's? As thoughtful, long-term investors, we agree with Mr. Buffett—and hope you do, too. Acxiom's decision to exclude institutional shareholders from its board must not be allowed to stand. It is time to make changes to a board whose directors have, in our opinion, lost their way as representatives of Acxiom's true owners—its shareholders.

Elsewhere on the Change @ Acxiom website, Ubben and his people explored, in vicious, almost demented detail, what they termed my "self-dealing." This included Acxiom's sponsorship of my and Rob's motorsports; financial ties between Acxiom and my family (example: We donated $30,000 to the symphony when Susie was chair of the Symphony Orchestra Society); and the ongoing lease of my Falcon 20 jet to Acxiom. They accused me of stacking Acxiom's board with friends, and detailed the personal connections ("board interlocks," they called it). They speculated about the "web" of Acxiom ties to a golf facility called Querencia that Rodger Kline, Jim Womble, and I had purchased in Cabo in 2004, and the supposed cost to Acxiom stockholders:

According to SEC filings, between April 2004 and April 2005, Mr. Morgan sold over $15 million worth of Acxiom stock. During that time, Acxiom's share price declined 13%, wiping out $260 million in shareholder value. In July of 2004, it was announced in a press release that Mr. Morgan and two other Acxiom executives, James Womble and Rodger Kline, bought a luxury residential golf club in Cabo San Lucas, Mexico....

None of us at Acxiom had ever witnessed such orchestrated vitriol, much less been on the receiving end of it. They made me sound like an arrogant, selfish, feather-nesting felon. This was the "wolf pack" mentality at work. In fact, ValueAct's public tarring became so outlandish that the SEC stepped in and made them take down some of the more egregious charges.

In the article by Thomas Briggs about hedge fund tactics, there's this quote from Martin Lipton, a prominent mergers and acquisitions lawyer: "The current high level of hedge fund activism warrants the same kind of preparation as for a hostile takeover bid." That's precisely how Acxiom viewed these attacks by Jeff Ubben and ValueAct. We hired a big-time, high-priced law firm, Wilson Sonsini Goodrich & Rosati, and for the next few months I was forced to spend hours and hours meeting with attorneys.

I was touched by the fact that Speer came and spent the summer of 2006 doing what he could to help me. "This is the kind of loving thing brothers should do for each other," says Speer. "I used my rhetoric to try to help Charles in any way I could—writing press releases, papers, speeches, whatever."

But none of us could really do much. I became virtually paralyzed, locked up, handcuffed by this stupid proxy battle. I couldn't do anything I was supposed to be doing at Acxiom. Meanwhile, we couldn't respond, couldn't say, "This is bullshit"; the SEC wouldn't allow it. So we kept spending tens of thousands of dollars a month for lawyers and I was held captive in my own office. I just wanted to throw up.

THEN ONE DAY as we neared voting time, I got a phone call from Jeff Ubben. I think he realized he was going to lose the proxy battle. "Can I come see you?" he said.

"What about, Jeff?"

"I just need to talk. I need an hour—will you give me that?"

He said he'd rather not meet at Acxiom, which I thought was the smartest decision he'd made so far. "I'll be flying in on a private jet," he said. "Maybe you could meet me at the airport and we could get a conference room where nobody would see us." By now, he'd been in the press, I'd been in the press; for us to be seen together would raise eyebrows and possibly even affect Acxiom's stock.

"Okay," I said, "I'll meet you at the Dillard's private hangar." Bill Dillard, CEO of Dillard's Department Stores, was on our board. In other circumstances, Jeff Ubben would've made a scandal of our using his hangar.

On the day of our meeting, Jeff arrived with one of his colleagues. It may have been his CFO, Ronald Yee, who was later indicted for insider trading, involving Acxiom stock. In any case, this guy made himself scarce while Jeff and I met in a little office inside the Dillard's hangar. I had my guard up. "All right, Jeff," I said, "what is it you want to discuss?"

"I give up," he said. "You've won. You beat me."

I just looked at him, concentrating on my poker face. But I liked the way this meeting was starting. In hindsight, I realize that Jeff Ubben was slicker than the motor oil in my Acxiom-sponsored race cars.

"I really screwed up," he said. "My partners are about to kill me, or at least throw me out of the firm. I wasted a lot of money and we're not going to win this.

It's just a terrible mistake. I can't apologize enough for being so stupid. You guys really do know what you're doing."

He was practically on the floor groveling, and he wouldn't stop. He kept up the self-flogging to the point of making me embarrassed for him. Then he made his play. "Charles," he said, "I know I have no right to ask you this, but can you let me get out of this mess with just a small bit of my personal honor left?"

"What do you mean?"

"If you would just appoint me to a one-year term on your board, I would agree that it would be just a twelve-month deal. Then I'd be gone and you'd never hear from me again. If I could get on your board, I could say I haven't lost everything. I *guarantee* I will be your biggest supporter."

He was all cry, cry, cry, beg, beg, beg. And in a moment of total stupidity I agreed to his request.

"I wasn't surprised," says Susie. "Charles doesn't look at people and think, *They're going to screw me over*. If you tell him something, he wants to believe what you tell him. I'm the one in the background going, *That doesn't sound right. Are you sure about this?* Because Charles doesn't harp on the negative. He's always trying to move forward."

"Charles was tired of the nasty fight," says Rodger Kline. "He was besieged, he wanted to end it. And you had Ubben playing the role of trying to convince everybody that he was a good guy, a white hat. I was a step removed from where Charles was—they weren't writing nasty things on that website about me, thank God, but they were about Charles. So I understood the momentum driving Charles' decision.

"However, I was extremely skeptical. I didn't say a lot to Charles about it because I've learned over the years that when a decision is made, all you can do is try to make the best of it. By this time it was done. They had agreed. But I didn't trust Ubben."

"There's actually a funny family saying that came out of the Jeff Ubben episode," says my daughter, Carrie. "I had never heard of Ubben, but my husband had been watching him buy up Acxiom stock over a period of months. Rod told me all about him—said he was really bad news. So I went to Cabo with my dad—this was at the point where it had become a critical issue. And I remember saying to Dad, 'Oh, yeah, Rod said to ask you about some guy named Jeffrey Ubben.' And my dad's exact words were 'Yeah, it's a problem.'

"So now in our whole family, when anything goes wrong, we say, 'Yeah, it's a problem.' And when we say it's a problem, it's a problem of real magnitude."

□ □ □ □ □

WE SENT OUT a press release announcing the proxy détente between Acxiom and ValueAct and the imminent board membership of Jeff Ubben.

Partly because of a technicality, Jeff ended up serving two years. Acxiom had a certain cycle for electing board members, and we were somewhere in the middle of that cycle when Jeff and I had that conversation in the Dillard's hangar. As we actually started looking at the details of his board service, we figured out he would have to serve either six months or two years. With quarterly board meetings you can't accomplish much in six months, so we opted for the longer term. Besides, it takes time to really get to know a company. We didn't want Jeff to make decisions or push changes before he was far enough along in the learning curve. We felt the two-year term was actually in Acxiom's best interest.

On September 27, 2006, Jeff attended his first Acxiom board meeting, in New York. His first order of business was to apologize to everyone for all the trouble he and ValueAct had caused. "I'm sorry," he said. "And I'm so glad to be here. I'm here to help." We were all skeptical, to varying degrees, but Jeff was on his best behavior. He didn't assert himself. He clearly wanted to give the impression of being a true member of the team.

During the proxy battle, one of ValueAct's prime criticisms was that an "Arkansas Mafia" was running Acxiom, and we had taken that complaint to heart. Jim Womble was stepping down from the board, and at this meeting we were adding more "independents"—outsiders with no connection to either Acxiom or Arkansas. Under our agreement with Ubben, we would support one candidate of his choice, and he would support Acxiom's slate of new board nominees.

Jeff's selection was Halsey Wise, president and CEO of Intergraph, a leading global provider of spatial information management software. Among our nominees were two independents, William J. Henderson, former Postmaster General, and Michael Durham, former American Airlines CFO and, briefly, CEO of Sabre, the airline reservations system. I had worked with Bill Henderson on projects related to postal addresses and data, but we weren't close. As for Mike Durham, he'd been appointed the previous March to fill the seat of a board member who had resigned; now he was running for his own two-year term. I hadn't known Mike before his appointment, but our board member Mack McLarty had been on a board with him and said he thought Mike would be good for Acxiom. In my due diligence on Mike, I didn't hear exactly glowing reviews, but he was considered "competent" and "meticulous in his duties." And I trusted Mack McLarty.

In many ways, then, this board meeting could've been seen as a kind of renewal, even a rebirth. But I, personally, didn't feel reborn. I felt worn out, depleted. All I had done for months was meet with lawyers and field inquiries from stockholders. *"What's going on over there?"* To say that I wasn't having fun is an understatement. For 34 years I had enjoyed this job, but now I seemed to have lost something inside myself. And I was having a very hard time finding it again.

No way did I feel that I was running the business anymore; now it was running me. Not only had we been in a chaotic business environment for most of the decade, but now we also had the Sarbanes-Oxley Act of 2002 to contend with. Sarbanes-Oxley laid out new and "enhanced" standards for all U.S. public company boards of directors, management, and public accounting firms. Look it up—it'll make your eyes glaze over, especially if you're the CEO of a public company.

Sarbanes-Oxley is big on procedures, committees, certifications. Boards now spend much of their time on busywork—on *compliance*. And the intrusions into the business, in the name of protecting the public, are beyond irrational. I almost lost it when our auditor told me we now had to certify all our computers according to the Sarbanes-Oxley requirement. "We have to run an audit on every computer," he said. "We have to be sure the data it's collecting is correct and isn't being tampered with. We've got to be sure all the accounts are coming in right and the customer is being billed correctly. There's a forensics team that will help us do that for only two hundred thousand dollars."

"Are you fucking kidding me?" I said. "We've got *twenty thousand computers!*" Between proxy battles and Sarbanes-Oxley, I was about at the end of my rope.

Maybe Jeff Ubben read my mood, because sometime in his first few months on the board, he said to me, "You know, Charles, we ought to just take this thing private. We could keep it private for a couple of years, then take it back out and double our money."

At first I was lukewarm to the idea—maybe because it came from Jeff. I figured his real plan was for us to take it private with *him* running the show; after all, he had twice tried to buy the company. But as the weeks dragged on, and the distracting, expensive, onerous nature of being public grew ever weightier, I began to rethink my position. Every time Acxiom's stock dropped, for whatever reason, some disgruntled shareholder filed a lawsuit. That was the litigious world we now lived in—and it wasn't going to get better. For half a decade we'd been stuck playing a dispiriting defense, and I yearned for the nimble offense—the offense of innovation and achievement—that we'd played so thrillingly in the past. Going private began to sound like heaven.

So I began talking with my team—Jim, Rodger, Jerry Jones—about finding a private equity firm and getting ourselves focused back on the business. There was a lot of opportunity, if we could just take advantage of it. They liked the idea. I also brought a couple of other board members into the fold, including Jeff Ubben and Mike Durham.

By this time I had discovered that Mike was *made* for Sarbanes-Oxley. His recommendation as "meticulous in his duties" was a polite way of saying "anal beyond belief." I also realized he was kind of a professional board member, someone who gets on as many boards as possible to reap more pay. He was probably on four other boards while he was on ours. And if he could chair a board committee for extra compensation, he was all for it. Mike was the kid in the front row waving his hand at the teacher. Without much else to do, he lived to read every detail of every piece of paper circulated. He especially relished Sarbanes-Oxley certification documents.

I had come to dislike Mike. He was a nitpicker who loved to hear himself talk. In our board meetings, fully two-thirds of the discussion was now driven by Mike Durham. "Well," he would say, "I read the minutes of the last meeting, and I find that we didn't characterize the discussion accurately." Or, "I need more information on that. I'm not comfortable that I have enough to say we're doing that right." Or, "I object. I refuse to vote yes." Board meetings that used to take half a day were now stretching toward 5 p.m.

One day during a break in a meeting in which Mike was being especially argumentative—not just to me, but to everyone—I walked up to him and said, "Mike, I've come to realize you're a complete asshole."

"What?" he said. "What do you mean by that? I carry myself in the most professional manner."

"It's just the way you deal with people, Mike," I said. "You bring up all this bullshit that doesn't matter, disrupting the meetings. You talk disrespectfully to people who don't share your opinions. You're just an asshole."

"Well," he huffed, "I'll never forgive you for saying that."

And he didn't. I tell you that story as necessary background.

□ □ □ □ □

THE PRIVATE EQUITY firm we selected was based in Toronto. They had recently bought Beech Aircraft, and we thought they would be a good fit for Acxiom. Our team had agreed that we would accept an offer of $27 a share, a nice premium over the $20 or $21 that the stock was then selling for. These private equity guys seemed fine with that, so we entered into a process with them. The future looked bright. For the first time in years I was feeling like my usual, hopeful self.

But after months of back and forth, and just as we thought the deal was all but done, the private equity firm offered $22 a share. We couldn't believe it. We tried to negotiate them upward, but they wouldn't budge. And then they just disappeared—*Well, we made you an offer, so long!* In hindsight, I don't think they were bad guys. I think they were just having a hard time understanding our business, and they got cold feet.

We, though, were booted back into our own harsh reality. By now it was early 2007. "Charles," said Jeff Ubben one day—this was a conversation just between the two of us—"what would you think if ValueAct came back with an offer of twenty-seven dollars a share?" He went on to say he was friendly with the people at Silver Lake Partners, a private equity firm. "They're good guys, and they like this business. I think I could get them to go in on this."

The irony—now I was listening. What a difference a few hard years can make.

Jeff and I discussed the deal at length, and I agreed to go forward, with certain conditions. We would be acquired by and merged into companies formed to buy us; and Acxiom, the surviving corporation, would continue as a private enterprise. By mid-May, we had a formal offer. It was all cash, at the price of $27.10 a share. The deal was valued at $3 billion. Now we just had to make it happen.

Because Jeff and I had a "relationship," we had to be extremely careful not to run afoul of any SEC rulings. As it was, our next-largest institutional investor—MMI Investments LP—was already opposing the deal, complaining that the share price was too low and that new buyer Ubben, in his role as Acxiom director, had had an unfair advantage by being part of the initial go-shop to evaluate potential buyers. What we needed was a special board committee to own this process. And it had to be totally unassailable, impervious to auditors and lawyers. That meant independent board members only—no Acxiom employees could take part in any way.

I remember talking to Halsey Wise, Ubben's selection, about the special independent committee. "I'm good with this, Halsey," I said. "But for the love of God, don't let that asshole Mike Durham have anything to do with it."

I'm sure you can see where this is going. The trouble with independent committees is that they're independent.

So our independent directors went into executive session to decide who was going to be on this special committee. Actually, there was already a committee comprised of our independent board members, chaired by Bill Dillard. I had hoped Bill would head up this special committee, but it came at a terrible time for him— he was facing his own proxy battle. "I need this Acxiom thing like I need a bullet in the head," he said. He agreed to be on the committee but he couldn't take charge of it. Long story short, nobody wanted to be chairman—except You-Know-Who. "I'll do it! I'll do it!" said Mike Durham. When they came and told me, I thought: *A fate worse than death.*

Mike was now in his element. "I have to hire my own lawyers," he said. "I have to hire my own investment bankers." We already had Stephens, Inc., on retainer, but Mike had a buddy at Merrill Lynch, and the next thing I knew, this guy was Durham's investment banker. Not only that, but Mike had promised to pay him no matter what happened with ValueAct and Silver Lake. I've never heard of such an arrangement, before or since. Those deals are always success based. If the merger falls apart, the investment banker gets nothing. "What the fuck, Mike?" I said, as Jerry Jones and I grilled him about this sweetheart deal that Acxiom was going to have to pay for. Mike ended up hating Jerry as much as he did me.

So the process got off to a rocky start. Not only that, but the timing was terrible; remember, this was the summer of 2007. The financial world was starting to crumble, pieces of it chipping off here and there. Our big bank customers were getting skittish: *We better cut back on our marketing. We better put that off till next month. We need to wait and see how things shake out.* As a consequence, our revenues were becoming a little soft.

We also started hearing about big deals failing to secure financing. Money was tightening up, rates going higher. We had a firm commitment from UBS for $2.2 billion, but now UBS was told that that money was going to cost them hundreds of millions of dollars in fees. In deteriorating financial markets marked by increasing uncertainty, how much was UBS's word worth to them?

□ □ □ □ □

FOR ME, THE bright spot in this otherwise precarious scenario was that I had made a big decision—to get the hell out of there. I was 64 years old and had been doing this since I was 29. It had been a great adventure, but now even going private didn't strike me as worth it anymore. Too much had changed, and I couldn't change it back—not in this job, anyway. I felt a little like I had in the early '70s when I worried that IBM would promote me out of what I loved. I wasn't thinking of quitting Acxiom to sit around the house or to play golf all day. I wanted to go create something *new*, and I wanted to have fun doing it. Once we got this deal consummated, I would of course stay to help choose my successor—and the sooner the better. I was exhausted.

Not wanting to create additional waves in the buyout deal, I hadn't told the board about my decision. But I had told Susie that the very moment this deal closed, I wanted to start looking for my replacement. Now she and I began laying the foundation for our new life. In May 2007, just after Ubben's team had submitted their offer, we bought a condo in Dallas. I figured this deal would take six months to complete, and I wanted to establish my official residency in Texas, where there is no state income tax. My plan was to sell a lot of Acxiom stock and diversify my portfolio. I would keep some stock, but I wanted to spread my risk.

During that summer of 2007, though, my biggest risk was the slow slide of Acxiom's stock price, reflecting the failing business climate. In the three-month period between the first of June and the end of August, the last time our stock closed higher than the agreed-upon deal price was June 15, when it hit $27.55. By July 16, it was at $26.25. By August 15 it was at $22.60. Little did I know that Mike Durham and his Merrill Lynch crony were busy using this stock softness against me.

In late September, the bottom dropped out: It became clear that we would post a net loss of $11.5 million in the second quarter; the news sent our stock below $20. Then Silver Lake, seeing the handwriting on the spreadsheet—and I mean that in the broadest, most global sense—told us they were backing out of the privatization deal. ValueAct couldn't go it alone, so that was the end of that. We had spent months, and millions of dollars, preparing for this change that now wasn't going to happen. We had basically stopped being a public company, practically withdrawing from the industry. Now we had to reboot. The thought made me sick.

But it got worse. On a Sunday at the end of September, in Dallas, I got a phone call from Bill Dillard, who said that Mike Durham had visited all the independent board members on a mission to convince them that I should be fired. Then, on that very day, he had convened a secret meeting of the independent directors, in Dallas, to put it to a vote. Durham, along with his Merrill Lynch analyst, had told them that the stock drop and consequent loss of the privatization deal was my fault, that I had lost credibility in the investment community, that Acxiom's fortunes wouldn't rise until I was gone. According to Dillard, Durham wanted to fire me outright and have security escort me to the Acxiom door carrying a cardboard box of my belongings. Naturally, Jeff Ubben and Mike Durham were locked arm in arm.

I was shocked, of course. And I felt betrayed. Apparently the question on the table wasn't *if* I was leaving, but under what conditions. Durham had made it seem that inevitable. All of the independent board members I thought I could count on—Dillard, Ann Die Hasselmo, Mack McLarty—had seen which way the wind was blowing and had blown along with it. At least Bill Dillard had given me a warning. "There's nothing I like about what they're doing," he said. He told me that he and others had reluctantly agreed to my being exited out of the company, but not in the way Durham wanted to do it. Bill Henderson, the former Postmaster

General, had reportedly stood up and said, "Over my dead body we're going to humiliate Charles like this. We're going to give him an honorable exit."

Some of the directors came over to meet with me. I told them I had already planned to retire—I was *there*, and now they'd done this. It was a grim meeting, marked by anger and shame. They said Durham wanted me off the board as well—no doubt his plan was to ascend to the chairmanship. In fact, I had no desire to remain on the board; I preferred to be free to divest myself of Acxiom stock. But now I said I intended to *stay* a board member—I'd been elected by the stockholders and Mike couldn't just throw me off. In this way my board membership became a bargaining chip in my exit package.

Late that afternoon Susie and I flew back to Little Rock. I had to meet with Cindy Childers to make a plan for communicating these developments to our leadership team, to our associates, and to the press. I would announce the failure of the privatization deal. I would announce my voluntary retirement. I would say I intended to remain until we found my successor.

The sun was low as we made our descent into the Little Rock airport. Looking out the window, I could see the new Acxiom building glowing red in the setting sun. I felt numb. I dreaded the charade I would have to perform once I touched the ground. "Charles had been such a fighter through all of this," says Susie. "Now I saw him taken down. That was tough. I saw a very vulnerable Charles that night. All that he had built, and it was such a thankless ending."

FULL CIRCLE

1 0 0 1 0 1 0 0 1 0 1 1 0 0 1 0 1 0 0 0 1 0 0 1 0 1 1 0 0 1 0 1 0 1 1 0 0 1 1

I HAVE ALWAYS been an agent for change. On the frontier's edge, where I grew up, the very air felt charged with the spirit of exploration, of trailblazing, of transformation. For a boy as curious as I was, the possibilities for change were all around me. And as a professional, I've surrounded myself with forward-thinking people who can see beyond the status quo.

So while I may not have liked how my transition from Acxiom came about, I was, in any case, ready for a change. And once I accepted the inevitability, I was determined to make the best of it.

Mike Durham and Acxiom didn't make it easy. A lame duck, I remained in my job for four months. My relationship with the board—now chaired by Durham—was rocky at best; it's hard to be comfortable around people who've just stabbed you in the back. And here I want to bring forward the story about the Falcon 20 jet, the one I agreed to buy when Acxiom refused to take on more debt; the one that prompted Jeff Ubben's and Mike Durham's repeated claims that I had "taken advantage of Acxiom" by leasing it back to company.

Ever since we embarked on that deal, I had tried hard to make the cost to Acxiom lower than market rate. To do that, I took all the income Acxiom paid me for my business trips, and I used that to pay down the principal and interest on about a $7 million loan. In the early years, taking accelerated depreciation, I derived some significant tax benefits from this arrangement. But in the later years, once the plane had been depreciated to zero, I kept receiving that income but the only expense I had was my interest. Not so good, tax-wise.

When I left Acxiom, I still owed $3 million in principal on the airplane and it was probably worth only about $2.2 million. I tried to sell it back to Acxiom, but Mike Durham would have no part of that. I kept putting off the selling because if someone actually bought it for $2.2 million, it would cost me about $1 million to do the deal—$600,000 to the bank for interest, and around $400,000 in capital gains tax. Meanwhile, the jet was costing me $40,000 a month in maintenance— even if I didn't fly it! I finally unloaded it for $1.7 million. So when I say that this was the worst deal I ever made, you now know why. And to be trashed for it simply added insult to injury.

In those first weeks after announcing my retirement, I concentrated mostly on finding my successor. There were several people internally whom I urged to apply, but the board seemed bent on going outside. They hired the executive search firm Heidrick & Struggles to cast a wide net and bring us their three top CEO candidates; we would then choose my replacement.

They presented us a woman and two men. One of the male candidates seemed to have no qualifications whatsoever; I couldn't understand why he'd even been a finalist. The woman, whom I liked best personally of the three, was a professional manager, but she had no real knowledge of our kind of work. Data to her was just information on a spreadsheet.

That left a man named John Meyer, who'd held high-level positions at Ross Perot's EDS and at the French communications giant Alcatel-Lucent. Susie and I went to dinner with John and his wife in Dallas. Meyer talked a big game, but his patter rang hollow. Susie was horrified. "The whole time we were at dinner," she says, "I was going, *Oh my God, this guy is an asshole.*" Later, back at home, we commiserated over how awful Meyer was. Unfortunately, Mike Durham had imposed a very stringent process on the selection team—we *had* to vote for one of the three. John Meyer struck me as the least unqualified of the bunch.

My last day at Acxiom was Meyer's first day—February 4, 2008, my 65th birthday. By then, Jim Womble and Rodger Kline had also gotten the silent ax, and the three of us were ushered out with a joint "retirement party." Six years later, I can say without equivocation that that retirement party was one of the worst days of my life. Not only was it crushing to my pride, but I also sensed that many people who'd counted on me for years now felt betrayed: *Hey, we're in trouble here, and you're cashing in your chips and leaving us behind?* But I couldn't tell them the truth.

As part of my severance, I had a three-year consulting deal with Acxiom, but I soon learned that John Meyer preferred to keep me at arm's length. Meanwhile, he set about to dismantling everything I had worked so hard to build. He brought back titles, because he loved being at the top of a vast hierarchy, and he began cleaning house—especially of people closely associated with me—in the name of "cutting expenses." Meyer actually told me that his first order from Mike Durham was to "fire that son of a bitch Jerry Jones." Jerry survived, and does to this day, but many didn't. Meyer hired a hatchet man who slashed the careers of lots of good people; others jumped ship as soon as they could find a safe landing—or sometimes even before.

One in the latter category, Jeff Stalnaker, often regales old Acxiom hands with his story of spending a week on the road with John Meyer. Stalnaker, then president of Acxiom's Financial Services division, convinced Meyer (who didn't much like leaving the office) to accompany him on an intensive round of meetings with Citibank, Chase, and other big bank customers. The purpose was for Meyer to get to know the bank executives and for them to get to know Acxiom's new CEO.

After almost every meeting, Jeff says he received a phone call from the bank customer saying, "Don't ever bring that blowhard out here again." But for Jeff, the worst part of the trip were the nights he had to spend alone drinking with Meyer, listening to his gleefully recounted boasts of escapades in hot tubs with women. By the time Jeff got home, he knew that John Meyer had no respect for *anyone*, from women to employees to customers, and so he submitted his resignation.

"The 'era' of John Meyer would be spelled 'e-r-r-o-r,'" says a former colleague of mine. "He was a tyrant who created an extraordinarily oppressive environment. I had grown men in my office crying after a session with him. He would just rake people over the coals, and he liked to do it publicly: '*This is the kind of shit you're bringing me? Not acceptable. What the hell were you thinking? Don't you know I can get someone to replace you in a heartbeat? Get your ass out of here!'* All of that in front of a group."

Just nine months into Meyer's reign, the Acxiom board decided to replace him, but it would take them another two years to finally pull the trigger. "The most dysfunctional group of people I've ever seen," one board member told me, describing how ineffectual that body had become. "It's a complete nightmare. Nobody likes anybody. It's just awful."

□ □ □ □ □

WHILE ACXIOM WAS whirling out of control, I looked for ways to stay busy and be happy—in other words, I looked for projects. I began spending more time in Cabo in my capacity as chairman of Querencia, our golf development there, and I attended to my occasional duties as a board member of Hendrix College in Conway. But in the meantime, and in my usual fashion, I conceived of a very personal project to really throw myself into: my own money.

Six months after my last day at Acxiom, I was free to trade my Acxiom stock. Figuring that John Meyer would do nothing but wreck the company, I was eager to diversify my holdings, and the sooner the better. I was already invested with a young man named Ken Lee, the son of my cousin Reaves Lee (the one whose toys I tore up out of mechanical curiosity during my Fort Smith childhood). Ken had split from a successful Wall Street career to start his own firm, Bridgehampton Capital Management. Not wanting to trust anything so important as my investing to anyone I didn't know, I had turned to Ken.

Now I wanted to learn to do it myself, with Ken's able assistance. For the first year after leaving Acxiom I spent three to five hours a day working with Ken on investing, and he taught me plenty. Eventually, I became Bridgehampton's co-chief investment officer, and together Ken and I built a small hedge fund that has a mutual fund as one of its products. We did well enough that when we decided to sell late in 2013, we had half a dozen suitors. As I write this, Ken has nearly completed the sale to Tocqueville Asset Management, a quality Wall Street firm providing investment management services.

Another project arose out of a friendship. In Dallas, Susie and I became close to a couple named Bill and Beth Conner. Bill, who grew up in Arkansas, is a bright guy who ran a digital security company called Entrust, and our paths had first crossed during my Acxiom days when he and his team had pitched the idea of a partnership between Entrust and Acxiom. I was impressed then with their digital security product solutions. They used very advanced software to protect companies' data from hackers and other unwanted intruders.

In July 2009 when Entrust went private, Bill asked me to join the board. So I began spending a day or so a month on that, having a lot of fun working with Bill and his management team to help grow the business. In late 2013, Entrust was sold at a price that gave the investors in the private company a 77 percent internal rate of return.

I also joined the board of a small Internet marketing and technology company called Inuvo. This came about as the result of a request from Rich Howe, Acxiom's former Chief Marketing Officer, who was also on Inuvo's board. At the time, the company was located in New York, but in 2013 we moved it to Conway. Today Rich Howe is Inuvo's chairman and CEO, and I'm its lead outside director and one of the company's largest investors. Inuvo has become intertwined with my life. The office I now go to every day is in Inuvo's space—which brings me to the most pivotal post-Acxiom project of all.

I've already told you how the 1990s saw the dramatic rise of people using data for irresponsible reasons. That trend continued in the decade of the 2000s. So in 2008, when I heard about a new start-up called First Orion, I was intrigued enough with the company's potential to invest in it. The brainchild of a guy in Boston, First Orion's idea was to sell a call blocking service to large telephone carriers, such as Sprint: "Your customers get lots of calls they don't want, so here's call blocking for their home phone."

My initial investment was about $1 million, and I told them I would maybe double that if they signed a contract within the first year. Well, at the end of the year they hadn't signed anyone. I gave them a little more money and a little more time, and finally I took over the company. That coincided with Jeff Stalnaker's departure from Acxiom. He intended to retire in his early 40s, but once I heard he'd resigned, I phoned him and said, "Hey, Jeff. I've got your next job."

Under Jeff's leadership, we changed the name of the company to PrivacyStar and converted the original product idea into a suite of smartphone applications that include call blocking, text blocking, caller ID, directory assistance, reverse phone lookup, and complaint filing. We're largely on Android systems, but some of our services are also available for iPhone. On both operating systems, our complaint feature is a key element, giving customers a way to file directly with the Federal Trade Commission against telemarketers, scammers, debt collectors, and companies that violate the Do Not Call registry. As our personal data has become increasingly available online, people are looking for ways to protect themselves and their privacy. To me, PrivacyStar is a zeitgeist idea.

Today I'm PrivacyStar's majority owner. We have about 35 employees, and our office looks a little like Old Home Week: Sharon Tackett still keeps me organized, and Jeff Stalnaker and other familiar faces from Acxiom play key roles in tech and marketing. Occasionally, Jim Womble or Rodger Kline stops in to say hello—both are investors. Even Susie's son, Aaron, is on our marketing team. Across the hall, Rich Howe and his Inuvo team handle our IT work.

No start-up is easy, and we've had our rough patches. We bled money for a while. But we've continued to pivot and innovate, using many of the tools and tricks we learned at Acxiom. Our primary customers are Sprint, T-Mobile, and Metro PCS, and after a two-and-a-half-year effort we just signed with TracFone, the fifth largest carrier in the U.S. That's a huge milestone. We're really helping our customers control their environments.

And today we're profitable. As I write this, in the spring of 2014, we've just closed out Q1, and revenue was up 323 percent over the same quarter in 2013. This year we're averaging between a five- and a 15-percent increase month over month. I believe we're in the right business at the right time, providing a useful service with a bright future ahead of us, and I'm having as much fun as I did 40 years ago at Acxiom. I couldn't be a happier guy.

□ □ □ □ □

THAT EXTENDS TO my personal life as well. Susie and I have now been married 16 years, and we've come to what I consider a very healthy understanding. We can have bad days without having bad weeks, or months, or years. If I think she's acting "bitchy," I can simply say so; she may not like my saying it, but she usually comes back and admits that indeed she was acting that way. And then it's all done—there are no eggshells to walk on in our house.

Eggs themselves are something else. "Charles is *very* picky about the way he likes his eggs," says Susie. "Early on, he told me that Jane had done something he didn't like with his eggs, and she never cooked eggs for him again. He likes to flip his eggs, and he makes really good ones. But I don't do his eggs—or his rice, for that matter, because he's really picky about rice, too. If I were insecure, I would take offense. I think the reason Jane got okay with me is because at some point, in the early part of our marriage, I told Carrie: 'I want you to know that your mother was not all wrong. I live with your father. He's very difficult. If I wasn't as secure as I am, it would be very hard. And I just want you to know that the things that bothered her, I can see those things. It's just that we handle them differently.'"

Susie has channeled her competitive, go-getter side into ballroom dancing, flying off to Dallas and Chicago and Orlando to compete in Arthur Murray events. I've attended a few of those contests, and she's amazing. "I did my first competition and, just like I expected, I *needed* to hear my name win," says Susie, laughing. "Dancing has opened up the past for me, because I do love competition. It's taken me a long time to get comfortable with not having a job and no one expecting me to deliver on something. But I finally figured out that if I'm happy, Charles is happy. And I gave myself permission to have fun and not be thinking that I was supposed to be doing something bigger. I said to myself, *Keeping up with Charles Morgan is job enough.*"

Time has also softened my feelings toward Jane. The anger I once felt about the divorce—specifically about her participation in what I still think was a totally unnecessary and very traumatic experience for me, for the children, and for Jane herself—has now been transferred to Steve Engstrom. I continue to regard his approach as self-serving. I sense no feeling of caring about our kids or even about the long-term damage that this prolonged agony might have done to Jane. As long as Jane wanted to keep punishing me, Steve could find excuses, and ways, to keep up the pressure. In my fantasy world, he continued to encourage her in order to generate more fees.

But it's easy, now, for me to understand how hurt Jane was. She was embarrassed. Her self-worth was under attack. There are a lot of reasons that a person lashes out in anger, and I know I certainly played a part in that. I did things in the marriage that embarrassed and hurt her. The way I approached some things probably wasn't the wisest or the best. Divorce is never just one person's fault.

Jane moved back to Fort Smith many years ago, and her health isn't good. She never remarried. When she was having a health problem some time back, I helped her find medical assistance and got her into the Mayo Clinic, to a specialist. She's been extremely appreciative of that, and I was happy to be able to do it. Today, I feel that I can phone her at any time and it'll be okay with her.

Jane and I have even worked together on issues related to the children. In fact, not only has my relationship with Jane moderated in a most dramatic way, but also our entire family seems to have settled into a remarkable contentment in the last few years. When I think of that, I feel very lucky—many kids of wealthy parents lose their way.

Carrie remains married to Rod Ford, and their children, Yale, 13, and Jules, 11, are smart and funny kids. They live in Little Rock. Somewhere along the way, Carrie seems to have figured out that I'm not always judging her, and that's made her a much happier person. She went back to school and got her Ph.D in marketing and now teaches and consults. She's whip smart. She's also 27 years sober, and I couldn't be prouder of her for *all* her accomplishments.

Rob still lives in California, in Newport Beach, and he and Vici now have three wonderful children—daughters MaKenna, 13, and Lainey, 10; and son Chase, 3. Rob no longer races, but he's found a way to stay in the game. His company, TruSpeed Motorcars, in which I'm an investor, primarily focuses on Porsches—buying and selling and servicing them. Rob also works with a partner to provide "racing service" for clients; this entails hauling these hot cars to the racetrack and also providing crew and management for their racing clientele. Both arms of the business fall under the TruSpeed banner.

Susie's son, Aaron, and his wife, Ashley, have two beautiful children—a daughter, Morgan, age 4, and a son, Carson, age 2. In all, Susie and I have seven grandchildren!

Unfortunately, my mother didn't live to see them all. Mother died in November 2007, at age 94. It was the month after I announced my "retirement," but I spared her the gory details. She was already upset about our moving to Dallas, and I didn't want to upset her more. She was probably worried enough about how I could keep up my extravagant spending without a job.

Mother was pretty spry until the last couple of years. She was even driving into her late 80s, but one day she fell asleep at a stoplight and backed up traffic for blocks; a friend called and told me about it, and I had no choice but to relieve her of her car keys. The woman who once fell asleep and drove Jane's new Porsche into a mailbox never *ever* admitted her narcolepsy.

I did tell her I would come over from time to time and let her drive with me in the car. The last time was when she was about 92. "Mom," I said, "would you like to drive a little bit?"

"Oh, I would love that," she said. "That would be so fun." And so we got in her car and at first she was worried that she couldn't do it. We had mapped out about a three-block loop, and by the time she'd gone half the distance, she said, "Oh, I *can* do this now." And she drove just fine all the way back to the house. Mother lived out the rest of her life at home in Conway; I hired a person to help her so she wouldn't have to go to a nursing home. Money does have its benefits.

□ □ □ □ □

IN 2011, ACXIOM finally got rid of John Meyer. A board member, Jerry Gramaglia, stepped in as interim CEO while the company searched for a new chief executive. Within a year Mike Durham would be gone as well. "The skies cleared," says Cindy Childers. "It was like a breath of fresh air."

Soon I received a phone call from Gramaglia. "I'm only going to be in this office a short time," he told me, "but I can't just be a caretaker. This company needs fixing bad, and I've got to take some action. I need all the advice and help I can get." He asked if we could meet in person.

Susie and I were still living in Dallas then, but I was back and forth a lot. Gramaglia and I soon met at a restaurant called Dugan's Pub, about a block away from Acxiom headquarters. There he told me that he'd been traveling around to all the company's locations to talk with people and find out what was going on. "It's not a pretty picture," he said. "Morale is horrible." He picked my brain about things he might do to get the company back on track.

We met at Dugan's several times. During our second meeting, Gramaglia said, "I need to send a strong message to the associate population that we've made a lot of bad decisions about getting rid of people and running people off. Who is the one person who could make a difference if I could rehire them?"

It didn't take me long to say, "Terry Talley." Terry had been our chief tech scientist, intimately involved in the development of both AbiliTec and the grid. He'd jumped ship when Meyer took over, and now had a very cushy deal where he was. But from all I knew about trends in technology, combined with what I'd heard about Acxiom, I thought they desperately needed Terry's leadership.

"Done," said Gramaglia, himself a tech guy. "Who else?"

"Alex Dietz," I said. I told him that Alex was a very smart guy, the one person who'd helped me avoid wrong decisions over the years—to the extent that I'd avoided them. I told him the story of Alex coming into my office and forcing me to focus on core competencies.

"Great," Gramaglia said. A few months later, I heard that both Terry Talley and Alex Dietz were back at Acxiom. Alex, now in his 70s, works from home a lot, but they won't hear of his retiring. Of the Demographics/CCX/Acxiom old guard, he's the Last Man Standing.

Symbols are important, and it's vital for leaders to understand that. In July 2011, Acxiom hired a young new CEO who certainly does understand. So—clearly—does Jerry Gramaglia, who spearheaded Acxiom's recruitment of Scott Howe, corporate vice-president for Microsoft's Advertising Business Group, to guide the company into its next incarnation. Howe's background in emerging digital systems immediately sent one important message—Acxiom was going back to basics.

Before long, Howe began sending messages of his own. The first thing he did was to set off on a nationwide odyssey to meet all of Acxiom's clients. He called his focus on client issues "maniacal," but "a good crazy." He also announced that Acxiom would launch a $30 million research and development initiative—one that would require the hiring of some 400 new employees, largely from universities in central Arkansas. It all sounded encouragingly familiar.

I began to hear from Scott Howe regularly, and to meet with him from time to time. His story echoed Gramaglia's: "I've been here a few weeks now and I've had sessions with all the senior people. I'd like you to tell me what you think of them." So we went down the list until we got to the guy who'd been John Meyer's hatchet man. "I kind of like him," Scott said, "but I'm trying to figure out how to deal with him."

"You've got to fire him," I said. "I've met him and he does seem like a nice guy. But he went out and ruthlessly slashed, burned, and pillaged. He's a reminder of that bad time. As long as he's around, people are going to wonder when the next spate of burning and pillaging will begin."

Shortly after that, I heard that the Hatchet Man was history. I wasn't sorry, but I did make a note to be more careful about what I told Scott about people.

One day in late 2011 I got a phone call from Scott asking if I would attend a meeting at Acxiom. Scheduled for December 8, it was to be a celebration of retired employees, and Scott wondered if I would say a few words. I agreed, and dutifully prepared my little talk.

On the appointed day I arrived at Acxiom to find a full auditorium. This struck me as strange, and I remember the fleeting thought that maybe something was afoot beyond a celebration of retired employees. I made my way to my place on the stage next to Rodger Kline and Jim Womble and Alex Dietz. Soon the program began, and that's when I spotted Susie in the back of the hall with the rest of our wives. *Why are they here?*

In short order, I learned why. There were several speeches, laudatory words, about the glory days of Acxiom and the importance of a strong company culture. Then Scott Howe unveiled a huge oil painting of Jim, Rodger, Alex, and me. This, he said, was to hang in Acxiom's lobby in perpetuity, a reminder of the team that built this company, and of the teamwork and dedication that sustained it.

Even in that moment, I recognized this as a masterful exercise in symbolism by Scott Howe. Less than five months after arriving at Acxiom, he was sending a clear message to all, both inside and outside the organization: *Hey, we forgot our roots for a while, but now we're bringing back the best of that. We've come full circle. And we're building on that illustrious past, in R & D and customer service and employee excellence.*

But he wasn't quite finished. As a finale to an amazing day, Scott announced that this vast hall we were in would thenceforth be known as the Charles D. Morgan Auditorium. After that my memory is a blur, except for the tears.

ACKNOWLEDGMENTS

.

LIVING A LIFE is a messy business, and telling the story of that life requires much outside help. Numerous relatives, friends, and colleagues from all phases of my time on this earth have therefore contributed to making this book a reality, and I thank each of you for sharing your memories and your insights. There are too many of you to name, but of course you're already in the book—because you're part of the story.

I'd like to extend a special thanks to my ex-wife, Jane, who put aside our past troubles and agreed to sit for several lengthy interviews; Jane passed away in November 2014, just as this book was going to press. Many thanks to my children, Carrie and Rob, who added greatly to making this the unvarnished memoir I wanted it to be; and to my brother, Speer, a prize-winning novelist, for his eloquent and sometimes hilarious depictions of our growing-up years—it's amazing we survived them. Thanks, too, to Sharon Tackett, not just for her stories in this book, but for keeping me organized for 37 years and counting. In great measure it was Sharon's doing that allowed me to carve out so much time to work on this book with the very talented James Morgan (no relation that we know of!). Jim and I had a good time doing it, which I think shows on every page. I also want to thank Janell Mason, who organized and designed our photo sections. She made a tough job look almost easy.

Finally, I want to acknowledge the many contributions of my lovely wife, Susie, who has been a partner in this project every step of the way. I'm proud to dedicate the end result to her.

ABOUT THE AUTHOR

CHARLES D. MORGAN is the visionary former Chairman and CEO of Acxiom Corporation, world leader in data gathering and its accompanying technology, with 1,500 separate pieces of information on some half a billion people around the globe. A gadget geek from childhood, Morgan has raced motorcycles, flown jets, and built and driven his own race cars in a professional career that includes victories at both the 12 Hours of Sebring and the 24 Hours of Daytona, along with 17 other wins. Now CEO of his latest tech venture, PrivacyStar, he lives in Little Rock, Arkansas, with his wife, Susie.

CPSIA information can be obtained
at www.ICGtesting.com
Printed in the USA
JSHW021318161021
19611JS00002B/125